GERMANY UNDER DIRECT CONTROLS

Germany

Nicholas Balabkins,

Under Direct Controls

ECONOMIC ASPECTS OF INDUSTRIAL

DISARMAMENT   1945 – 1948

Rutgers University Press | New Brunswick, N. J.

To the memory of Gundega Balabkins, née Miesnieks
1 9 3 2 – 1 9 6 2

ACKNOWLEDGMENTS

To the publishers of the following journals the author expresses his thanks for permission to reproduce partly or fully:

To Kyklos Verlag for "Repressed Inflation in West Germany, from 1945 to 1948. Some Qualitative Observations," *Kyklos,* vol. 15, Fasc. 4 (1962), used in Chapter 2.

To J.C.B. Mohr (Paul Siebeck), Tübingen, for "The Interdependence of Industry and Agriculture: West Germany, 1945–1948," *Zeitschrift für die gesamte Staatwissenschaft,* vol. 119, Fasc. #1. (January, 1963) used in chapter 3.

PREFACE

The economic resurgence of West Germany is a well-known fact. From its wartime devastation and postwar stagnation, West Germany has risen like a phoenix to an enviable economic position in Europe. But despite the interest this resurgence has attracted there have been surprisingly few treatises devoted to the performance of the German economy in the British and American zones of occupation prior to the onset of economic reconstruction by the occupying powers. The currency reform of June, 1948, accompanied by sweeping economic reforms, was the beginning of its rapid economic upsurge. Prior to this reconstruction, the Allied powers had concentrated on reversing the economic and political bases of the Third Reich. Industrial disarmament, sweeping decentralization, demilitarization, and denazification were some of the more specific policy objectives; these were all designed to prevent Germany from waging future wars.

This volume is primarily concerned with the effects of the industrial disarmament policy on Germany. In particular, it examines the role of direct controls in the execution of the above-mentioned policy objectives in the American and British zones. No effort is made to extend the discussion to either the Soviet or French zones of occupation.

The writing of two fellow immigrants, the late Dr. Gustav Stolper and Dr. M. J. Bonn, initially aroused my curiosity in the subject. I have never met either of these two scholars, but I wish to acknowledge here my appreciation for their intellectual integrity and courage.

This volume has been written in many places, but two deserve particular mention. I have mined ruthlessly the collections of the *Hoover Institution on War, Revolution, and Peace* at Stanford University and many gaps of my work were closed there. Mrs. Agnes Petersen, the Curator of Western Collections at the Hoover Institution, took a personal interest in the study, and I owe her thanks for many favors. The major part of this work was written at the *Bibliothek des Instituts für Weltwirtschaft* in Kiel, West Germany, in 1960–61. It was there that I sifted through veritable mountains of German literature on the immediate postwar years. Excellent working conditions were helpful, and Dr. Frieda Otto, Dr. Gerhard Teich, and Dr. Gustav Hampel bore willingly some of my burdens. I owe them more than I can say. Dr. K. Passarge, of Hamburg, put me in touch with many former administrators who helped me to iron out some misconceptions about the wartime and postwar system of controls. Herr K. Surenhöfner of *Hamburgisches Weltwirtschaftliches Archiv* assisted and guided me through the initial stages of research in the fall of 1960.

Needless to say, my colleagues at Lehigh University have frequently raised questions regarding this work, and I owe them a debt of gratitude for assistance, advice, and valuable criticism.

In particular, I would like to thank Professors Leon R. Krouse, Joseph B. McFadden, Eli Schwartz, and Thomas J. Orsagh.

No words could adequately express my debt to my late wife, Gundega, for her encouragement and unfailing support in this undertaking. Her tragic and untimely death, however, prevented her from seeing the finished product. I dedicate this volume to her memory and our years together, when hope, joy, and humble affection guided our lives.

Nicholas Balabkins
Lehigh University
December, 1963

CONTENTS

GERMANY UNDER DIRECT CONTROLS

1

THE MUDDLING THROUGH

Scores of books have dealt with the breakdown of Allied rule in Germany after World War II. There has been little agreement on the cause among the authors—some have blamed the militant Soviet ideology, some the anti-Soviet attitudes of the Western powers, others the thorny reparations issue. In historical studies divergent interpretations of the available records are hardly new. It is virtually impossible, of course, to achieve perfect objectivity in evaluating historical phenomena because a particular writer's social and political preferences are bound to influence the interpretation.

Another source of difficulty arises from the fact that in big-power politics analytical concepts generally have been relegated to the background.[1] With very few exceptions the works on postwar Germany have failed to distinguish between *normative* and *positive* issues. This failure is more likely to generate heat than to cast light. In the social sciences, *normative* concepts usually refer to a set of criteria designed to show what ought to be.[2] All blueprints dealing with future or ideal social, economic, and political arrangements belong to this category. Such visions are not subject to verification. They may be scrutinized for their assumptions and logical consistency, but in general they tend to become articles of faith and are frequently used to fire the imagination. *Positive* propositions, in contrast, deal exclusively with "what is." Positive economics attempts to expound purely economic principles in an apolitical manner; it is concerned with analysis and not with the right or wrong of the policies pursued.

It would be pretentious to claim that the separation of normative from positive propositions will eliminate all the analytical difficulties encountered by writers on postwar Germany, but it is hoped that such a device will be useful. A framework of assumptions and postulates is basic to the investigation of any subject. In the case of Germany, wartime prejudices and wishful thinking frequently colored public opinion and influenced policy makers as well. Therefore, to put the postwar economic and political developments in Germany into proper perspective, it is necessary to set up a sensible premise about what determined the economic activity in the Western zones of Germany during the years 1945–48.

1. The Disunited Allies

The Allies decided during World War II to make sure that Germany after her defeat would never again disturb the peace of the world. In the prevailing wartime atmosphere Germany was considered the eternal felon among nations and the sole threat to world peace. Putting her in chains seemed the surest way to eliminate the scourge of war forever. To deprive Germany of the sinews of war required the destruction of her military power and "industrial war potential." This necessitated a substantial across-the-board reduction of German manufacturing capacity.

In May, 1945, the armies of the Third Reich surrendered unconditionally to the Allied Powers. The last legitimate government of the Third Reich went out of existence and the British forces took its members into custody.[3] On June 5, 1945, the four Allied Powers established the control machinery for the occupation and assumed supreme authority in Germany.[4] Elimination of the central German government called the inter-Allied government into being. Under the Allies' agreement Germany was to be divided into four zones with the respective commanders-in-chief supreme in each. In matters that affected Germany as a whole the four commanders would constitute the Allied Control Council in Berlin, which would jointly and unanimously exercise the supreme legislative, judicial, and executive authority within Germany.

The Potsdam Conference, held three months after the surrender, outlined some of the Allies' principal aims. The agreement called for a drastic reduction of German heavy industry. Germany was to have only light, "peaceful industries" and a highly developed agriculture. Germans were to be farmers and dairymen, not engineers, chemists, and steelmakers. During the occupation Germany was to be treated as an economic unit with central administrative agencies for industry, agriculture, finance and banking, transport and communication, and exports and imports. The Potsdam blueprint also called on the Allied Control Council to work out a "level of industry" plan within six months to indicate the industries to be left in Germany and to earmark the firms and the capital equipment for reparations.[5] The agreement said nothing, however, about the question of Germany's future social and economic system. This significant omission became the point of discord among the Allies.

At first the postwar prospect both dazed the victors and stimulated their imaginations. Nations looked hopefully toward a warless future, and the generals at the Allied Control Council were to translate this dream into reality. The four powers at first agreed that holding down Germany was the surest way to secure permanent peace. Such unity of purpose also seemed the best way to preserve the wartime alliance.

Generals Dwight D. Eisenhower and Lucius D. Clay, the American representatives in the Allied Control Council, were both determined to make the quadripartite government in Germany a success.[6] They felt that with forceful determination it would be possible to convert the Germans into a peaceful and democratic people. They were convinced that the Germans had violated basic principles of international morality and that it was time to exorcize the people's evil spirits. As firm believers in human progress, the Americans assumed that at the end of the occupation the "re-educated" Germans would be converted into "peace-loving democrats." Impatient with detailed work and wanting to get things going, the principal American spokesmen advocated policies "with more enthusiasm than knowledge."[7] Americans were frequently disposed to favor toughness rather than clemency. They were bent on a considerable deindustrialization of Germany without regard to the consequences.

To the more sober-minded British representatives, such punitive attitudes of the Americans amounted to "utter lunacy."[8] The British policy implied firmness toward the defeated enemy, but firm dealing did not call for vengeance. From long experience the British believed that extreme measures were futile in international affairs. Therefore, they showed a strong preference for moderation. They were more calm, more balanced, and less crusading than the Americans. The British members of the Allied Control Council spent much time and effort in opposing the more extreme policy measures of some overzealous Americans. In over-all policy the British aimed essentially at two things: the preservation of the wartime alliance and the prevention of Germany's starting another war. The British never wavered from these goals for more than brief periods.[9]

Apart from these differences another source of difficulty was the negative attitude of the United States War and State Departments toward the British. Some of the high policy makers in Washington at that time were more suspicious of the British than of the Russians because they felt that too close ties between Britain and the United States might prevent close postwar co-operation with the Soviet Union. Another explanation for the Anglo-American rift was the economic rivalry between the United States and the United Kingdom.[10]

The French approach to the postwar German problem was matter-of-fact. The French did not propose razing most of the German heavy industry but they insisted, with directness and consistency, that the Germans pay heavy reparations in kind. To weaken Germany as effectively as possible the French insisted on a sweeping decentralization of economic and political life. While the former enemy was on her knees the French tried to re-establish themselves as a dominant power on the Continent.[11]

The Soviet Union was the most intelligent, the most determined and, at the same time, the most enigmatic member of the Allied Control Council. After the wartime pro-Soviet sentiments in the United States and Great Britain, the Western officers were frequently baffled above Soviet moves in East Germany. There was no question that the Soviet Union was determined to eliminate the German menace from central Europe. On this point all four Allies agreed; but on others the Soviets and the Western Allies were worlds apart. Ideological differences, so diligently and persistently overlooked during the war, suddenly came to the surface as soon as the Allies sat down to implement wartime agreements.

The Soviet military government lost no time in revamping its zone in accordance with Communist ideology. Working from a well-planned blueprint, the Russians quickly nationalized all basic industries but left small businesses, for the time being, in private hands.[12] The land reform of 1945 with one sweep destroyed the economic base of the Junker class and thus drastically altered the property relation in agriculture.[13] In political life, Communists called the tune. All strategic posts in administration, police, and education went to them. Some bourgeois political parties and administrators were installed, but the real power was firmly in Communist hands.[14]

The ruins of the Third Reich were still smoldering when the East-West tug-of-war in Germany started. The principal disagreement among the Allies concerned the implementation of the Potsdam Agreement. The Western Allies quickly sensed that remaking Germany along the lines of the agreement would set up a society that would resemble the Soviet social order much more than the American. The Americans realized, for instance, that the social changes implied by the Potsdam blueprint would depress the entire German middle class.[15] American administrators were also surprised to discover that the most ardent anti-fascists in most cases were Communists. Fear of such far-reaching social changes made Americans recoil from their enthusiastic anti-fascist policies. This realization marked the Americans' early retreat from Potsdam.[16] Or, to put it more bluntly, "the ceaseless fight against socialism was the principal reason for the breakdown of the quadripartite government in Germany." [17]

Since all four powers believed that holding Germany down was important, they quickly agreed on such matters as the punishment of war criminals, denazification, and the destruction of German military forces. But on the constructive side—if anything within Potsdam could be so termed—the record was dismal. During the first two years the Allied Control Council registered all the conflicts among the four powers. It was able to reconcile some minor differences, but such major problems as reparations, the future social order, and the export-import program remained unsolved.[18] With the passage of time the conflicts grew, the lines hardened, and the Allied Control Council became the "fantastic circus" of Berlin.[19] In March, 1948, the Soviets walked out of the Allied Control Council and the last vestige, or rather the façade, of Allied unity in Germany crumbled. The Allies' split was complete; the quadripartite administration ended; the cold war was on in earnest.[20]

2. Some Allied Goals for Postwar Germany

During the war, some influential pressure groups in Washington and what passed for public opinion in the United States and Great Britain viewed Germany in general and the Ruhr in particular as a conglomeration of steelworks, coal mines, and engineering and chemical plants run by warmongers who for centuries had threatened world peace. To make the world safe from future German aggression, American planners for peace were determined to destroy German war potential in all its forms. The story of wartime planning for postwar Germany on the diplomatic level is rather well known and needs no recapitulation.[21] On the economic level, Henry Morgenthau's vision for a peaceful Germany of the future is notable as one of the truly curious types of normative economics.

THE MORGENTHAU PLAN

Morgenthau's thesis was that as long as Germany possessed heavy industry there could be no peace in the world. The Morgenthau Plan called for a complete destruction of the German metallurgical, chemical, and electrical industries within six months after the cessation of hostilities. All factories should be razed or dismantled and sent to the victorious countries as reparations, and all mines should be closed. Germany was to become an agricultural country. Morgenthau argued that without heavy industry Germany would never again wage war.[22] It is known that this proposal was officially accepted by President Roosevelt and Prime Minister Churchill at the Second Quebec Conference in September, 1944, as the program for postwar Germany.[23]

The public reception in the United States of the Morgenthau Plan was adverse but not wholly unfavorable. Although the American government never formally adopted the blueprint in its original, more stringent form, its basic principles nevertheless dominated the official thinking in Washington. After the retirement of Cordell Hull as Secretary of State, Morgenthau's influence on postwar planning for Germany gathered momentum. The fact that Morgenthau, the Secretary of the Treasury, could see Roosevelt frequently and informally gave him a considerable advantage over other Cabinet members who opposed him.[24] It is likely that in these informal talks Roosevelt became gradually converted to Morgenthau's views on Germany. It is known that Roosevelt held that the German people were collectively guilty of war and that he tended to favor a harsh postwar policy for Germany. The favorable disposition of Roosevelt to Morgenthau's views was of crucial importance in setting a new course in planning for the occupation of Germany.

THE PROGRAM OF THE FOREIGN ECONOMIC ADMINISTRATION (ENEMY BRANCH)

In late September, 1944, Roosevelt instructed the Chief of the Foreign Economic Administration to accelerate work designed to see to it "that Germany does not become a menace again to succeeding generations." [25] Under the terms of the Presidential order the Enemy Branch of the Foreign Economic Administration, in close co-operation with the Technical Industrial Disarmament Committee, presented in the summer of 1945 its final report, called *A Program for German Economic and Industrial Disarmament*.[26]

The basic reasoning of the FEA report was that there would be no security against German aggression "until the economic base on which German military might rests is rendered powerless to support war." [27] To bring about a peaceful and harmless Germany, the industrial disarmament program was to be cast in terms of stringent controls over the German economic and industrial base, scientific research, and economic institutions which were useful for economic mobilization for war. The report did not suggest a complete elimination of German heavy industry, as did the Morgenthau Plan. However, it recommended severely cutting the level of German industrial activity except for textiles and some other light consumer goods.[28] It also claimed that a disarmed Germany would "free the surrounding countries of Europe from German economic domination." [29] The FEA apparently felt that a prohibition of the export products of heavy industry would constitute a great blessing to Germany's neighbors.

THE PLANNING WORK OF THE MONETARY RESEARCH DIVISION OF THE TREASURY

The Treasury's influence on the planning work for postwar Germany was pervasive. No paper of any importance dealing with German occupation could be released until approved by the Treasury; the State and War Departments were virtually subservient to the Treasury Department in this respect.[30]

Although Henry Morgenthau was the Secretary of the Treasury, Harry Dexter White, his chief assistant, determined the course of events. White, who joined the Treasury in 1934 and remained until 1945, was an able man and a technically competent economist, and his influence extended well beyond the Treasury.[31]

The Monetary Research Division of the Treasury, under the direction of White, drew up a detailed plan for the future of mankind through the permanent elimination of Germany as a potential troublemaker. Two drafts of the Monetary Research Division's plan are presently in the Harry Dexter White collection at the Princeton Library. Examination of these drafts shows that the basic theme of the plan advocated "strong Europe, weak Germany." Germany was to be completely deindustrialized, her factories razed, and her coal mines flooded. This manuscript was subsequently published, with minor changes, as a book by Henry Morgenthau under the title *Germany Is Our Problem*. It was the gist of this plan that was discussed and approved by Roosevelt and Churchill at Quebec.

The plan proposed as a measure of political security the greatest machine-smashing action ever attempted in time of peace and argued that the European economy would not suffer from it. In a memo that White wrote on September 7, 1944, he claimed that European prosperity did not depend upon Germany because the United States, Great Britain, France and Belgium could easily provide what Germany had supplied before the war.[32] The fallacies of Morgenthauism, or perhaps more correctly Whiteism, in all its variations were an important contributor to the postwar collapse of Western European economies. It took a Marshall Plan to restore the economic unity of Western Europe. Can anyone today envision a European Common Market without an industrial Germany?

But the question does remain as to how an economist of such technical skill as H. D. White could overlook the most essential relationships of the economic life of Western Europe. Two reasons lend themselves as possible explanations.

The Nazi atrocities produced an understandable animus and bias against Germany in many people.[33] In the case of White and Morgenthau, E. F. Penrose has observed that the Treasury people "were not open to reason when it came to postwar German questions." [34] Morgenthau and White apparently were convinced that Germany was the scourge of nations and that only harsh and repressive policies would be able to cope with her.

Or suppose that White's motives were not purely, or predominantly, emotional. Might it yet not be that the intellectual fascination of his normative system so blinded him to the realities of positive economics that he inextricably confounded these two essentially dissimilar branches of economics?

White's normative views on these matters and the strength with which they were held are still shrouded in mystery to a great extent. From R. F. Harrod's observations it is known that White was a "reformer of genuine convictions . . . single minded in the pursuit of his aims." [35] It seems to this writer that in his crusade for a better world, free of the German menace, White freely substituted normative views for positive propositions, and that out of this mixture arose his "scientific" outline for the treatment of postwar Germany. With the Treasury carrying such an enormous weight in determining American policies toward Germany all the fallacies of logic, the evasions of issues, and the deliberate disregard of essential economic relationships were overlooked.[36]

THE DIRECTIVE OF THE JOINT CHIEFS OF STAFF, JCS 1067

After the Morgenthau Plan was officially withdrawn (because of the severe criticism it provoked, in September, 1944) White and Morgenthau continued to have strong voices in all decisions regarding the German occupation. A joint State and War Department directive of September 22, 1944, issued with the blessing of the Treasury, was to become the basis of the future JCS 1067.[37] The secret JCS 1067 directive was issued by the Joint Chiefs of Staff to General Eisenhower in April, 1945.[38] In a way this directive became an official but diluted version of the Morgenthau Plan.

JCS 1067 did not require the destruction of all German industries and the flooding of all mines, but it limited German industrial activity to a level needed to prevent "disease and unrest." [39] In terms of the directive the U.S. occupation authorities were instructed to build a strong Europe with a weak and peaceful Germany. The objectives for the initial post-defeat period were industrial disarmament, demilitarization, denazification, and decentralization of German administration through regional and local autonomy.

Industrial disarmament was to be practiced in three forms: reparations in kind, i.e., removal of German plants and equipment; outright destruction of German production facilities; and statutory neglect of plant and equipment. The U.S. Military Governor was required to impose "controls to the full extent necessary to achieve the industrial disarmament of Germany." He was forbidden to take "steps (*a*) looking toward the economic rehabilitation of Germany, or (*b*) designed to maintain or strengthen the German economy." Only minimum production of iron and steel, chemicals, non-ferrous metals, machine tools, radio and electrical equipment, automotive vehicles, heavy machinery, and important parts thereof was permitted. This minimum level of industrial operations designed to prevent disease and unrest was undefined and ambiguous. As it turned out its application varied directly with the intensity of the cold war between East and West. But in the initial post-surrender period such provisions were designed to weaken the German industrial economy as thoroughly as possible.

To cripple permanently the German pre-eminence in physics, chemistry, and engineering and to eliminate German technological "know-how" as a factor for industrial war potential, JCS 1067 spelled out in great detail ways and means for "technological disarmament." Since technology and advances in technology depend to a great extent on research, detailed provisions on this score are quite interesting and consequently are reproduced in full. Paragraph 31 stated that as an additional measure of industrial disarmament, pending agreement in the Control Council, the U.S. Military Governor would adopt the following measures in the U.S. zone of occupation:

a) prohibit initially all research activities and close all laboratories, research institutions and similar technical organizations except those considered necessary to the protection of public health;

b) abolish all those laboratories and related institutions whose work has been connected with the building of the German war machine, safeguard initially such laboratories and detain such personnel as are of interest to your technological investigations, and thereafter remove or destroy their equipment;

c) permit the resumption of scientific research in specified cases, only after careful investigation has established that the contemplated research will in no way contribute to Germany's future war potential and only under appropriate regulations which (1) define the specific types of research permitted, (2) exclude from further research activity any persons who previously held key positions in German war research, (3) provide for frequent inspection, (4) require free disclosure of the results of the research and (5) impose severe penalties, including permanent closing of the offending institution, whenever the regulations are violated.

Such drastic measures were evidently designed to enforce the envisaged industrial disarmament of Germany. From an economic point of view the United States could hardly have done worse than to subscribe to such a mass-scale *industrial pogrom,* because an impoverished country is always a poor customer. In the field of international relations, the United States still had to learn that extreme measures never work. In comparison to the White-Morgenthau Plan even the Soviet-sponsored Varga Plan was mild, and in its destructive zeal the former had little resemblance to the latter. Careful reading of E. Varga's proposal for the postwar treatment of German industry and reparations, "Restitution for Damage caused by Hitlerite Germany and its Allies," shows that Varga advocated *reparations in kind,* in terms of machinery, equipment, sequestration of German property abroad, reparations from current production, and the use of German labor for reconstruction purposes.[40] Varga did not advocate large-scale deindustrialization of Germany as did White and Morgenthau. He was merely interested to avoid the repetition of another "German reparations muddle" of the post-World War I type. It is known that the Versailles Treaty imposed heavy reparations on Germany. Yet at the same time, the recipients of reparations refused to buy German goods. Hence, the only way for Germany to pay reparations was to borrow on a large scale from American and European bankers. As soon as loans were called in, Germany suspended paying reparations. The concept of deindustrialization of Germany was White's contribution to the economic literature. It could have been disregarded as a curiosum had it not been so costly in terms of dollars, human life, and diplomatic ineptness. The Russians were much more interested in transforming East Germany into a Soviet type of society than in carrying out a large-scale industrial disarmament program of White's type.[41]

In this stringent form, the JCS 1067 probably determined the policy for a few months in 1945. From the fall of 1945, a

drift in policy ensued which eventually led to its formal repudiation in July of 1947. However, as long as JCS 1067 was
not formally revoked, the lower administrative echelons had
to enforce its harsh provisions. Since the instructions of JCS
1067 were commands, the rank-and-file administrators frequently interpreted its provisions rigidly and applied them
zealously.

THE FIRST ALLIED PLAN FOR REPARATIONS
AND LEVEL OF THE POSTWAR
GERMAN ECONOMY, MARCH 26, 1946

The level of industry plan of March, 1946, called for a severe
reduction of Germany's industrial capacity and proposed no
significant contribution by German production to European reconstruction.[42] Production was to equal 55 percent of 1938, or
about 70 or 75 percent of 1936 production. Heavy industries
such as steel, chemicals, machinery and heavy equipment were
subject to particularly severe restrictions, and it is estimated
that the plan projected wiping out three-fourths of their capacity.[43]

More concretely, the plan prohibited the production of arms,
ammunition, and implements of war, and all types of aircraft
and seagoing ships. It stipulated that all industrial capital
equipment for the production of synthetic gasoline, oil, rubber
and ammonia, ball and taper roller bearings, heavy tractors,
primary aluminum, magnesium, beryllium, vanadium produced
from Thomas slags, and radio-transmitting equipment would
be eliminated. In the so-called restricted industries, steel production was to be limited for Germany as a whole to 5.8 million
tons a year. The production of basic chemicals was to be
limited to 40 percent of the 1936 capacity. Only 11.4 percent
of the 1938 machine-tool capacity was to be left in Germany.
In heavy engineering industries the retained capacity was es-

tablished at 31 percent of the 1938 capacity. The so-called unrestricted industries, such as building materials, furniture and woodwork, flat, bottle and domestic glass, ceramics, bicycles, and potash, were free to develop within the limitations of available resources. The excess capacity was to be eliminated in the form of reparations in kind. The plan, however, was a skeleton agreement that required quadripartite implementation.[44]

The rationale of the plan was the reduction of the German standard of living to an undefined European average, excluding the Soviet Union and the United Kingdom. German economists estimated that with the permissible retained capacity the German standard of living would actually have been about 15 percent below the 1932 level and that industrial output, taking into consideration the interdependence of the various branches of the economy, would have been about 40 percent of the 1936 level.[45] However, even this level of industrial operations seemed improbable. The severely truncated machine tool and steel industries were likely to become major bottlenecks.[46] Considerable unemployment was likely; Seume estimated that, if industrial output was about 51 percent of the 1936 level, from 3 to 3.5 million industrial workers would be out of work, and that, if the built-in bottlenecks reduced the output to 40 percent, unemployment would go up to 4.5 million. In that case industrial unemployment would have been greater than in 1932, when only 4 million were out of work.[47] The forecasts of these German economists, biased though they may be, could not have been too far from the mark, and later developments seemed to bear out the inadequacies of this first plan.

To a number of American administrators the allied economic policy was unique or ran counter to the normal behavior in economic life. One disillusioned American official admitted that "the task of deliberately reducing production and holding down the standard of living . . . went contrary to all habits of thought in the western world." [48] And in the eyes of *The London Economist,* the plan was, "without exaggeration, a plan for dislocation and impoverishment. It is negative, restrictive and basically unworkable." [49]

EUROPEAN ECONOMIC PLIGHT

It did not take long to prove that the Allied attempts to build a strong Europe with a weak Germany was a chimera. Germany traditionally exchanged manufactured goods for raw materials and necessary food imports. For the last century and a half Germany had been a food-deficient country. Before the last war, even after the Nazis had made wholesale attempts to increase self-sufficiency, Germany had imported about 20 percent of her foodstuffs. Most home-produced food had been grown in the eastern part of Germany—an area now under Polish control. Industrial exports had always provided the needed foreign exchange to pay for the food imports.

Before the war Germany had been tied to the European economy in an intimate fashion.[50] The prosperity of Italy, the Low Countries, Denmark, Sweden and France had been inextricably tied to the prosperity of Germany both as a supplier and as a market. Germany had supplied a great variety of industrial goods, especially machinery and coal. Thus, for example, Germany had been a major source for Italy, supplying some 26.4 percent of her imports. Switzerland had bought 24.8 percent, Sweden 23.7 percent, Holland 23.3 percent, Norway 17.6 percent, Belgium 11.5 percent, and France 7 percent of their imports in Germany.[51] If Germany could not produce and sell her industrial goods to her neighbors then the Italians, the Dutch, the Danes, and the French could not sell their products to the Germans. In such a case the intra-European division of labor, the basis of European prosperity, would be disrupted. An attempt to deprive Germany of her heavy industry would not inflict pain on Germany alone but would penalize Europe as well.

But purely economic considerations carried little weight in the immediate postwar period. By political decision Germany was to be deprived of her war-making ability—heavy industry. This goal was considered to be of utmost importance for the future peace in Europe, overriding all other considerations. During the two years of neglect of her industry, Germany for all practical purposes disappeared as a significant factor in European economic life. The Allied policy of industrial disarmament of Germany was responsible for cutting up European economic integration and intra-European division of labor. Elimination of Germany as a buyer and seller led to the realization that "Europe cannot hope to prosper under any arrangement which would leave it half rich and half poor." [52] The Allied policy of depriving Germany of her heavy industry was bound to impoverish not only Germany but all European countries. [53]

The day-to-day administration of Germany, instead of being unified, continued to be divided into four zones, causing economic and social dislocation. Such four-zone administration delayed and obstructed efforts to commence rehabilitation of Germany even under the terms of the Level of Industry Plan of March, 1946. [54] As the impasse continued and the Allied Control Council failed to resolve any important issues the German economic situation continued to deteriorate.

During the course of 1946 Germany, the occupied enemy, became the subject of Allied wooing. The Soviet Union was bidding particularly hard for German favors, and it became obvious to the Western powers that their previous disregard of ideological differences between East and West could not continue. [55] In 1947 it was an open secret that the United States was engaged "in competition and very real competition with communistic ideology all over the world." [56]

The United States gradually realized that unless it met Soviet competition it was likely to lose control over Germany. The Soviet Union's policy was "national-interest oriented," and no time was lost in launching an intelligent political and ideological drive to win Germans and other Europeans to its side. The war-shattered Soviet Union was too weak economically to offer material assistance, but American policy had persisted in indulging in illusions and myths. In contrast to the Soviet Union, the United States had sought to solve all European problems by purely economic means, i.e., by substantial deindustrialization of Germany. Under the pretext of preserving wartime Allied unity, American policy had intended to keep Germany weak.

Such policy offered no hope, no future.[57] No myth has done more damage to American interests abroad than the concept of a deindustrialized Germany. It was unquestionably proper to advocate harsh measures against Germany, but it was dead wrong to refuse to face realities. There was no need to mortgage American and German hopes for a better future just to win the fleeting favor of the Soviet Union. An economically prostrate Germany resembled a huge vacuum in the heart of central Europe.[58] As the Soviet Union attempted to fill the vacuum the American government slowly recognized the strategic importance of Germany. It was this realization, and nothing else, that made Washington change its former negative and repressive policy. Germans were in no way responsible for this reversal.

The first and most important corrective step was the fusion of the American and British zones of occupation. This merger took place on January 1, 1947, and it was expected that pooling the economic resources of the two zones would permit a considerable economic reconstruction. The British and Americans argued that the merger should be considered as a first step toward the economic unity of all Germany. It was also felt that the two zones would be able to make a substantial contribution to the economic rehabilitation of Western Europe under the terms of the Marshall Plan.

JCS 1779

From such considerations General Clay was given a new directive, JCS 1779, on July 15, 1947.[59] The tenor of the directive was positive, but it represented only a limited departure from the purely negative provisions of the JCS 1067. To be sure, under the pretext of preventing starvation, disease, and unrest a great deal of assistance had been rendered to the Germans while JCS 1067 was still formally in effect, and JCS 1779 abolished this pretense completely.

On the positive side, JCS 1779 called for the creation of stable economic and political conditions in Germany. It was thus recognized that democracy could not develop and even permissible reconstruction could not take place in a starving, economically disorganized Germany. The listed economic objective, however, still called for the elimination of the entire German armaments industry and the enforcement of the Potsdam provisions concerning industrial disarmament.

The Western zones were to proceed with economic reconstruction toward achieving a self-sustaining economy. The permitted level of industrial operations was to be determined by another level of industry plan. But the directive still called for reparations in the form of capital equipment to eliminate Germany's war potential, though the extent and zeal of such removals was to be smaller than planned a year earlier.

To prevent disease and unrest, Congress had voted special funds to pay for the imports of foods, feed, seed, and some petroleum products. The U.S. Military Government nevertheless was required to prevent all nonessential imports. Raw materials were not considered essential for the German economy and no congressional funds were provided for this purpose.

Because West Germany has no raw materials except coal, industry was bound to remain idle.

On the whole, the new directive failed to break the bonds of the restrictionist Morgenthau-like mentality. It was a half-hearted departure from the earlier norms, although constructive intentions were definitely in evidence. The wartime visions of an economically weak Germany still plagued policy makers in Washington, and without a clear-cut break with the Morgenthauist past, German and European economic prostration was to continue.

REVISED PLAN FOR LEVEL OF INDUSTRY
IN THE BRITISH AND AMERICAN ZONES

On August 29, 1947, the U.S. and U.K. Military Governments presented a new proposal designed to settle the future of German industry in the bizonal area. It was officially admitted that Germany could not regain economic health under the plan in force and that Germany could not contribute her indispensable part to the economic rehabilitation of Europe.[60] The Revised Plan for Level of Industry of the Bizonal Area stipulated the retention of sufficient industrial capacity to approximate the 1936 level of output. Because the two objectives of the revised plan were to provide for a self-sustaining economy and to enable the area to contribute to the rehabilitation of Western Europe, substantial increases were allowed in retained capacities in the metal, machinery, and chemical industries. The American and British military authorities asserted that these capacities would permit production at levels averaging about 5 or 10 percent less than in 1936.

More specifically, the new plan, like the old, did not permit the production of ball bearings, synthetic ammonia, synthetic rubber, or synthetic gasoline and oil. The previous prohibition of the production of aluminum, beryllium, vanadium and magnesium was to continue, but no plants in these industries were to be made available for reparations removals without further review.[61]

In the restricted industries, the first plan's incredibly low ceiling of 5.8 million tons of steel a year for all Germany was scrapped. Immediately after the publication of that plan German economists had protested that the entire plan was in jeopardy because bottlenecks in steel and mechanical engineering were likely to frustrate all attempts at even permissible reconstruction.[62] But the Allies had turned deaf ears to these protests. The new plan set the annual limit in the two zones at 10.7 million tons a year.

The production of all chemicals was limited to approximately the 1936 capacity, which raised the ceiling by about 42 percent. The machine tool ceiling was raised from 11.4 percent of the 1938 output to 65 percent of the available capacity. Retained capacities were set at 80 percent of the bizonal total in heavy machinery industries and at 119 percent of the 1936 level in the light machinery industry. The excess capacity was scheduled for removal as reparations.

On the whole the Revised Level of Industry Plan, like the new occupation directive, was more generous than the first but still exhibited the old restrictive mentality. Germans were still to be kept in economic chains and at the same time were to contribute to the riches of the rest of Western Europe. The extent of the new restrictions was clearly seen when the second part of the revised plan, the reparations plan, was promulgated in the fall of 1947.

The plan, a list of plants or portions of plants available for reparations, scheduled 682 facilities in the bizonal area for dismantling.[63] Four hundred ninety-six plants in the heavily industrialized British zone had to go, the majority steel producers or processors, and 186 plants in the American zone.[64] Factories earmarked for removal were classified either as "war plants" or "surplus" industrial plants. This classification did not imply that "war plants" could not be adapted for peacetime uses—in the British zone, for instance, many plants which were listed as "war plants" had been successfully converted to peacetime production. All plants in the two Western zones with capacity exceeding the needs to produce at the 1936 level of output were labeled surplus.

But in calculating capacities the experts did not take into consideration that Germany in 1936 had a viable economy without bombing damage, without millions of homeless refugees, and no scarcity of raw materials.[65] The European economy desperately needed more steel, but the reparations list called for the demolition of steel facilities in the most industrialized area—Germany. The publication of the reparations list was a considerable blow to all who had hoped for a speedy restoration of the intra-European trade.

The very essence of the Marshall Plan was to eliminate as quickly as possible the basic causes of postwar dislocation and economic distress in Western Europe, especially Germany. During the extensive congressional inquiry into the European Recovery Program it was repeatedly emphasized that Germany was the hub of the entire recovery system and that the Ruhr constituted the economic heart of Europe.[66] Secretary of the Army Kenneth C. Royall testified: "German recovery is not only important to Germany. The other nations of Europe need German industry and exports for their own rehabilitation and progress. Historically it was the central and principal industrial nation of Europe." [67] Philip D. Reed, chairman of the General Electric Corporation, said that Germany's "well-being is probably the key to European prosperity," [68] and William Green, president of the American Federation of Labor, remarked that "the crux of the European economic crisis lies mainly in Germany." [69]

Richard M. Bissell, a member of the Presidential Committee

on Foreign Aid, elaborated on the controversial question of whether the European Recovery Program would be an all-out "Germany first" program. He insisted that if the program as a whole could be more rapidly advanced by giving needed raw materials to the Germans instead of to other countries "the choice should be in favor of Germany." [70] John Foster Dulles, later Secretary of State, testified that "Western Germany is the bottleneck of European recovery." [71] The overwhelming consensus supported the view that if Germany should remain in economic chains, Europe would remain in rags.[72]

However, there was no unanimity of opinion on whether the dismantling of German factories should be stopped. Congress favored immediate discontinuation of dismantling, whereas the State and War Departments wished to continue the removal of German industrial facilities.

The departments justified their position on moral and economic grounds. Secretary of State George C. Marshall pleaded for the continuation of reparations for moral reasons.[73] He called for compensation of the victims of German aggression. On the economic side, it was argued that severe shortages of food, coal, and raw materials and transportation difficulties would not permit an appreciable increase in German production for four to five years. Royall insisted that since Germany would not be able to operate the existing industrial capacity even at the levels permitted by the Revised Level of Industry Plan, the excess plants could be dismantled without harming either the German or the Western European economy.[74] General Clay, the Military Governor of Germany, defended this analysis and the continuation of dismantling. But he also added casually, and the remark is of utmost importance, that "a reduction of Germany's industrial output was also a security measure." [75]

Taken at face value before the inception of the European Recovery Program, such arguments would have carried weight and would have justified considerable removals of German plants. But the arguments were presented after it was decided that Germany was to be included in the Marshall Plan. The reluctance of the State and War Departments to admit that the dismantling list was drawn up mainly with reference to self-sufficiency of the bizonal area [76] without examining its implications on the European Recovery Program showed that "Morgenthauism" died hard.

In steel, for instance, Clay in his memoirs termed the two zones' quota of 10.7 million tons an important security measure.[77] The Revised Level of Industry Plan contemplated the destruction of 4 million tons of steel capacity.[78] A number of German and Allied surveys insisted that the permitted level considered domestic consumption exclusively and disregarded the fact that before the war Germany exported roughly one-third of all metals produced,[79] and German inability to produce her traditional exports aggravated the European economic situation. Combined with the grossly inadequate steel capacity, the intended dismantling of facilities for various steel products such as plate, hot strip, seamless tubes, forgings, and electrical steel was to be so considerable as to cripple Germany's steel and machinery industries.[80] Such an artificial throttling of the Ruhr's industries would clearly wreak havoc on the European Recovery Program.[81]

But pressures for halting reparations mounted. After the George M. Humphrey Committee [82] recommended deletion of 167 plants from the reparations list, the U.S., U.K. and French Agreement on Revised German Reparations Program of April 13, 1949, permitted the retention of 159 plants previously scheduled for removal as reparations.[83] Even after this partial retreat the most important and efficient German steel producing units remained on the list for eventual removal. But the Petersburg Agreement on November 22, 1949, led to a virtual suspension of reparations with the exception of a very few plants.[84] The death knell for reparations was sounded in April, 1951, when all reparations were stopped for good and the remaining links of the economic chains forged by White and Morgenthau were broken.[85]

SOME ECONOMIC IMPLICATIONS OF THE POSTWAR POLICY OF INDUSTRIAL DISARMAMENT

The advocacy of industrialization today is generally based on the argument that all advanced countries have a significant proportion of the working population in manufacturing. In under-developed countries the proportion is small. Because the income generated in manufacturing is higher than in agriculture, it pays to industrialize.[86] Another argument postulates that the growth of manufacturing is necessary to absorb the surplus population and to put partially idle hands into productive work. And another is that as real incomes grow people tend to spend increasing proportions of their incomes on nonagricultural products, which is likely to foster the growth of specialization in economic activity. Production of specialized outputs for the market is the inevitable concomitant of economic growth.

In postwar Germany the previously existing pattern of specialization was to be broken and unemployed industrial workers were to be sent to farms. The policy of industrial disarmament was a blueprint not for economic progress, higher output, and better standards of living, but the opposite.

To put the 1945–48 deterioration of German economic status in perspective, an attempt will be made to discuss the industrial disarmament in terms of stock of capital goods, technology, natural resources, and the role of government. Most economists agree that these variables are of crucial importance for economic development. It seems reasonable, then, to assume that industrial disarmament, the inverse of development, must also depend on these variables and the functional relations among them.

CAPITAL STOCK

The shortage of physical capital is a salient feature of all underdeveloped countries, for without substantial capital formation, chances are slim for rapid economic development. The very poverty of physical capital, as represented by low productivity and low per capita income, frustrates attempts to achieve a higher level of capital formation. Low savings and low investing propensities make it extremely difficult to reduce the already low levels of current consumption for needed capital formation. Breaking this vicious circle of underdevelopment has long been recognized as one of the most important goals of all planners for economic development.

The Allied policy of reparations, destruction and neglect strove to reduce the existing stock of German physical capital. Reparations in kind were regarded as the best way to strip Germany of capital equipment and to reduce her war-making capacity.[87] The peace in Europe was to be brought about by forcing vanquished Germany to lower her level of economic status. The policy of industrial disarmament, per se, implied some deinvestment, some deindustrialization, and some economic retrogression in Germany. The early Allied preoccupation with eliminating the German war potential led many high-level policy makers in Washington to forget, or willfully to overlook, the fact that war potential constitutes also recuperational potential.[88]

The effects of this oversight became clearly visible in 1947. The rapidly deteriorating German industry put all Western Europe into economic stagnation. The fallacy of building a strong Europe with a weak Germany became obvious as Germany's neighbors clamored for the products of her heavy industries, not textiles and toys.

NATURAL RESOURCES

Inaccessible and untapped natural resources in relation to the size of population are a common characteristic of over-all economic backwardness. Lack of available natural resources, jointly with the conspicuous absence of modern technology, manifests itself in low productivity of factors of production.

Germany, the Ruhr Valley in particular, is one of the greatest industrial centers of the world, and yet this region is conspicuously deficient in natural resources. Huge deposits of high-quality coal form the only exception. Everything else, from iron ore to food, must come from abroad in exchange for Ruhr products. Deprived of its coal and its imports of raw materials, semifabricates, and foodstuffs, the industrial heart of the Ruhr would stop beating.

Yet this was precisely the policy pursued by the British and Americans. The policy sanctioned exportation of coal to the victorious and liberated countries. Timber and scrap were also exported in considerable quantities. Figures for 1946, 1947, and 1948 show that the American and British zones of Germany were transformed from a raw material importing into a raw material exporting area. This was a complete reversal of the prewar pattern of foreign trade and in itself it is an indicator of the postwar economic dislocation. In 1936, for instance, 80 percent of the Reich's exports consisted of manufactured goods; [89] only 9 percent were raw materials, primarily coal. In 1946, raw materials made up 91 percent of all exports from the bizonal area and manufactured goods came to a trickle of 4 percent.[90]

After World War I, Lord Keynes warned the victorious powers that forced coal exports from Germany would disable her industrial operations.[91] But after World War II, the envisaged industrial disarmament did not call for any German economic contribution to the well-being of Western European nations. Wishful thinking for quite some time obscured a more realistic assessment of the Ruhr's position in the Western European economy.

TECHNOLOGY AND RESEARCH

Primitive technology, high labor-output and capital-output ratios, high real costs of production are further obstacles to economic development. Without large-scale introduction of skills and without technological proficiency economic development is unthinkable. Taken by itself, technological proficiency represents an important determinant of the economic capacity of a nation. The more advanced the technology, the greater the economic capacity, and vice versa.[92] With given resources, advances in technology are conducive to raising productivity. The important point to keep in mind is that technology is a direct condition of productivity and that "know-how," per se, represents one of the most important variables in the contemporary theory of economic development.

Germany has been known for her spectacular exploits in the applied and pure sciences in the past. The Ruhr, despite its niggardly endowment by nature, was almost magically transformed in the nineteenth century into one of the greatest and most productive industrial regions of the world through its extraordinary research facilities.[93]

With these considerations in mind, a consistent industrial disarmament policy of Germany implied considerable reduction of Germany's technological skills. Because technology and advances in it depend to a great extent on research, a special scientific disarmament program of Germany was drawn up.[94] Drastic measures were contemplated to cripple permanently

German pre-eminence in physics, chemistry and engineering, as outlined earlier in this chapter, and all laboratories whose work had been connected with the "building of the German war machine" were to be destroyed.

GOVERNMENT

Government action or inaction is of particular importance to economic growth. The maintenance of law, public education, and public health are some of the primary functions of every government. In addition, of course, control of the aggregate level of investment, employment, and minimization of economic fluctuations are some of the other important tasks which, singly and jointly, contribute to economic growth. However, if the government does too much, or too little, or the wrong things, economic growth will be retarded and economic stagnation or retrogression may follow.[95]

W. A. Lewis has singled out nine factors which may bring about economic decay: failure to maintain order, plundering the citizens, promoting exploitation of one class by another, placing obstacles in the way of foreign intercourse, neglecting the public services, excessive reliance on laissez faire, excessive control of economic activity, excessive spending, and embarking upon costly wars.[96] With the exception of the excessive reliance on laissez faire and the burden of costly wars, these factors are highly useful for throwing light on the ways the British and American military governments fostered economic retrogression in the bizonal area of Germany.

In the U.S. zone of occupation, far-reaching decentralization of political and economic administration was attempted as early as the fall of 1945. The three new states, Bavaria, Hesse, and Württemberg-Baden, were made responsible for all economic and political matters, subject to the supervision of the U.S. military government.[97] By way of contrast, the British military government fostered the growth of extreme centralization in economic and political matters. Only in the fall of 1946 did the British agree to the creation of German administration on lower levels of authority.[98]

Thus three levels of administration of differing competence, ability, and objectives existed next to each other. At the very top the Allied Control Council was decisive and, where agreement was possible, quadripartite legislation prevailed. In purely zonal matters, the respective military governments were in control. Under them were the German Länder governments with administrations on subordinate levels. But during the first two years of occupation German administrations had practically no legislative or executive authority and the respective military governments determined the course of events.[99]

The policy of industrial disarmament of Germany was executed within a system of direct controls that stifled initiative and blunted all economic incentives. The existing economic legislation favored city dwellers at the expense of the farmers and forbade all personal or commercial contacts with foreign countries. Allied requisitions of German homes, patents, and production secrets, together with the uncertainty caused by the expected reparations program, lamed the will to produce. The expected currency reform caused the business community to hoard goods. Plundering of German citizens—figuratively speaking—took place under a variety of pretexts. The aggregate result of such a policy was to reduce Germany to an economic morass.[100]

2

THE THEORETICAL AND INSTITUTIONAL BACKGROUND OF DIRECT CONTROLS

The arrest of the Dönitz government in May, 1945 closed the annals of the Third Reich. Having taken over supreme authority in occupied Germany, the Allied military governments instituted immediate changes in administrative, political, and social institutions. But they preserved virtually the entire body of Nazi economic legislation dealing with the stabilization of prices, wages, and rents, the rationing of consumer goods and foodstuffs, central allocation of manpower and raw materials, compulsory delivery quotas for farmers, and housing controls.[1]

In recent history, such direct controls have primarily been associated either with economic mobilization during war or with postwar reconversion. After World War II, the United Kingdom and Norway used direct controls to accelerate economic growth and to work off gradually the accrued wartime demand.[2] But in the case of Germany, investment programs and the rebuilding of German industry and cities were definitely not on the victors' immediate agenda. The first order of business was the military and industrial disarmament of Germany. Implementation of the policy of industrial disarmament was attempted within the framework of direct controls. Thus far, however, the use of direct controls for such purposes has escaped the attention of economists, although the case merits examination.

The official reason for the continuation of wartime controls was to prevent open inflation. An official American source stated that open "inflation would strike at the heart of Allied hopes for a democratic Germany." [3] Such a statement implies the use of controls to achieve certain political objectives, but this does not stand up under examination. In fact, it turns out to be mere window dressing as soon as one considers the Allied aim to enforce the policy of industrial disarmament described in Chapter I.

Obviously direct controls were important for the furtherance of the Allied policy of industrial disarmament. An understanding of the theory of direct controls is, therefore, indispensable, but in itself insufficient. Since the Allies took over the system of Nazi direct controls lock, stock, and barrel, it is equally important to describe the Nazi institutional framework.

1. Direct Controls During a Major War

During World War II, all major belligerents drastically changed the structure and orientation of their market economies. The imposition of direct or physical controls partially or entirely suspended the operation of market forces. Instead of the price mechanism, price, wage, and rent controls, rationing of consumer goods, and direct allocation of housing, manpower, and raw materials became the main pillars of the new economic structure.

In times of peace, the so-called market economies are primarily geared to the satisfaction of consumer demand. The pricing mechanism is the sole rationing agent both in the factors of production and in the consumer goods market.

With the onset of belligerency, the economic policy of a nation aims at maximum utilization of material and human resources for victory. Winning the war becomes the primary social objective of the nation, and everything else is subordinated to this goal.[4]

The previously cherished social values, which normally guided economic behavior in the marketplace, change. The making of money, the measuring of one's personal success, and the drive for profits and conspicuous consumption go temporarily out of fashion, and the economy becomes geared to the satisfaction of governmental requirements for war matériel. Many things which are right in peace become wrong in war, and such a shift in attitudes changes the structure of wants and the composition of the gross national product.

Wars are collective efforts and governments have always, to a smaller or greater degree, assumed responsibility for their direction. Moreover, since the Industrial Revolution, wars have also become more and more industrialized. This has tremendously increased the importance of manufacturing industries in determining the relative strength of nations. It is inconceivable that modern war could be fought without large metallurgical, engineering, and chemical industries.[5]

Beginning with the Civil War, armed conflicts have tended to become total wars. Total war is a matter of victory or annihilation, unconditional surrender and nothing short of it. To fight such wars a huge administrative effort by the government is as indispensable as the possession of heavy industries. The days are gone when kings and princes made and unmade wars with specific national or personal objectives in mind and total destruction of the enemy was seldom sought. Today major war is a matter of victory or death, with the result that the existing manufacturing capacity must be mobilized quickly and totally. A task of such magnitude cannot be entrusted to the market forces, and consequently the government must suspend the market mechanism by subjecting the economy to direct controls.[6]

Given this single objective, the distribution of resources between private and public uses, or between "guns" and "butter," can be brought about by a relatively simple formula. To achieve maximum striking power, resources for the private sector can be drastically cut. But even the urgency of military requirements does not justify crippling the civilian sector, on which the public sector of any war economy rests.[7]

The civilian population should receive the indispensable minimum of food and consumer goods to maintain health and incentive and the remaining resources can go to the war-goods sector of the economy. Under no circumstances can too little resources be allocated to the civilian sector, because ill-fed and ill-clothed civilians may seriously undermine the entire war effort. For this reason the choice in any war economy is never between "bread" and "guns" but always between "guns" and "butter." To sustain high motivation for war, available resources must be divided judiciously between the private and public sectors.

THE THREAT OF INFLATION

In wartime, government demand is urgent, credit is virtually unlimited, and there is no limit on government spending to obtain the necessary resources.[8] With a fully employed economy, in terms of manpower and resources, the aggregate demand exceeds aggregate supply at constant prices. This excess is known as the inflationary gap, and its control constitutes the very crux of the problem of a wartime economy. In the absence of direct controls there would be practically no limit to the rise in wages and prices. Government as a bidder with unlimited resources would attempt to obtain all the resources needed for the conduct of war. Scarcity of consumer goods would be reflected in high prices and, most likely, in high profits for the producers of such goods. The better-off classes would then obtain scarce consumer goods, while the poorer and weaker bidders would go empty-handed. In such circumstances the production of consumer goods would tend to be particularly lucrative, and the prospect of high profits would make producers of goods unessential to the war generous bidders for manpower and resources. Such continuous bidding would send prices and wages upward. The "real" income of the receivers of wages and fixed incomes, including the millions of servicemen's families, would decline, while the income of profit takers would tend to rise sharply. Declining real wages would surely promote labor unrest, for war profiteering has always been the object of particular resentment.

Continuously rising prices would tend to distort the distributive justice of scarce goods among the civilian population and diminish the motivation for war. The declining will to fight, in turn, might jeopardize the entire war effort. Apart from the social effects of a continuous wartime price-wage spiral, unrestrained price advances would greatly increase the cost of war and would probably degenerate into a hyperinflation.[9] All hyperinflations lead inevitably to a substitution of goods for money, reflecting the society's repudiation of the existing monetary unit. Absence of an effective unit of account makes a monetary economy impossible and a clumsy barter system replaces it. Because barter is incompatible with the division of labor and industrial specialization, breakdown of the monetary economy would have disastrous effects on total output.[10] No war economy can be kept going on a barter basis, and avoidance of such a calamity is one of the most important tasks of wartime administrations.

The surest way to avoid monetary chaos with all its consequences is by checking the excess demand of wartime by direct controls. Imposition of direct controls will prevent receivers of income from spending their money and will extract sufficient savings to match the wartime government expenditure. Only by preventing people from spending their earnings can consumption be curtailed and the necessary real savings, equal to the amount of factor incomes employed in the war sector, be obtained. Without such a policy open inflation during wartime is inevitable.[11]

Direct controls are a government's most powerful weapons for curtailing aggregate spending. Price, wage, and rent controls, coupled with rationing of goods, services, and housing space, allocation of factors by governmental agencies, and strict control over exports and imports are the most effective means for such purposes. Fixing of maximum prices, wages, and rents also keeps the costs of living stable and thus preserves the "real wage" of the labor force. Such stability eliminates the pitfalls of the wage-price spiral and minimizes social frictions during the war.

Furthermore, stability of prices and wages, together with a strict rationing, assures "rough justice" in the distribution of consumer goods.[12] Rationing of food generally takes place more on the basis of physical need than on demand. For instance, to determine rationing scales the available data on food requirements for different ages, sexes, and occupations can be used. Such criteria are also useful for the determination of supplementary food rations. Rationing of gasoline, electricity, and dwelling space is also based primarily on physical needs and not wants.

However, such egalitarian rationing can be assailed for its effects on labor incentives. Maintenance of incentives and raising the productivity of factors are important considerations during wartime and cannot be taken lightly. Consequently, a number of methods have been used in the past to set rationing quotas in accordance with the varying needs of individuals.

One method, known as differential rationing, was widely used in the United States to ration gasoline during World War II. The respective driving needs determined whether an individual would hold the A, B, or C card. Doctors, for instance, had C cards and were entitled to almost unlimited quantities of gasoline at fixed prices, while the so-called Sunday drivers, the holders of A cards, could buy limited quantities only.

Another way to ration scarce consumer goods is by point rationing. This method permits some freedom of choice in the spending of ration coupons for some specific goods. For example, butter, fats, and meats were so rationed that a buyer could choose among these items and spend his points as he wished. Point rationing was used in Nazi Germany up to 1942 for clothing.

Still another method is so-called value rationing. Great Britain, for instance, used this method for meat rationing. Under such a system, the consumer was permitted to spend a specific sum of money per week for meat. The sum varied weekly, depending upon the availability of meat. If the customer chose to buy cheaper cuts he could buy much greater quantities of meat than a customer who bought more expensive cuts.[13]

Without subjecting the various methods of rationing to detailed criticism, it can be noted that all of them suffer from certain drawbacks. For instance, the method of rationing based on needs offers great administrative conveniences, but it lowers the incentives of labor and does not offer any scope for individual choice. Differential rationing takes into account the varying needs of individuals, but it causes many administrative headaches and fosters corruption. Point rationing likewise permits some choice but cannot include too many items for it would then cause almost insoluble administrative problems. Value rationing offers advantages insofar as it permits thrifty individuals to obtain maximum benefit from the ration, but it ties the consumer to a given market. This, at least, was the British experience during World War II.[14]

No matter what method of rationing is used, both rich and poor get the most important consumer goods in limited quantities at a fixed price. Such wartime egalitarianism preserves the distributive justice and assures social peace at home.[15] With ample food rations, an assured supply of consumer goods, and a tax system which does not blunt incentives, price controls and rationing keep the aggregate civilian demand, in relation to the inelastic full employment output, to the minimum. In this way maximum amounts of resources can be channeled into the war sector.

However, sheer availability of resources is not enough. To make sure that deliveries of war material are made as fast as possible, the government also directs and commandeers the utilization of plants, stocks of raw materials, and all means of transportation.[16] In a total war nothing can be withheld, and governments assume sweeping powers to ensure that everything is done to maximize the war effort.

The key to wartime planning is the so-called bottleneck planning.[17] In the United States, for instance, priority allocations existed throughout the war for resources in short supply. A number of special commodities, such as steel, aluminum and copper, were subjected to minute administrative control.[18] Scarcity of manpower is generally the major bottleneck of any war economy, and for this reason manpower has to be husbanded most carefully. To meet the all-around increased demand for more manpower, governments generally conscript the entire working-age population and allow no one to take or leave a job without permission from the labor office.[19] Such compulsion appears to be necessary either to prevent or to limit the production of nonessentials during wartime.

Subjecting the war economy to direct controls is designed to check the tidal wave of demand. Under such a system of controls, physical dispositions become of paramount importance while the monetary factor is reduced to secondary importance. Direct controls do not eliminate excessive monetary demand but merely prevent it from influencing prices of consumer goods and factors of production. Rationing of consumer goods directly affects society's propensity to consume, while direct allocation of manpower and raw materials keeps in check the propensity to invest. The existence of the entire gamut of physical controls in conditions of excess monetary demand is, by definition, repressed inflation,[20] or, to use Galbraith's term, a disequilibrium system.[21]

Under repressed inflation, earning a monetary income does not automatically entitle its receiver to claim goods and services. Goods can be purchased only if currency is accompanied by rationing coupons, special purchase permits, or points. Monetary income, as far as it can be spent on legal purchases and rations, retains stable purchasing power. Those portions which cannot be spent legally due to a lack of coupons or points are deprived of legal purchasing power and must, perforce, be either saved or spent illegally. Thus, under a system of repressed inflation, two kinds of monetary incomes exist: first, incomes endowed with legal purchasing power; second, incomes rendered powerless for legal purchase. This excess income may, of course, be used for paying taxes and fees or for accumulating savings. The difference between income endowed with legal purchasing power and income without it constitutes the monetary overhang, or waiting purchasing power.[22]

Depending on the degree of repressed inflation or the comprehensiveness of direct controls, the waiting purchasing power will be large or small. The more universal the direct controls, the larger will be the amount of the waiting purchasing power and the greater will be the tendency for the marginal value of incomes above the legal expenditure level to fall to zero. In that case substitution of leisure for work will take place, with all the inevitable consequences of declining productivity and falling gross national product. On the other hand, if only a part of the economy is subject to direct controls while the other is free, incomes beyond legal expenditures can be used for purchases of goods in the uncontrolled sector of the economy at prevailing prices. Of course, the greater the free market, the greater the importance of making money and the greater the incentive to work.[23]

Although rationing of consumer goods and allocation of manpower and raw materials delimits physically the total aggregate civilian demand, taxation, direct and indirect, is an indispensable part of direct controls. Taxation is used to absorb purchasing power further, to curtail civilian demand further, and to release additional resources for war-essential industries. However, taxation for such purposes must be used with care. Taxation will mop up purchasing power, to be sure, but if taxes take away too large a portion of incomes earned, incentives to work and to produce will definitely be blunted. For instance, if wartime income taxes reduce the marginal dollar for overtime to less than the standard hourly rate of pay, workers will prefer leisure to overtime work. If such shifts in workers' attitudes occur on a considerable scale, the entire war production may be jeopardized. Since the size of gross national product is primarily determined by the size of the working population and the productivity of the labor force, falling average productivity of labor, withdrawal of overtime work, and rising rate of absenteeism may result in greatly reduced over-all output of goods and services. No belligerent can afford this.

To prevent such an unfortunate turn of events, J. M. Keynes

devised an ingenious scheme of deferred pay.[24] Although he was acutely aware of the shortcomings of wartime taxation, he wanted to tax as well as to preserve incentives. The "deferred pay" plan was his answer to this problem. The plan proposed to place a portion of current incomes in special accounts to be released only after the war. "Freezing" a part of wartime incomes, rather than taking it away in direct taxes, would preserve the incentive to earn money incomes and discourage a withdrawal of labor from the labor market while cutting the civilian demand and thus release the additional resources for the war effort. Though Keynes's plan was implemented only partially, it dramatized the part taxation can play in an overall scheme of direct controls.

To sum up: During a major war, direct controls aim at mobilizing resources at stable prices. Price, wage, and rent fixing, rationing of consumer goods, foodstuffs, and housing space, subsidies, direct allocation of manpower and raw materials, and export and import controls are the main physical controls. Price and wage fixing, jointly with the various rationing measures, is designed to preserve distributive justice and to keep down the costs of war. Rationing of food must provide the indispensable minimum diet for the preservation of health and stamina, while assurance of minimum supplies of necessary consumer goods helps to maintain incentives. Meeting these minimum civilian requirements has absolute priority over everything else.

2. The Salient Features of the Nazi Direct Controls

To understand the economic and social landscape of the British and American zones of occupied Germany prior to the currency reform of June, 1948, it is necessary to sketch the salient features of the Nazi economic machinery inherited by the Allied occupation forces.

The structure and functions of the Nazi economic system were far more complex than the Nazi sham-philosophy of races and the totalitarian political system. The philosophy was based on the assertion that humanity can be divided into superior and inferior races and that the law of nature requires that superior races rule over inferior ones. The Aryans, in general, and the German race, in particular, were said to be superior to all other races and therefore destined to be masters of the world. It was furthermore asserted that the indispensable precondition for the maintenance of German superiority was the preservation of the purity of the German race. Therefore, the highest duty of every German was to guard the racial purity and to promote the power of the Nazi state. Nations of inferior races must either become servants of Germanic races or be eliminated.[25] Hitler's ruthless and brutal attempt to remake Europe in accordance with this vision doomed to death millions of people all over the continent.

Nazi political institutions were tailored to this racist-collectivist philosophy. As soon as the Nazis took over in 1933 the existing political parties of the Weimar period were eliminated, the parliamentary processes were scrapped, and one-man rule was substituted for majority rule. With the Nazi Party firmly in the saddle the "One Realm, One Nation, One Führer" slogan subordinated everybody and everything to the state. The individual was effectively deprived of his rights and given only obligations instead; he became a mere tool of the Nazi state.[26]

In the economic sphere the Nazis were rather conservative, for they upheld the existing economic institutions. Private ownership of the means of production was recognized—the Nazis never attempted wholesale expropriation. In this manner they avoided duplication of the Soviet experiences. However, the preservation of private property was subject to many qualifications. For instance, the Nazi concept of private property had nothing to do with customary subjective property rights. The Nazi property law safeguarded the rights only of those persons who had an acceptable status in the Third Reich. All politically unreliable Germans and all Jews were deprived of their property during the Nazi "co-ordination" process.[27] Without introducing central planning of the Soviet kind, this wholesale reorganization of the existing property structure subjected the German industrial and agricultural economy to the iron grip of Nazi control.[28] Even though German businessmen continued to operate their businesses they were subject to supervision by the various control agencies. The Nazi drive for self-sufficiency in many commodities resulted in a flood of administrative regulations concerning the use of raw materials and the standardization of commodities. In this fashion, behind the façade of economic conservatism, the Nazis were bending the existing "private property to governmental purposes." [29]

THE STRUCTURE OF GOVERNMENT AGENCIES IN CHARGE OF THE INDUSTRIAL ECONOMY

After the seizure of power in 1933, the Nazi Ministry of Economics carried forward essentially the work of the former Weimar Ministry of Economics. It controlled foreign trade, supervised Germany's commercial policy, exercised foreign exchange control, and kept an eye on the activities of cartels. This ministry, with the Four-Year Planning Office, was also primarily responsible for assuring Germany's self-sufficiency in strategic raw materials.

Immediately below the Ministry of Economics was the National Economic Chamber. This institution was created in November, 1934, to direct the activities of the existing industrial organizations. The Nazis simply took over the functional and territorial business organizations of the Weimar Republic, re-organized them along the lines of the "leadership principle," and made membership in the National Economic Chamber compulsory for every firm.[30] The functional and territorial organizations of the National Economic Chamber were organized on a hierarchical basis. Its principal task was to put government policy measures into practice speedily and with a minimum of interference. It was an autonomous agency of public law, and it financed its activities through levies on its members.[31]

Each branch of the functional, or vertical, division of the National Economic Chamber embraced all firms of a given trade or industry. The national groups (*Reichsgruppen*) represented the highest authority in each field of activity. In 1939 there were seven national groups, one each for industry, trade, banking, insurance, power (electricity, water, gas), the tourist trade, and handicraft. The economic groups (*Wirtschaftsgruppen*) represented the middle level of authority. At the end of August, 1939, there existed forty-six economic groups, thirty-one for the entire manufacturing industry, from mining to food processing, and fifteen for trade, banking, insurance, power, and tourist groups.[32] On a lower administrative level were the 328 trade groups (*Fachgruppen*), which controlled individual industries such as coal mining and potash mining (under the economic group for all mining). At the lowest level were trade subgroups—there were 323 at the outbreak of World War II—which directly supervised the individual mines, factories, etc. in given areas.[33]

Under such a hierarchical structure, the policy-control network became highly centralized and the Nazi administration acquired a firm grip over the entire economy. The dovetailing of the subordinate economic organs into the National Economic Chamber was the tangible manifestation of the revamping of the German economy in accordance with the Nazi "leadership principle." The centrally directed and hierarchically structured economic administrative bodies were endowed with the power to enforce decisions of the state from the top down. The lower administrative organs, on the other hand, had complete responsibility to the higher administrative authority. In other words, all administrative authority came from the top down, and all administrative responsibility went from the bottom up.

. The three salient features of the industrial economy of the Third Reich were compulsory membership, the leadership principle, and the organic view of the various branches in the economy.[34] The specific objectives of the various branches were:

a) To inform the groups and subgroups on new substitute raw materials, new production methods, and latest developments in the given field of technology.

b) To assist the subordinate groups to develop uniform cost accounting methods.

c) To keep all the members informed about the market situation and matters of similar import.[35]

One reason for such a highly centralized economic structure was the Nazi quest for economic self-sufficiency. It was expected that a powerful centralized state, with an economy organized along hierarchical lines of authority, would be able to improve the strategic raw material situation by developing close substitute materials, by eliminating wasteful utilization of scarce materials in the industry, and by rigorous stockpiling measures. But in addition to these tasks the various economic groups also carried on their former trade association activities. Postwar examination of the records of the various Nazi economic groups has shown that they were much more successful in advising their members on foreign trade regulations, on fees and discounts, and on how to establish uniform cost accounting systems than in developing Germany's self-sufficiency in strategic raw materials.

The other division of the National Economic Chamber consisted of territorial economic bodies. In the Third Reich every business, regardless of size, was required to be a member of the local chamber of industry and commerce as well as of the appropriate functional group.[36]

The activities of local chambers touched all aspects of business life. In the field of price fixing, for instance, all applications for price changes or for setting prices for goods not previously produced were first examined by officers of the local chamber of industry and commerce. Their findings were forwarded to the respective price formation offices, which then decided on each application. The local chambers also distributed government orders to the firms, made regular reports on local economic conditions to the Ministry of Economics, and maintained close contact with all government agencies and the local Nazi Party.

On the middle administrative level of this territorial hierarchy were the economic chambers, twenty-three in number in 1939.[37] The number of economic chambers corresponded to the number of economic districts in the Third Reich, which varied with the expansion and contraction of the Reich. The economic chambers were the most important administrative bodies on the operational level, for they co-ordinated not only the activities of the local chambers of industry and commerce but the activities of the various functional groups of the National Economic Chamber in their respective districts. Such a co-ordination was almost indispensable because the existing territorial and functional organization of the German industrial economy gave rise to overlapping authority and a lack of clearly defined responsibility. All territorial bodies came under the Federation of the Chambers of Industry and Commerce (*Arbeitsgemeinschaft der Industrie-und Handelskammern*), which was directly subordinate to the National Economic Chamber.

This network of control for the German industrial economy continued essentially unchanged up to the end of 1941. But after two years of belligerency, rapidly growing wartime demands on the economy called for a more streamlined control of industrial production. The existing dual responsibility and overlapping authority between the functional groups and economic chambers was frustrating and not conducive to an effective mobilization of all available resources for war. To eliminate this source of administrative friction and waste, the Nazi government in 1942 created regional economic chambers (*Gauwirtschaftskammern*).[38]

The regional economic chambers became the administrative centers for the industrial economy in a given region (*Gau*). The existing local and district economic chambers and the functional groups on the middle administrative level were merged into the new regional economic chambers. The decree also provided that there should be one economic chamber for each region and that political boundaries of each region were to correspond to the economic boundaries of the *Gau*. This provision was particularly important in avoiding friction and administrative uncertainty between the party and economic administrators. The national groups were deprived of their authority to issue binding regulations upon their subordinate bodies and thereafter were strictly limited to functional matters in a given field of activity.[39]

In matters of over-all economic policy the functions of the groups on the middle and lower administrative levels were taken over by divisions of the regional economic chambers. Four divisions, one each for industry, trade, crafts, and tourism, performed the functional tasks in a given region. Banking, insurance, and power were not represented by a special department but by a district representative from the respective national groups. The purely administrative divisions of the regional economic chambers were primarily concerned with matters of law, taxes, prices and consultation.[40]

After this reorganization of the German industrial economy, the regional economic chambers became the centers of unified economic command and were directly subordinated to the Ministry of Economics.

THE REICHSSTELLEN

This description of the Nazi industrial economy would be incomplete without briefly mentioning the principal instruments of raw material control. With the exception of coal, potash, and some magnesium, Germany is deficient in important minerals. The list of raw materials which must be imported is long, and Germany's position as an industrial power is precarious for that reason. Her major natural resource is coal, located both in the Ruhr Valley and in Silesia. The Ruhr coal is of high quality and is particularly suited for making metallurgical coke. The Ruhr can provide all the coal and coke needed to feed blast furnaces of the gigantic metallurgical industries there, but most of the iron ore must come from abroad because iron ore deposits of Germany are negligible and of low quality. Other special minerals, such as nickel, molybdenum, vanadium and tungsten, which are indispensable for special steels, must also come from abroad. Absence of domestic bauxite (the basic raw material of the aluminum industry), copper, lead, manganese, mercury, mica, platinum, tin, sulphur, and pyrites indicates the heavy dependence of German industry on foreign sources of supply.[41]

In addition to this heavy dependence on other countries for foreign raw materials, Germany was not self-sufficient in food. From her own sources she could cover 80 percent of her requirements of grain and potatoes, but in fats and meats her dependence on foreign sources of supply was particularly heavy.

As soon as the Nazi government came to power, steps were initiated to increase Germany's self-sufficiency in strategic raw materials and food. Although concentrated efforts on this score commenced only in 1936, with the beginning of the second

Four Year Plan, raw material control was initiated as early as 1933. A number of special supervisory agencies (*Überwachungsstellen*) were set up to control imports of strategic raw materials. A drastic reduction of nonessential imports served well to husband dwindling German foreign exchange reserves and thus enabled the Nazis to pay for the most needed imports.

These supervisory agencies like the National Economic Chamber, were not governmental bodies but institutions of public law which covered their operating expenses by special levies and charges on firms doing business with them. "Statutory trade associations" [42] is another name given to these agencies, which were nominally under the over-all supervision of the Ministry of Economics but in fact were quite independent. While, at first, supervisory agencies primarily controlled imported raw materials, with time their responsibilities and powers grew until ultimately they were in complete command of domestically produced raw materials as well. The respective supervisory agencies had complete responsibility for the production, purchase, distribution, and utilization of raw materials. Furthermore, they issued priority allocation procedures, inventory regulations, and conservation measures for each raw material.[43]

The actual allocation of raw materials among firms took place on the basis of licenses, of which there were two kinds. All firms producing war-essential items obtained raw materials on the basis of licenses marked "urgent" from the respective supervisory agencies. The producers of other goods could claim raw materials on licenses of lower priority called "ordinary." Producers of such goods frequently had to follow detailed instructions on conservation, by-mixing procedures, and the use of substitute raw materials.

In 1939 the supervisory agencies were transformed into commodity control boards (*Reichsstellen*) and continued to operate under this name until the end of the Third Reich. Their number varied from time to time. In 1941 there were twenty-four boards for industrial raw materials and commodities, while the rest administered agricultural raw materials. The boards for industrial commodities were nominally under the Ministry of Economics, while those administering agricultural raw materials were under the Ministry of Food and Agriculture. At the beginning of the war, commodity control boards were given additional powers, and for a particular raw material the respective board represented the final authority on all matters of production, distribution, utilization, price fixing, profit margins, and granting of export and import licenses.[44] In 1944 there were twenty-nine control boards in existence that were responsible for providing firms with the necessary raw materials.[45]

STRUCTURE OF NAZI AGRICULTURE

In the course of its reorganization of the economy in quest of self-sufficiency, the government subordinated the business community to its administrative organs without instituting central planning. The Third Reich created a directed instead of a centrally planned economy. In propaganda terms, all these changes were necessary for the purposes of strengthening the German *Volksgemeinschaft,* the national community. This task implied steps to reduce Germany's dependence on foreign sources of food as well as raw materials. In fact, the achievement of self-sufficiency in food became a sacred goal of the Third Reich. For all intents and purposes, such measures were designed to increase Germany's military preparedness.

The Reich Food Estate

The agricultural economy of the Third Reich was under the over-all supervision and regulation of the Reich Food Estate (*Reichsnährstand*). This agency was created in 1933 as an institution of public law, and its primary objective was to step up the domestic production of food.[46] Detailed planning of production, wholesale introduction of scientific production methods, and a vigilant propaganda were some of its methods.

The structural organization of the Reich Food Estate was similar to that of the Reich Economic Chamber, described earlier. All firms engaged in agriculture, horticulture, fisheries, hunting, food processing, and food trade on the wholesale or retail level were subject to mandatory membership.[47] The Reich Food Estate, like the Economic Chamber, consisted of territorial and functional divisions which reflected the unrestricted "leadership principle." [48] The functional division was in charge of the distribution and utilization of agricultural produce, while the territorial division controlled production through territorial farmers' associations.

The Vertical Organization of the Reich Food Estate

The functional division of the Reich Food Estate covered everyone concerned with producing, processing and distributing specific primary commodities. All such firms were vertically organized into market associations (*Marktverbände*), which for all practical purposes constituted a compulsory cartel. In 1943 there were ten central associations (*Hauptvereinigungen*), the highest division of the market associations, controlling the following: grain, meat and livestock, milk and dairy products, potatoes, eggs, horticulture, viticulture, hops and breweries, sugar, and fish and fish products.[49]

Subordinate to each central association were regional economic unions (*Wirtschaftsverbände*), which were the actual executive and administrative agencies on the middle level. The boundaries of these Regional Economic Unions corresponded to the boundaries of the *Land* peasants' associations, the territorial bodies of the Reich Food Estate.

In their day-to-day operations regional economic unions

maintained a close working alliance with the peasants' associations. For instance, the regional economic union for livestock and meat united all livestock farmers, dealers, butchers, producers, and processors of meat products of a given region. It also handled the distribution and consumption of meat products jointly with the *Land* peasants' associations. The regional economic union for milk and dairy products likewise embraced all milk producers and dealers of a given area. It assigned to each milk producer a specific dairy to which he had to sell milk and regulated the utilization of milk, fixed the price, and charged an equalization fee to those farmers whose milk could be sold in liquid form. The proceeds of such levies were used to pay subsidies to milk producers who were located too far away from the market and where it was necessary to turn milk into butter or cheese. Together with the central associations, the regional economic unions were responsible for determining the regional quotas to be allotted to the various *Land* peasants' associations.

On the lowest administrative level, the so-called subeconomic unions (*Unter-Verbände, Marktbeauftragte*) performed these functions at the grass-roots level.

Each market association had sweeping powers for the collection and distribution of a particular commodity. Again, the channels of command came from the top down and the responsibility went from the bottom up. Although membership in the functional division of the Reich Food Estate was mandatory, the market associations covered their operating costs through levies, dues, and fees.

While the market associations were primarily responsible for the distribution and utilization of the various domestically produced commodities, the importation of agricultural commodities was the responsibility of commodity control boards for corn and feed, milk and dairy products, fats and oils, meats and meat products, eggs, and fish. In their early period these boards protected the domestic market from cheaper foreign products by foreign exchange control and import licensing. However, after the outbreak of World War II, as more uniform regulations for the entire market became indispensable, the control boards were merged with the already existing central associations and functioned as divisions of the central associations.[50]

The Horizontal Organization of the Reich Food Estate

The other division of the Reich Food Estate consisted of purely territorial organizations of German agriculture. Its chain of command was also hierarchical. On the very top was the Reich Food Estate with its administrative apparatus, including the principal territorial organs of control. The territorial control was actuated through three departments. Department I, called "The Peasant," was concerned with social and political aspects of farmers' life. Department II, called "The Farm," was interested in raising the productivity of German agriculture by introducing new methods of production and making available better seeds and fertilizers. Department III, called "The Market," was in charge of sales, distribution, and storage of farm products. It is significant that this administrative structure was duplicated on lower administrative levels in all territorial organizations.

Below the Reich Food Estate were the *Land* peasants' associations (*Landesbauernschaften*), which maintained over-all production controls in their territories. Their specific task was to supervise the activities of the district peasants' associations (*Kreisbauernschaften*), which with the subordinate local peasants' associations (*Ortsbauernschaften*) operated at the grass-roots level and were the principal executive arms of the *Land* peasants' associations. The district peasants' associations were responsible for supply of farm labor, farm productivity, and tight control of farm records, which showed farmers' actual deliveries against assigned quotas. The local peasants' associations operated a system of homestead cards for the production and determination of the delivery quotas for the individual farm. They also checked the actual fulfillments of the delivery obligations by frequent farm visits. The orders of the territorial division of the Reich Food Estate were binding upon its lower echelons, and to the individual members they had the force of law. The Reich Food Estate had the power to impose fines of up to 100,000 Reichsmarks and to confiscate property as well. In 1938, there were 20 *Land* peasants' associations, 515 district peasants' associations, and 55,000 local peasants' associations.[51]

With minor modifications this system of regional control existed up to the very end of the Third Reich, and in the postwar period it was taken over by the four powers of occupation.

OFFICE OF THE PRICE COMMISSIONER

As soon as the Nazi government took over it launched massive public works programs to bring the economy out of depression. Countercyclical spending was designed to raise the level of national income and employment, yet it was hoped that monetary and fiscal authorities would be able to keep prices and wages stable. After the hyperinflation of 1923 the Germans remained particularly sensitive to price rises, and the Nazi government was determined to safeguard the stability of the Reichsmark at all costs. During the first three years of Nazi rule the existing network of prices of the Weimar period was adequate for such purposes; however, as employment continued to rise and industry reached capacity operations, labor shortages developed and pressures for higher wages and prices mounted. Existing legislation was inadequate to stem the rising tide. To assure price stability and to avoid a new wage-price spiral, all previous selective controls were superseded by a general wage freeze and a special Reich Commissioner for Price Control was appointed. On November 26, 1936, the Price Commissioner issued the Price Stop Decree, which became the basis of the entire price control system of the Nazi government.[52] The decree froze all prices for goods and services retroactively to October 18, 1936, which was also the beginning date of the Second Four Year Plan.[53]

The setting up of maximum prices alone does not assure price stability. Corollary measures, such as prohibition of combination sales and the production of inferior grade products at old prices, were adopted. The price fixing authorities knew from experience that attempts to freeze prices of goods below their potential levels always resulted in the appearance of so-called "new commodities," that is, items which had not been produced prior to the "freezing" date. From the manufacturers' point of view, production of "new commodities" was one way to obtain higher prices despite the general price freeze. The government decreed that items which had not been produced on October 18, 1936, would be assigned maximum prices applicable to similar commodities, with necessary adjustments for unavoidable cost increases. In the absence of a similar commodity maximum prices would be determined on the basis of legal maximum prices of raw materials and wages.

Although prices of agricultural commodities were nominally under the jurisdiction of the Price Commissioner, the actual price fixing in this field was delegated either to the Ministry of Food and Agriculture and the Reich Food Estate or to the market associations.

Some prices were uniform throughout the Reich or throughout certain sections. For instance, there were twenty regions for rye and wheat, fourteen for barley, and two for edible fall potatoes. Prices differed slightly in each of these, being lower in the east and higher in the west. As a rule, fixed prices were applicable only at the agricultural producers' stage, while in the later stages of production or distribution maximum prices were fixed either in terms of maximum wholesale and retail markups over costs or were predetermined.

The administered prices, cartel prices, and resale price maintenance agreements were put under the over-all authority of the Reich Price Commissioner. For instance, any new cartel price which, when compared with the old price, would cause disadvantage to the buyer required the approval of the Price Commissioner. During the prewar period, cartel prices were usually fixed on the basis of the highest-cost cartel member. After the outbreak of World War II the Price Commissioner ruled that, to keep down the costs of war and to reduce the cost of living, cartel prices would have to be based on the costs of the average-cost cartel member. Administrative pressures continued, and on July 27, 1942, some cartel prices went down.[54]

Prices in government contracts were determined on a cost-plus basis. The LSÖ regulations (*Leitsätze für die Preisermittlung auf Grund Selbstkosten bei Leistungen für öffentliche Auftraggeber*), used principally for munitions and armaments, spelled out the allowable cost items and prescribed steps for the determination of costs. Profits were restricted to a specified percentage yield on a rigidly defined "necessary" capital.

The earlier version of the cost-plus system was modified in February, 1942, when the Price Commissioner and the Minister of Armaments and War Production established a uniform price group system for government war contracts. Costs of the most efficient producers, classified as Price Group I producers, were used as the basis for fixing uniform prices for war-important items. For the higher-cost producers of the same item as many as five price groups were established. Firms belonging to Price Group I were given preferential treatment in terms of lower taxes and priorities in the allocation of labor and raw materials.

In 1943 this system was extended to certain consumer goods industries.[55]

In addition to these general provisions, the Price Stop Decree contained other regulations worth mentioning. At the retail and wholesale level, three types of maximum markups over costs were permissible:

a) Specified maximum percentages were used for wholesale and retail sales of furniture and shoes and for retail sales of textiles and apparel.

b) Base period percentages were used to determine wholesale trade margins as for instance in the textile industry. The actual percentage margins taken during a specified period of 1939 served as a base.

c) Prices were allowed to be fixed at stipulated "Mark-and-pfennig" amounts over costs. Subject to such "Mark-and-pfennig" markups were agricultural prices at the retail level as well as prices of matches, soap, automobile repair and towing services, bricks, wastepaper, scrap iron, and silver products.

According to official Nazi sources,[56] the drive for self-sufficiency, with its corollary economic and social objectives, necessitated the great price freeze of 1936. The social goals aimed at the maintenance of real wages and the avoidance of a continuous wage-price spiral with its inevitable social tensions and class warfare. On the economic plane, the price freeze attempted to prevent speculation in scarce commodities, to stimulate exports, and to protect domestic agriculture.

To assure an effective system of price control, a tight network of supervision was erected. The Nazi government did not wish to rely on moral suasion as a principal safeguard. From the outset the Reich Price Commissioner was authorized to prosecute violators quickly and severely. Violators were frequently prosecuted not on criminal charges but for economic and political offenses against the state. In cases of serious violations the Commissioner was authorized to declare the violator a nationally dangerous element (*Volksschädling*) and fine, close, or confiscate the violator's property.[57] Later on, especially during the war, flagrant violations of the price fixing regulations or evasions of rationing controls were made subject to the death penalty.[58] "Economic misbehavior" was regarded from time to time as a capital offense.

The administrative structure under the Reich Price Commissioner, like the other agencies considered, was hierarchical, with regional, district, and local offices. Regional price control, which in most cases extended over the administrative limits of a German state or Prussian province, was entrusted to the price formation offices (*Preisbildungstellen*). The number of price formation offices was constantly in a state of flux, but there were thirty-six in 1942.[59] These agencies were generally attached to the offices of Nazi national governors and Prussian provincial presidents.

To avoid undue centralization, prices for goods of regional importance were fixed by price formation offices and not by the Reich Price Commissioner. These offices were also responsible for fixing prices of new products and for setting higher prices in case the 1936 price caused financial hardship. Yet the price formation offices were responsible neither for prices of agricultural goods, as noted earlier, nor for prices of industrial goods of cartels, which were set by the commodity control boards (*Reichsstellen*).

On the lower administrative level were the price supervision offices (*Preisüberwachungsstellen*), the number of which was seventy-three in 1942. These agencies were generally attached to the offices of the Subprovincial Presidents (like the *Regierungspräsident* of Schleswig-Holstein) and had two principal tasks. First, through continuous price supervision and reporting, they supplied the necessary data to price formation offices to enable them to determine prices.[60] Second, they were charged with the enforcement of existing price legislation and the apprehension and punishment of violators. They were authorized to use the police and to impose unlimited fines,[61] but they could not fix or change prices.

Subordinate to the price supervision offices were the price offices (*Preisstellen*), 1,140 in number in 1942. Price offices in the cities were usually attached to the offices of chief mayors and in the countryside to the offices of county managers. They were primarily concerned with the day-to-day enforcement of the existing price regulations and could impose fines of up to RM 1,000 and close operations of the violator for ten days, or both.

After the introduction of the price freeze of 1936, market forces were suspended but not completely eliminated. The determination of prices, new and old, was usually done by administrative fiat on the basis of cost plus a reasonable profit. To simplify the process of price fixing many products were standardized, many luxury items were completely eliminated, and high profit margins were forbidden. In many cartelized industries, the Reich Price Commissioner ordered the establishment of so-called guiding prices to eliminate unjustified profits.

TABLE 1. German Wholesale Prices and Cost of Living Indices.

(1913–14 = 100)

Year	Wholesale prices of industrial goods (means of production and consumer goods)	Cost of living index
1936	104.1	124.5
1937	105.9	125.1
1938	105.7	125.6
1939	106.9	126.2
1940	110.0	130.1
1941	112.3	133.2
1942	114.4	136.6
1943	116.2	138.5
1944	117.6	141.4

Source: Länderrat des Amerikanischen Besatzungsgebietes, *Statistisches Handbuch von Deutschland, 1928–1944* (F. Ehrenwirth Verlag, 1949), pp. 460, 463.

Despite the price freeze many price adjustments were made, but on the whole, as shown by Table 1, prices remained remarkably stable up to the very end of the Third Reich.

In 1936, when all prices of goods and services were frozen, the cost-of-living index stood almost 25 percent higher than at the beginning of World War I, while the wholesale price index stood only 4 percent higher. From 1936 to 1944 the two indices moved almost in step; the wholesale price index went up 13 percent, the cost-of-living index 14 percent. This was rather remarkable in view of the terrible destruction of German cities and the losses which Germany suffered in the last two years of war.[62]

WARTIME ADMINISTRATION

Shortly before the outbreak of hostilities in the late summer of 1939, sweeping administrative changes took place in the Ministry of Economics and the Ministry of Food and Agriculture. To strengthen and unify the chain of economic command for war the decree of August 27, 1939,[63] subordinated to the Plenipotentiary for the Four Year Plan the Ministries of Economics, Food and Agriculture, and Labor, and the Reich Price Commissioner as well. The decree also placed the Reich Food Estate under the over-all direction of the Ministry of Food and Agriculture. Thus with one stroke of the pen Göring became the economic dictator of the Third Reich.

With the introduction of wartime rationing of goods and services, the Ministry of Economics became responsible for the production and distribution of all essential goods to the civilian population and the armed forces. The actual production of munitions and armaments was administered by the armed forces' War Economy and Armament Office and the Ministry of Armament and Munitions.[64]

THE SYSTEM OF ECONOMIC OFFICES

To discharge tasks of such magnitude it was necessary to give the Ministry of Economics subordinate administrative organs on the middle and lower levels of authority. Only with a direct chain of command all the way down to the consumer would it be possible to have a closely knit administration. With these objectives in mind, a few days before the outbreak of actual hostilities *Land* economic offices were created as direct administrative arms of the Ministry of Economics on the middle level of administration.

The *Land* economic offices represented the highest authority in economic matters in all German states or Prussian provinces. As such, they were either attached to the offices of the national governors or to the presidents of various states or provinces. Fig. I indicates the administrative structure of wartime economic command.

As can be seen from the organizational chart, the wartime industrial economy was under the joint over-all direction of the Ministry of Economics and the commodity control boards for industrial commodities. Each commodity control board had the entire responsibility for the control, production, supervision of inventories and distribution of a given raw material. In such a manner, commodity control boards were the principal control organs of the Ministry of Economics.

The *Land* economic offices, twenty-nine in number in 1941,[65] supervised manufacturing, trade, banking and insurance, rationed the consumption of coal and oil, and administered scrap collection and utilization. Since they were also responsible for industrial production, their principal activity was to secure the needed raw materials from the commodity control boards and to distribute them among the various claimants. They were also

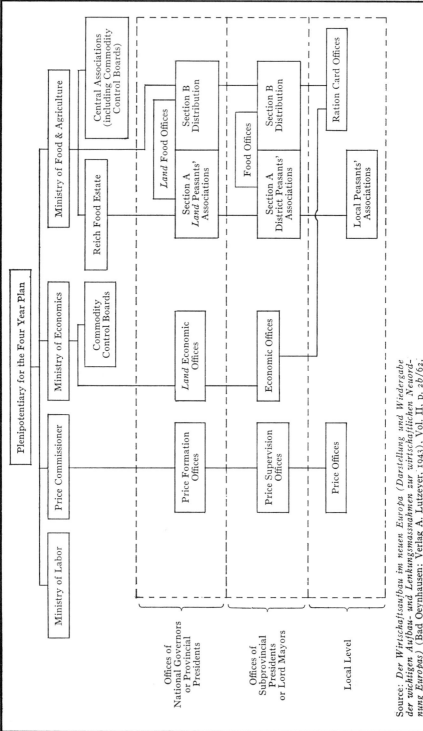

Source: *Der Wirtschaftsaufbau im neuen Europa (Darstellung und Wiedergabe der wichtigen Aufbau- und Lenkungsmassnahmen zur wirtschaftlichen Neuordnung Europas)* (Bad Oeynhausen: Verlag A. Lutzeyer, 1943), Vol. II, p. 2b/62.

responsible for adequate supplies of labor, equipment, power, and transportation.

On a lower administrative level the work of the Ministry of Economics was performed by economic offices (*Wirtschafts-ämter*). They functioned on a subprovincial level, and as such were either part of the county offices or the lord mayor's offices in the cities. The principal duties of the economic offices consisted of the supervision and distribution of rationed industrial goods and the collection and utilization of scrap.[66] On the grass-roots level of administration, the various card-issuing offices formed the last link in the hierarchy.

THE CHAIN OF FOOD OFFICES

Without a closely knit administration an efficient rationing of food is impossible. Because the Ministry of Food and Agriculture did not have agencies of its own on the middle and lower levels of administration, reorganization along the lines of the Ministry of Economics was effected shortly before the outbreak of hostilities in 1939.

The Ministry of Food and Agriculture, jointly with commodity control boards of agricultural products, represented the highest authority in the field of agriculture. To avoid administrative overlap the Reich Food Estate's merger with the Ministry was completed on the middle and lower administrative levels, but at the very top the main administration of the Reich Food Estate remained intact throughout the war.[67]

On the middle level of authority were the *Land* food offices, which were directly subordinated to the Ministry of Food and Agriculture. Each *Land* or Prussian province had one such office, and it represented the final authority in all food matters on this level. On a lower administrative level were the food offices, which were generally attached to the offices of the subprovincial Presidents and lord mayors. On the lowest level, thousands of offices for the distribution of ration cards formed the final and most important link between the Ministry of Food and Agriculture and the wartime consumer.

All food offices consisted of two sections, A and B. Section A was responsible for the over-all supply of agricultural products and section B was in charge of distribution and rationing. In the *Land* food offices section A was formed by the *Land* peasants' associations and the corresponding sections of the lower food offices were the district peasants' associations. Section B, on the *Land* level, was set up by the highest administrative organs in the *Land* or province, and on the district level by the lord mayors in the cities or district presidents in the country. Chiefs of the *Land* food offices were the *Land* peasants' leaders, who at the same time were also in charge of section A. On the district level, the district peasants' leader similarly was in charge of section A as well as the entire food office. In such a way, a tight and closely knit system of production control and distribution was available at the beginning of World War II.

Before the war, commodity control boards had the authority to buy and sell on their own account, while central associations, primarily concerned with production and purposeful utilization of agricultural produce, had no such powers. With the outbreak of hostilities some commodity control boards, such as those for grain and grain products, were merged with the corresponding central association as its business agent. The Ministry of Food and Agriculture worked directly with central associations and prepared the production and distribution plans for the various agricultural products.

Section A of the *Land* food offices was responsible for the implementation of these plans. But all administrative instructions to Section A of the *Land* food offices and to the *Land* peasants' associations still came from the Reich Food Estate. This agency's personnel were incorporated into the various Section A's and coped with such problems as maintenance of agricultural productivity, timely deliveries of the produce, and supply of agricultural labor, machines, gasoline, seeds, and equipment.[68]

However, the distribution arm, Section B, of the *Land* food offices was directly subordinated to the Ministry of Food and Agriculture, and these sections issued direct instructions to the Section B's below. This arrangement gave rise to much inconvenience and double authority.

The basis for the wartime rationing of food was the decree of August 27, 1939, which requisitioned all agricultural products for the state except certain amounts for the farmers' use, seed, and fodder. The link between the farmer-producer and the non-farmer-consumer was forged through food ration cards. All farmers were assigned delivery quotas based on the size of the farm, quality of the soil, and the nature of the crops. To assure effective control over production and delivery, Section A of all food offices kept the so-called Homestead Cards. Frequent farm visits were made by appointed fellow farmers, usually members of the Nazi Party, to check actual deliveries, and during the war delivery quotas were met scrupulously. The fact that fellow farmers and not policemen controlled farm production and deliveries was one of the reasons for the system's unqualified success. Another reason was that throughout the war there was no appreciable shortage of agricultural workers because of the use of prisoners of war and foreign workers.

Agricultural machinery and spare parts were produced in great quantities up to 1943. The Ministry of Food and Agriculture negotiated directly with commodity control boards and thus was able to obtain considerable quantities of steel and iron for farm equipment.[69] Likewise, up to the very end of the war German agriculture was well supplied with fertilizers.

Consumers surrendered rationing coupons to retailers to obtain weekly allotments of rationed foodstuffs. Retailers submitted the coupons to the respective food offices in order to obtain a purchase permit to replenish supplies. This process was repeated in each rationing period. The flow of returned coupons enabled the Ministry of Food and Agriculture to determine requirements for the various foodstuffs and to take timely steps to avoid bottlenecks.

The rationing levels for the normal consumer remained adequate until the transportation system was disrupted in the last weeks of the Third Reich. Before the war Germans consumed an average of roughly 3,000 calories daily. From 1941 to 1942 the rations stood close to 2,500 calories per day and in 1943–44 went down to 2,200 calories per day. In January, 1945, the food ration of the "normal" consumer declined to 1,721 calories, but workers still received 2,150 calories per day.[70]

3

AGRICULTURE IN A SYSTEM OF
POSTWAR ECONOMIC CONTROL

The purpose of this chapter is to explain how the postwar system of agriculture control worked and to examine more carefully the implications of postwar food shortages to the German economy.

Throughout the war German agricultural production was maintained at relatively high levels, both in terms of total output and in terms of yields per hectare.[1] It was only in the last year of war that the average yields per hectare declined 10–15 percent below the prewar yields, primarily because of lower allocations of fertilizers.

An assured, adequate supply of farm machinery, consumer goods, and fertilizers, together with price policies were chiefly responsible for the high agricultural output during the war. The closely knit administration of wartime agriculture also played a decisive role in maintaining an efficient system of food collection.

Tight supervision over the entire distribution system was, in turn, responsible for the preservation of reasonably adequate rationing levels almost to the very end of the Third Reich.

After the defeat, the ensuing administrative vacuum threatened to disrupt the previously existing system of farm production, collection, and distribution. The elimination of the Reich Ministry of Food and Agriculture at the top and the division of Germany into four watertight zones of occupation created uncertainty and wrought administrative havoc. On the middle level of administration, the existing territorial and functional bodies of the Reich Food Estate either disintegrated with defeat or could not resume operations for sheer lack of personnel. In the immediate post-surrender period the antifascist crusade was pervasive. Many competent but Nazi-implicated administrators and technicians either were arrested or went into hiding.

Farming operations were hampered by extensively mined fields, damaged buildings, and a shortage of farm hands. Former POW's, displaced persons, and elements of ill repute roamed the countryside, burning, robbing, pillaging, and murdering. Under such circumstances farmers were primarily concerned with the preservation of life and property. Only toward the end of summer, 1945, could farmers resume full-time farming.

In cities and towns the situation was even more desperate. At the end of hostilities most German cities were in ruins. The Third Reich's total defeat was clearly reflected in the utter collapse of all city administrations. Life had to be started anew, so to speak. In the West this task fell to military government teams of the Anglo-American forces. To get life going again amid the rubble was a difficult task; here the British and American engineers frequently performed veritable miracles in restoring essential public utilities. The military government also appointed the first public officials, reorganized police forces, and instilled life into inert city administrations.

The most important task of all newly appointed city administrators was to feed the population. In the absence of any clearly defined authority, towns and cities simply took over the already existing institutions of food collection and distribution. The British and American military governments kept, on an ad hoc basis, all functional and territorial agencies of the Reich Food Estate as well as the wartime system of food offices. The entire gamut of Nazi institutions for food production, collection, and distribution survived the unconditional surrender virtually intact, although frequently without the personnel who had staffed these institutions.[2]

From the beginning of the occupation the shortage of food was the most pressing problem in the American and British zones. In the food surplus areas, such as Bavaria and Württemberg-Baden, the situation was not as desperate as in the highly industrialized Ruhr Valley or the major ports, such as Hamburg and Bremen in the British zone. To alleviate the immediate post-defeat food shortages the Allied forces released some 600,000 tons of grain from military stocks for the German population in the American, British, and French zones of occupation. Half this amount was distributed in the American zone, while the rest went to the British and French zones. But in spite of this generous emergency assistance, the actually distributed rations fell to less than 1000 calories per day.[3] This level of nutrition unquestionably was highly inadequate.

In the summer of 1945, officials of the American and British military governments realized the need for a central German administrative apparatus to cope with the almost desperate food situation. The approaches to this task differed widely between the two powers. The Americans favored the decentralized method, according to which the newly created states in the respective territories would perform the duties of the Reich

Ministry of Food and Agriculture. The British insisted on tight centralization with direct executive organs all the way down to the lower levels. With the conflict unresolved, two distinct systems developed in the two zones.

1. German Central Office for Food and Agriculture in the British Zone [4]

In the British zone, full utilization of agricultural resources and a balanced distribution of food were the two most pressing problems at hand. An over-all food plan was necessary to create order out of chaos. British military government officials knew that without the assistance of German food experts it would be futile to hope for a considerable improvement.

In the summer of 1945, the British military government set up a team of German food specialists—the German Inter-regional Food Allocation Committee, or GIFAC for short—to assist it.[5] GIFAC had no executive functions of any kind. Its principal task was to produce an adequate food distribution plan for the British zone. The existing food surpluses were to be channeled into food-deficient areas such as the Ruhr Valley and Hamburg. This was an extremely difficult task because in the summer of 1945 food autarky was spreading rapidly in all districts, each of which had an export embargo on food.[6]

GIFAC worked hard to put an effective end to such practices, and on October 15, 1945, uniform rationing scales were introduced for the entire British zone of occupation. Rationing levels, however, remained extremely low. In the absence of any substantial food imports, and with no responsible German administrative agency in existence, the food situation deteriorated rapidly. To improve matters, the British Military Government decided to create a German Central Food Administration.

In January, 1946, Dr. H. Schlange-Schöningen, the Minister of Food and Agriculture during the Weimar Republic, was appointed to head the new agency.[7] At first this agency was to serve only in an advisory capacity, but the terms of reference to Schlange-Schöningen indicated that his agency was soon to assume executive functions similar to those formerly exercised by the Reich Ministry of Food and Agriculture and the Reich Food Estate. On July 10, 1946, Schlange-Schöningen's agency was vested with executive authority over all *Land* food offices, *Land* peasants' associations and marketing associations, including their subordinate agencies. As of August 1, 1946, the German Central Office for Food and Agriculture in the British zone, known as ZEL, became responsible for the production, collection, distribution, rationing, and price control of agricultural products and for the supply of farm implements and machinery to the agricultural community in the British zone.[8] The agency also had authority over German food and agriculture at the *Land* and lower levels of administration.

To revitalize the agricultural market structure, ZEL ordered the formation of eight new central boards (*Hauptstellen*) to replace the central associations (*Hauptvereinigungen*) of the Reich Food Estate. New Central Boards were set up for grains and feeds, cattle and meats, milk, fats and eggs, potatoes, garden produce, sugar, fish, and liquors and beer.[9] As described in Chapter II, Central Associations were functional divisions of the Reich Food Estate, which embraced all producers of a specific commodity on all stages of production. Each functional agency of the Reich Food Estate was endowed with sweeping powers over the production, collection, and distribution of the particular commodity. In the hierarchy of Nazi economic order, with all the authority coming from the top, this system worked smoothly and efficiently.

The new central boards resembled the central associations, although there were some differences. In contrast to the central associations, the central boards did not require all firms to maintain membership in them; nevertheless each central board embraced all concerns producing or distributing a particular product. The new boards were corporations of public law, and they paid their way through levies, fees, and dues. The central boards were not legally successors of the central associations, but in terms of functional tasks the similarity between them was unmistakable. In the provinces, central boards controlled the activities of the economic boards (*Wirtschaftsstellen*),[10] which were supposed to do the work of the former regional economic unions (*Wirtschaftsverbände*). The administrative continuity between the old and new agencies was preserved simply by endowing the central boards with the rights and obligations of the central associations.

The postwar reorganization of the agricultural market structure adapted the wartime system of the Reich Food Estate to postwar conditions. But in the course of postwar administrative reorganization ZEL was not given direct executive organs in the provinces and had to rely on the administrative organs of the newly created *Länder* of the British zone for the execution of its directives. ZEL thus was handicapped in enforcing its instructions down to the farmers. It was an open secret that the *Land* administration frequently violated and resisted ZEL's directives.[11] The absence of a direct chain of command was to some extent responsible for the uninterrupted flow of foodstuffs into illegal channels.

Industrial stagnation, decentralized administration, and acute, widespread food shortages wrought havoc with the instructions of ZEL. The *Länder* simply refused to be subservient to ZEL, because administrative obedience amounted to giving up food surpluses and receiving nothing in return. Also, after the postwar introduction of the ballot, public officials in charge of food and agriculture paid considerable attention to the

wishes of the electorate. Agricultural areas such as Niedersachsen grew more and more "food autarky minded," while the
Ruhr Valley was absolutely dependent on food imports.
Schlange-Schöningen led a ceaseless struggle against the "food
autarky" attitude but never really managed to pull the tug-of-
war in ZEL's favor.

From the beginning of the occupation it was obvious to the
Anglo-American authorities that without substantial food imports starvation would be inevitable in their zones. In the
summer of 1945 considerable shipments of grain from the
SHAEF stocks had already been made. In 1946 these emergency measures were replaced by a regular large-scale food
importation program. The size, nature, and origin of these imports were determined exclusively by the American and British
food officers in their respective zones of occupation. After the
fusion of the two zones on January 1, 1947, all such decisions
were made by the Bipartite Board of Food and Agriculture.

In the British zone, ZEL took possession of imports only
after their arrival in German ports. For purposes of speedy and
balanced distribution of imported foodstuffs among the various
claimants, ZEL set up six import boards (*Einfuhrstellen*),
which resembled to some extent the commodity control boards
(*Reichsstellen*) of the Third Reich. As of September 1, 1946,
import boards for grains and feeds, cattle and meats, fats and
eggs, potatoes, fish, and garden products became solely responsible for the importation and storage of the respective products.[12] Although the import boards were not legal successors
of the former commodity control boards, they took over the
equipment, buildings, and claims of the latter. Unlike the Nazi
boards they had no foreign exchange at their disposal—the
British or American governments paid the bill. Since virtually
no food reserves of any kind existed, speedy channeling of imported grain into the industrial emergency areas was the most

important consideration. During the first three postwar years Germans lived virtually from "ship to mouth," to use an epigram of Schlange-Schöningen.[13]

A description of postwar German agriculture would be incomplete without mentioning the former territorial organs of the Reich Food Estate, which were also taken over. Minor changes were made in them during the postwar reorganization of the German administrative structure, but their functions remained essentially the same as during the war. The principal difference arose from the division of Germany into four military zones of occupation.

In the American zone, three new German states were set up in the fall of 1945, and the respective Ministers of Food and Agriculture took over most of the functions previously performed by the Reich Ministry. In the British zone, the Food and Agriculture Branch of the British military government exercised these functions well into 1946. After the creation of Niedersachsen, Schleswig-Holstein, Nordrhein-Westfalen, and Hamburg as independent states, the functions were taken over by these states' ministers of food and agriculture.

In the course of these administrative changes, the former *Land* peasants' associations were transformed into ministries of food and agriculture, while district and local peasants' associations remained unchanged.

The officials of the Nazi system of food collection and distribution were appointed. The great majority were members of the Nazi Party, and they enjoyed considerable authority over subordinate agencies and bore all responsibility to superior authority. But in the postwar period essentially the same system of food collection and distribution was staffed by elected officials. This step, necessary for fostering the growth of German democratic institutions, led to a considerable weakening of the administrative vigor of the entire food collection system. Because they depended on the farmers' votes, most of the officials of the district and local peasants' associations were reluctant to enforce tight controls and were frequently lenient toward those farmers who had not met their assessed delivery obligations.[14]

Another factor which negatively affected the administrative vigor of the entire postwar food economy was denazification. For political reasons denazification was absolutely indispensable; there can be no question about that. But in the early stages of denazification many competent men with a Nazi past were removed from office and replaced by reliable but incompetent non-Nazis. An antifascist creed alone was insufficient to obtain the co-operation and trust of the farmers,[15] and trust was particularly needed to restore the shaken system of food collection.

The determination of the farmers' delivery quotas was based on estimates of yields and acreage planted, and cattle censuses. Farmers were told how much land to plant in what crop and the entire harvest, except approved seed and feed requirements, had to be surrendered at fixed prices to food collection centers. Although the Nazi collection system was not flawless it functioned satisfactorily until the end of the war. As long as the authority of the Reich was not shaken and the local peasants' leader maintained the respect of the farmers, the assessed delivery obligations were met. Farmers knew that diversion of farm produce into illegal channels was subject to stern punishment, including death for gross violations. For this reason black-market activity in food was very small. For money incomes received, farmers could buy the most essential farm supplies, implements, consumer goods, and fertilizers.

After the defeat all this changed drastically. Gone was the Reich with its closely knit administration, gauleiters, and henchmen. The Allied Control Council and the respective military and state governments were all responsible to some extent for postwar German agriculture. The old system of food production, collection, and distribution was to continue under new managers and all crops remained subject to requisitioning at fixed prices, but farmers could not now buy farm implements, spare parts, fertilizers, or many other needed farm items on a regular legal basis.[16] With industry in low gear and with most industrial goods entering illegal channels, farmers were virtually compelled to use part of their produce illegally to obtain farm supplies.

In the absence of a strong administration the farmers exploited every administrative loophole to reduce delivery quotas. For instance, postwar meat quotas were based on the cattle census data, without taking into consideration the pasture area. Because no delivery obligations were imposed upon pastures, farmers tended to keep as much of the land as possible under pasture and as little as possible under tillage.[17] Another reason for these practices was low grain prices, which in 1946 were fixed even lower than the wartime levels.

To overcome these drawbacks and to create incentives for the efficient farmers, German administrators pressed for a new food collection system based on so-called grain values. Under this proposal, the basis for assessing a farmer's delivery obligations would be his total agricultural land and not the acreage under a specific crop. Yearly delivery quotas, depending upon soil fertility, location, and other relevant factors, would be assessed in terms of so many tons of grain. How the farmer would meet his quota would be his own affair. He would be told what his obligations were in time to adjust his production accordingly. If his soil was suited for grains, he would concentrate on that; if he had more pasture, he would raise more cattle. All products were assigned definite grain values, and the administrators hoped that the new system would provide incentives to the efficient farmer at the expense of the negligent. Every farmer would have to explain to his marketing board and food office why he had not met the assessed delivery obligations, and failure to do this would mean sanctions and fines.

This system was put into operation for the years 1947–48.[18]

The postwar system of food distribution also showed very little change from the wartime pattern. In the British zone, the system of food offices—*Land* food offices, district food offices, and ration card places—was retained. The wartime division of food offices into Sections A and B was also preserved. Section A retained authority over production and collection of farm produce, while Section B performed purely administrative functions. They were responsible for the issuance of rationing cards and purchase permits and for the collection of the used rationing coupons from retailers.

In the American zone of occupation, the system of food production, collection and distribution was similar to that of the British zone. The principal difference between the two zones arose from a far-reaching administrative decentralization in the American zone. The Ministries of Food and Agriculture in the newly created states of Bavaria, Hessen, and Württemberg-Baden had almost complete authority over all food matters. There was no institution comparable to ZEL in the British zone. The Special Committee for Food and Agriculture under the *Länderrat* was much too weak to cope with the rapidly deteriorating food situation.[19]

To improve food collection and distribution General Clay appointed Hermann R. Dietrich as Special Food Commissioner. Dietrich was given authority to issue *binding* orders to the ministers of food and agriculture of the three states and to channel surplus foods into food-deficient areas. Nominally he held as much authority in the south as Schlange-Schöningen in the north but his work, like his counterpart's, was greatly handicapped by an inability to enforce decisions at the *Land* level. Both Schlange-Schöningen and Dietrich had to call frequently on the Allied regional food officers to secure compliance. For all practical purposes the *Länder* did as they pleased.

During 1946 the economy of the British and American zones, in general, and the nutritional status of the German population in particular, deteriorated markedly. Differences about the political, economic, and social future of Potsdam Germany resulted in a deadlock at the Allied Control Council in Berlin. In 1946 no progress was made toward solving any major problems. Drastic shortages of almost everything made a new beginning imperative. The first and the most important corrective step was the fusion of the American and British zones of occupation which took place January 1, 1947.

After fusion, the two zones had 71.5 percent of all prewar German mining industry, 75.7 percent of her iron and steel-making capacity, 53.6 percent of her machinery-making industry, 40 percent of her electrical industry, and 49.1 percent of all her chemical industry.[20] In terms of 1936 output, the bizonal industry contributed 57 percent of the Reich's national income.[21]

The area's principal economic shortcoming was that it could provide only 50 percent of its food requirements from its own sources.

2. *The Council for Food and Agriculture at Stuttgart*

Five new German administrative agencies were created with the unification: the Council for Economics at Minden, the Council for Finances at Frankfurt, the Council for Food and Agriculture at Stuttgart, the Council for Transport at Bielefeld, and the Council of Posts at Frankfurt. Each agency was headed by an executive committee consisting of a representative of each of the eight *Länder*. The bizonal councils for economics, finances, and food and agriculture were not vested with any executive authority over the *Länder*. Decisions and ordinances of these councils were to be sent to the respective ministries of the eight *Länder* for implementation, not directly to the middle and lower administrative organs. On the other hand, the councils for transport and posts were given executive authority and their ordinances went directly to all subordinate organs in the *Länder*.[22]

A control group of American and British officers was attached to each of the councils and five bipartite panels in Berlin formulated policy guidance for them. The Anglo-American Bipartite Board was the highest policy making body of the new administrative structure.[23]

An unusually severe winter paralyzed Germany and made the task of the new administration much more difficult. The harvest of 1946 had been considerably below the average. Most Germans were hungry, eking out an existence on about 1000 calories per day. Food imports from the United States were stalled because of a prolonged strike of American seamen. Lack of coal kept industrial wheels idle.

The bizonal Council for Food and Agriculture was headed by Schlange-Schöningen. All decisions were reached by a simple majority vote of the eight members and were to be implemented by the *Länder* administrations. Nominally, the bizonal Council for Food and Agriculture was responsible for all food matters in the "Bizone." It was empowered to channel all available food stocks to feed areas where hunger was most intense. But, like earlier agencies in the two zones, the council had no executive organs of its own. The council was to legislate and the *Länder* to execute.

The legislative measures of the Council for Food and Agriculture were most unpopular in the food growing areas such as Bavaria and Niedersachsen. Prior to the fusion, the *Länder* in the American zone were looking forward to greater supplies of coal and industrial products from the industrial British zone and the British zone hoped to obtain more food from the south. However, for the time being coal, steel, and other industrial products were scarce, and the agricultural states naturally resisted unilateral transfers of food without reciprocity. In these circumstances, the *Länder* simply disregarded the Stuttgart agency and refused to surrender food surpluses. The "progression of the negative" continued.[24] By March, 1947, rationing levels had fallen to 900 calories per day.

After the failure of the Moscow Conference on Germany in March, 1947, the American and British military governments began negotiations on strengthening the bizonal administration. But differences deadlocked the talks for a time. The British demanded a centralized German economic administration and the Americans insisted on a decentralized structure with the *Länder* retaining control over the economy. Since political unification of the two zones was not to be attempted, the emphasis was solely on the development of a more unified economy. An agreement to this end was signed by the two Military Governors on May 29, 1947.[25]

Under the terms of this proclamation, the previous five bizonal executive committees were drawn into a single bizonal structure consisting of an Economic Council, an Executive Committee, and five executive directors. On the military government side the existing Bipartite Board, a new agency called "Bipartite Control Office," and a number of bipartite panels were set up to supervise the activities of the new German economic agencies.

The Economic Council consisted of fifty-two members elected by the legislatures of the *Länder* in proportion to their division by parties and in the ratio of one member for each 750,000 of population.[26] It was to issue the necessary ordinances in all permitted fields of economic reconstruction. These ordinances were binding upon the *Länder* for implementation, because the new bizonal agencies still had no executive organs of their own. But every piece of its legislation had to be approved by the Allied Bipartite Board.[27]

The Executive Committee consisted of one representative from each *Land*. Its main function was to propose economic legislation for the Economic Council and to supervise the execution of this legislation by the *Länder*. Five new departments —Economics, Food, Agriculture and Forestry, Finance, Transport, and Communications and Post Office—replaced the former bizonal executive committees. The executive directors of the departments were appointed by the Economic Council from nominations made by the Executive Committee. Directors were responsible to the Economic Council, but they operated under the immediate supervision of the Executive Committee. Dr. Schlange-Schöningen became Director of the Department of Food, Agriculture and Forestry and Dr. J. Semler of Munich was appointed to head the Department of Economics, the most important post. All the departments and their military government counterparts were situated in Frankfurt, a grouping together that represented a considerable improvement over the previous scattering of offices.

3. The Department of Food, Agriculture and Forestry

The new economic administration was hardly viable until August, 1947. Because food was one of the most acute problems of the bizonal economy, most of the Economic Council's early work was devoted to it. Everybody knew that revival of the bizonal economy depended upon improved nutrition—acute food shortages lowered industrial output because workers were too weak to work efficiently. But in the fall of 1947 all hopes for rapid improvement were dashed.

The food crisis of 1947–48 registered all the conflicts between the bizonal agencies on the one hand and the *Länder,* on the other. Frankfurt tried to legislate but the *Länder* refused to execute. Nominally, the *Land* parliaments and cabinets were stripped of all real power in economic matters and were reduced to field organs of the bizonal administration. But the *Länder* continued, openly or secretly, to defy bizonal agencies. In the absence of sanctions, this conflict was never resolved in Frankfurt's favor.[28]

How to survive the oncoming winter was in everyone's mind in the fall of 1947. While the harvest was still being gathered ominous signs of potato, meat, and fat shortages loomed. In spite of an incredibly dry summer the harvest turned out to be better than that of the previous fall, but farmers' food deliveries were almost 20 percent lower than in the preceding year for reasons that will be examined later.

To improve and above all to unify the food collection and distribution system, the Economic Council passed three important ordinances.[29]

One law, dealing with public control of deliveries of farm produce, required all villages to list for public inspection all individual farmers' delivery records. Special attention had to be paid to deliveries of grain products, potatoes, milk, and meat. The "potato law" requisitioned the entire potato crop of 1947, with the exception of seeds, non-edible potatoes, and stipulated amounts for the farmer's own use. The "meat law" ordered uniform meat rations for the bizonal area and subjected the delivery of animals to tight control.

The activities of the bizonal Department for Food, Agriculture and Forestry during the winter of 1947–48 can be cast in terms of "potato and meat wars" with the *Länder.*[30] This struggle came to an end only after the currency reform, when the revival of German economic activity laid the basis for a rapid increase in agricultural output.

4. Postwar Agricultural Production

One of the major errors of Allied economic planning in Germany was an almost unqualified disregard of the interdependence of industry and agriculture while seeking a new, peaceful Germany with a flourishing agriculture and a severely truncated industry.

The American and British military governments exerted considerable pressure on the farming community to till every inch of soil to increase agricultural output. For instance, the Western Allies in the fall of 1946 wanted a considerable increase in the acreage under grains and potatoes. German farmers were ordered to plow up pasture land, but no provisions were made for additional fuel or plows, tractors, and other farm machinery. On the contrary, the production of plows and tractors remained low due to a lack of coal and raw materials.

Shortage of fertilizers was the principal reason for low agricultural yields. But again, instead of stepping up the production of fertilizers, the Western Allies continued to export coal and to reduce the capacity to produce fertilizers. Because nitrogen is basic for munitions as well as for fertilizer production, fear of German "war potential" apparently necessitated the throttling of German fertilizer production.

The unsettled currency situation was another factor which affected agricultural production negatively. It was generally expected that currency reform would be inevitable and that in the course of any future currency conversion holdings of Reichsmarks would be scaled down to a small fraction. These expectations were responsible for the postwar "flight out of money" and for the hoarding of industrial goods by producers. Farm supplies were produced, but they were virtually unobtainable for Reichsmarks. To get supplies farmers had to turn to illicit sources, mostly on a barter basis. Under these circumstances considerable quantities of food were diverted into illegal channels, and a spreading barter system sapped the energies of the German economy. By January, 1948, the bizonal economy had reached "dead center." [31]

The quantitative performance of postwar agricultural production may be best assessed against prewar and wartime outputs. Table 2 shows outputs of four selected staple products in the bizonal area of Germany.

TABLE 2. Agricultural Output of Selected Staple Products, Bizonal Area of Germany. (In thousands of tons)

Period	Rye	Wheat	Potatoes	Sugar Beets
1935–38	2,689	2,186	16,053	3,877
1939–43	2,373	1,885	15,573	4,736
1945	1,492	1,303	12,298	2,182
1946	1,679	1,328	11,207	3,264
1947	1,827	1,038	12,815	3,624

Sources: Verwaltung für Ernährung, Land-und Forstwirtschaft, *Statistik der Land- und Ernährungswirtschaft, U.S.-Britisches Besatzungsgebiet Deutschlands, 1935–1947*, I (1948), for rye, p. 34; for wheat, p. 38; for potatoes, p. 56, and for sugar beets, p. 57. For the year of 1947 this volume recorded two sets of data. The first set, provided by German statistical services, understated production up to 25 percent for individual staples. This table has used the revised data.

Agricultural production fell off sharply after 1943 for reasons already outlined. On the average, the agricultural output of the bizonal area in 1946 was roughly 70 percent of prewar output. [32] The over-all decline of postwar food production is set forth in Table 3.

These data show that the output of plant foods in the postwar period was declining but still quite satisfactory. The production of animal foods, however, shows an almost precipitous

TABLE 3. Postwar Food Production in Bizonal Area of Germany.

(1935–39 = 100)

Period	Plant Foods	Animal Foods	All Foods
1946–47	89	60	67
1947–48	84	50	58
1948–49	109	69	79
1949–50	106	89	93

Sources: O. Thiel and K. Padberg, "Produktion, Verkaufserlöse und Betriebsausgaben der westdeutschen Landwirtschaft," *Berichte über Landwirtschaft,* Vol. XXX, N.F. No. 1 (1952), p. 6. Herbert Hoover estimated the 1946 agricultural production in the American and British zones at 65 percent of prewar; see *The President's Economic Mission to Germany and Austria, Report No. 1: German Agriculture and Food Requirements* (1947), p. 4.

decline. The principal reason was a serious deterioration in quality and numbers of postwar herds. In terms of over-all food production, three years after the end of hostilities the production index stood at less than 60 percent of the prewar level.

5. The Interdependence of German Industry and Agriculture

LACK OF FERTILIZERS

With the exception of the last year of the war, the German agricultural community received smaller quantities of fertilizers but enough to preserve the productivity of the soil. Significant cuts in fertilizer allocations occurred only in the summer of 1944. However, even such greatly reduced availability was still tolerable. After the end of hostilities, a considerable nitrogen production was possible in the British zone of occupation. During the war the Ruhr produced roughly 240,000 tons of nitrogen, and most of this capacity survived the war intact.[33] But for a number of reasons the available capacity was not used.

Industrial disarmament of Germany called for the removal of some fertilizer producing equipment and imposed production ceilings on the retained capacity. The shortage of coal was another factor which kept nitrogen production in low gear. Estimating roughly, the agriculture of the British zone of occupation in the prewar period required 200,000 tons of nitrogen yearly. In the first postwar year (1945–46) only 22,000 tons of nitrogen, or 11 percent of the required amount, were actually distributed for the entire British zone.[34]

In the American zone of occupation, the Trostberg plant was in a position to supply a considerable amount of the nitrogen requirements of the zone, but again the coal shortage kept its operations in check. In the second postwar year considerably greater quantities of fertilizers became available, but they still fell far short of actual needs.

It was estimated that just to maintain agricultural yields at their postwar levels, the united Anglo-American zone needed 230,000 tons of nitrogen, 250,000 tons of phosphates, and 400,-000 tons of potash per year.[35] But the actual amounts distributed came to a fraction of requirements: 75,000 tons of nitrogen in 1946 and 125,000 tons in 1947; 75,000 tons of phosphates in 1946 and 100,000 tons in 1947; and 170,000 tons of potash in 1946 and 218,000 tons in 1947.[36] Thus, in the first postwar year about 30 percent and in the second over 50 percent of the estimated nitrogen requirements were made available for distribution. For phosphates the situation was less favorable, mainly because of stagnating steel production and lack of phosphate imports.[37]

The data do not indicate whether these quantities of fertilizers were actually sold to farmers or whether distributors hoarded part of the stocks. There is considerable evidence that only a portion of fertilizers available reached its ultimate destination. Table 4 is designed to show the actual amounts of fertilizers used.

TABLE 4. Fertilizer Consumption Per Hectare of Agricultural Land, United States and British Zones, 1938/39—1948/49.

Year *	Nitrogen		Phosphates		Potash	
	Kg.	1938/39 = 100	Kg.	1938/39 = 100	Kg.	1938/39 = 100
1938–39	24.5	100	28.7	100	45.1	100
1945–46	2.8	11	2.5	8	16.2	35
1946–47	13.2	53	10.5	36	22.8	49
1947–48	18.7	74	16.7	57	31.7	68
1948–49	24.9	101	31.0	104	43.5	93

* Reckoned from July 1 to June 30.
Sources: "Düngungsmittelversorgung der Landwirtschaft," *Wirtschaft und Statistik*, Vol. II, No. 5 (1950), p. 731. See also Verwaltung für Ernährung, Land- und Forstwirtschaft, *Statistik der Land- und Ernährungswirtschaft, U.S.-Britisches Besatzungsgebiet Deutschland, 1935-1947*, I (1948), 191.

The drastic fall in fertilizer consumption per hectare in the first two years was alarming. Only 11 percent of the nitrogen and 8 percent of the phosphates used in 1938–39 were applied in 1945–46. The cut in potash consumption was considerably less. Only after the currency reform, when economic conditions returned to normal, did fertilizer consumption approach the prewar levels.

The principal reason for the drastic postwar shortage of fertilizers was unquestionably the industrial disarmament policy of the Western Allies. But postwar reorganization of the fertilizer distribution system added further strains to an already tight situation. During the war, fertilizers were allocated centrally to each *Land* peasants' association on the basis of the so-called quota system (*Kontingentierungsverfahren*). District peasants' associations saw to it that farmers were able to buy amounts of fertilizers available. But in the postwar period, three separate organs were set up to allocate the available fertilizers: The Potash Board, in Elze; the Nitrogen Board, in Bochum; and the Phosphate Board, in Düsseldorf. *Land* peasants' associations divided the amounts received among the district peasants' associations, and these issued purchase warrants to farmers.[38]

Yet it frequently happened that farmers could not obtain fertilizers even though they had purchase permits.[39]

Low agricultural productivity was the inevitable consequence of the fertilizer shortage. The unsatisfactory state of postwar German agriculture is shown in greatly reduced average yields.

T A B L E 5. Agricultural Yields Per Hectare, United States and British Zone of Germany. (In hundreds of kilograms)

Grain	1935–39	1939–43	1945	1946	1947
Rye	18.6	18.8	13.1	13.8	14.1
Wheat	22.7	21.8	16.9	16.7	13.8
Barley	21.4	20.8	15.5	14.6	13.7
Oats	21.0	20.6	14.8	14.7	13.7

Source: O. Thiel, "Getreideerträge auf dem tiefsten Stand?", *Neu Mitteilungen für die Landwirtschaft,* Vol. II, No. 6 (1947), p. 221.

Taking the data of the above table at face value, postwar yields for grains were roughly 30 percent below the prewar level.[40] A similar trend in the grain yields was also observed in the Soviet occupied zone.[41] However, caution is required in interpreting the above data. The chaotic postwar conditions and the peculiar German way of estimating yields were responsible for understating yields 10–15 percent.[42]

In the postwar period, German estimates of crop yields were made by honorary crop reporters who covered three or four villages (*Gemeind⋅⋅⋅*) and made one estimate a month on yields of principal crops. Final estimates of yields for grains were generally made in January and, for root crops, in November. Output was estimated by multiplying the reported yields per hectare by the acreage obtained from the land-use census. Of course, discrepancies were frequently present between the land-use statistics and actual acreage under different crops.

In the postwar years reporters used to understate yields of

main crops to prevent unduly large delivery obligations upon farmers and farming areas. Similar tendencies were evident even during wartime, but were kept in check by the fact that economic misbehavior was subject to capital punishment. Since Anglo-American law does not call for capital punishment for economic misbehavior, the tendency to understate became more widespread as food shortages grew more acute. To check the accuracy of German data on grain yields, officials of the American military government made sample surveys in 1947 and discovered considerable discrepancies between actual and reported yields.[43]

BARTER—THE SOURCE OF FARM SUPPLIES

In a highly developed country such as Germany, agricultural production is heavily dependent upon its industrial counterpart and vice versa. The farming community must be able to obtain farm supplies and fertilizers on a regular basis, while the industrial community must have sufficient amounts of food for sustenance.

It is estimated that from mid-1945 to mid-1948 the German farming community in the American and British zones of occupation was able to satisfy legally roughly one or two percent of its requirements for farm machinery, spare parts, and fertilizers.[44] The rest had to be obtained either illegally, mostly on a barter basis, or not at all.

Reliable German sources estimated that for the two united zones, replacement and spare-parts requirements for agriculture alone amounted to 2 million tons of rolled iron. Since in 1947 the production of iron and steel in the zones was less than 3 million tons per year, virtually the entire steel output had to be used exclusively to meet the demands of agriculture.[45]

In these conditions of almost fantastic scarcities, barter was the only reliable way out for both the hungry city dwellers and the supply-starved farmers. Fixed swap terms developed between industry and agriculture less than a year after the surrender. Common terms were: [46] One sack of twine for 150 kilograms of wheat, 200 kilograms of rye, or 12 pounds of bacon; 60 horseshoe nails for 1 pound of fat; 100 bricks for 50 kilograms of potatoes; 50 kilograms of fertilizer for 150 kilograms of potatoes; 1 sowing machine for 4,000 kilograms of potatoes plus the legal price; 2 grain sacks for 50 kilograms of wheat; 1 electric bulb for 1 kilogram of fat.

The existence of barter deals between industry and agriculture was widely known, but the German and military government administrators accepted their existence as a necessary evil and relatively little was done to reduce its scope. It continued to flourish until monetary incentives were re-established by the currency reform in mid-June of 1948. The hungry city dwellers were also scouring the countryside and bartering away possessions for food. From both sources the German farming community received industrial supplies and consumer goods to keep going. The widespread barter reflected the fact that industrial disarmament and flourishing agriculture were incompatible objectives.

AGRICULTURAL PRICES

All through the war the yearly average prices paid to farmers for rye and wheat remained practically unchanged. To stimulate early deliveries in the fall, Nazi price control agencies paid higher prices in the fall and lower prices in the spring. The Nazis offered special premiums for early fall threshing in addition to subsidies.

After the German defeat the Allies kept intact the existing price legislation for all agricultural commodities. As a result the postwar rye and wheat prices show remarkable stability (Table 6).

TABLE 6. Rye and Wheat Prices, United States and British Zone of Germany.
(In Reichsmarks per one thousand kilograms)

Product	1938–39	1944–45	1945–46	1946–47	1947–48	1948–49
Rye	187	187	189	189	190	240
Wheat	204	204	206	202	206	260

Sources: W. Doebel, "Zwei Jahrzehnte staatlicher Agrarpreisbildung," *Berichte über Landwirtschaft,* XXXI (1953), 484–85. The 1938–39 and 1944–45 prices are the yearly averages for the entire Reich, without special premiums.

In the fall of 1945 farmers were paid the prices for rye and wheat set by the Reich authorities on July 1, 1944.[47] In the fall of 1946 rye prices remained unchanged and wheat prices showed a small decline.

Nominally, the yearly average prices for rye and wheat changed little from wartime levels. But all averages are deceptive, and the actual prices farmers received were considerably below the average figure. Postwar shortages of agricultural machinery, spare parts and supplies frequently hampered early threshing and thus farmers were unable to make farm deliveries at higher fall prices. Deliveries made after November were made at lower prices.[48]

Another factor was the Allied insistence on a greater acreage in root crops, especially potatoes. In addition to purely technical difficulties to complete early fall threshing of grain mentioned above, potatoes had to be harvested at a time when grain prices were the highest. After the root crops were in, winter and spring deliveries of grains could be made only at lower prices. Farm subsidies were also partly eliminated in the spring of 1946. To avoid penalizing farmers who extended the acreage under root crops, prices for wheat, rye, oats, and barley were made uniform for the entire year of 1947–48.[49] Under this system, one price prevailed in a given price area from July 1 to the end of the following June. To obtain a more thorough picture it is necessary to consider briefly the postwar price policy for other agricultural staples.

Table 7 tells essentially the same story as Table 6. With the exception of prices of potatoes, butter, and a few other products, the average postwar prices paid to farmers remained roughly at their wartime levels.

TABLE 7. Some German Agricultural Price Movements.

		Price (Reichsmarks per 50 kilograms)		
Product	*Place*	*1938*	*1944*	*Mid-June, 1948*
Potatoes *	Hamburg	2.66	3.25	3.95
Potatoes	Munich	2.80	3.40	4.05
Cattle †	Hamburg	43.80	46.00	46.00
Cattle	Munich	41.20	43.00	52.30
Hogs	Hamburg	50.90	56.30	56.30
Hogs	Munich	52.30	57.00	64.00
Butter	U.K. Zone	133.85	158.25	226.00
Butter	U.S. Zone	133.85	158.25	226.00

* For human consumption only.
† Live bulls.
Source: Statistisches Amt des Vereinigten Wirtschaftsgebietes, *Wirtschaft und Statistik*, Vol. I, No. 1 (1949), p. 38.

Frozen prices and lower productivity brought about a sharp decline in farm incomes. Farms that had been profitable either scarcely paid their way or suffered losses. At the same time, prices of agricultural machinery, farm supplies, and consumer goods rose considerably. The postwar relationship between agricultural prices and industrial prices had a tendency to act to the disadvantage of the farmer. The divergence between the farm prices received and prices paid for the means of production is known as the "price scissors." Opening of the "price scissors" reflected the unfavorable financial situation of the postwar German farming community. With declining incomes and rising farm expenditures, farmers were either compelled to enter black markets to make ends meet or to lose money. Yet in this unfavorable milieu the American and British military governments urged German farmers time and again to maximize agricultural output.

Price changes in agricultural machinery and supplies between 1938 and 1947 throw useful light on the profitability of postwar German agriculture. In the Ruhr Valley in 1947,[50] prices of farm supplies such as nails, barbed wire, twine, and chains had risen to 259 percent of the 1938 levels. Fuels like coal, briquettes, and wood stood at 248 percent, building materials at 237 percent, and farm vehicles, such as tractors, at 233 percent of 1938 prices. Tools such as forks, spades, brooms, and scythes rose to 214 percent, while spare parts stood at 169 percent of the 1938 levels. During the same period work clothing rose to 283 percent and work shoes to 247 percent. Prices paid by farmers to craftsmen for services rendered had also climbed by 1947. The wage for carpenters, for instance, was 186 percent, for locksmiths 170 percent, for electricians 155 percent, and for bricklayers 152 percent of the 1938 levels.

It has been estimated that during the first two postwar years the aggregate farm receipts in the American and British zones were roughly 30 percent below the prewar receipts.[51] The squeeze of low prices and declining receipts against high costs and acute shortages was responsible for the low volume of agricultural production.

Farm incomes from the legal sale of agricultural produce were frequently insufficient to meet the costs of farm operations. As long as the Allies did not raise prices, farmers were virtually driven into the gray and black markets to make ends meet.[52] Some German authors estimated that roughly 20 percent of the farm output was diverted into illegal channels [53] —American military government sources put the figure at 10 percent.[54] By way of contrast, West German industry sent only 20 percent of its total output into *legal* channels.

Postwar examination of the records of some 2,400 farms showed that in 1945–46 one-third operated at a loss, while during the war 95 percent showed a profit.[55] A similar study, designed to determine the farm profitability in Bavaria, showed that income for 1947 of a representative farm of 20 hectares came to RM 10,844, while expenditures amounted to RM 13,-503. The net loss per farm, RM 2,659 was staggering.[56]

A similar survey of 3,100 farms over five hectares in size in the British and American zones showed that farm income per hectare in 1946–47 was RM 543, an increase of RM 114 from the average of RM 429 in 1934–38. In the same time farm expenditures, also per hectare, increased by RM 139, from RM 289 to RM 428; however, this still leaves a net profit of RM 115 per hectare.

These findings seem to put the reliability of the Bavarian study somewhat in question. But part of the net profit of the farmers was due to a shift in the agricultural production mix and entailed a consumption of capital. In the postwar years the acreage in potatoes produced for direct consumption was greatly increased, and there was a corresponding reduction in the output of feed crops. This paralleled a stepped-up liquidation of the hog and cattle population, thus apparently increasing farm incomes but also reducing agricultural capital.[57]

Without trying to impugn either the findings or the techniques used in these studies, the profit squeeze in postwar German agriculture is beyond dispute. Many other investigators have independently arrived at similar conclusions.[58]

In the acute postwar food shortages, with black market prices more than a hundred times higher than legal prices, most farms had ample opportunities to make substantial amounts of cash by selling some food "black." Needless to say, participation in the black market reduced farm deliveries, with the result that less food was available for legal distribution.[59] However, black market sales substantially raised farm incomes, and it was not unusual for poorly operated farms with black market ties to make a better financial showing than conscientiously run farms without such ties.

However, despite some profit squeeze, the postwar German

farming community was relatively well off in comparison to the industrial sector. In contrast to the hunger and poverty in the cities, farmers continued to enjoy a reasonably high standard of living. One indicator of the strong over-all position of farmers is that from 1939 to 1947 the bizonal farming community reduced its mortgage obligations per hectare of agricultural land from RM 348 to RM 190.[60] This reduction in monetary indebtedness was mostly achieved by a reduction in livestock holdings and a failure to replace farm equipment. The real wealth position of the farmers probably declined. But the German farmer (as a net debtor) did relatively well under the conditions of repressed inflation after World War II, just as he did during the hyperinflation after World War I.[61]

6. Importation of Food

Allied wartime planning did not call for German food imports after the surrender. Germany would have to rely on her own agricultural resources in conditions of world-wide food shortages and in the prevailing climate of opinion. This was justified in terms of Germany's virtual self-sufficiency in food. In 1939 Germany produced 80 percent of all food consumed, and the Allies felt that with a minimum diet of 1550 calories a day for a "normal" consumer Germany should be able to maintain self-sufficiency. A sense of justice also required, after prolonged suffering and malnutrition in the German-occupied countries, that postwar German food rations "under no circumstances" be higher than in liberated areas.[62] The policy was to have been altered only to prevent mass starvation. The policy was made known to the Germans immediately after the surrender.[63]

However, as soon as the British and American military government officials had time to take stock this policy was scrapped.[64]

Two factors were mainly responsible for the reversal. First, the loss of Germany's former breadbasket, located east of the Oder-Neisse line and placed under Polish administration, aggravated the food deficit of the American and British zones. This territory produced 25 percent of Germany's prewar agricultural output.[65] Second, six or seven million German refugees and expellees settled in the two Western zones after the war, greatly increasing food requirements.[66]

The zones became one of the most food-deficient areas in the world. It was estimated that in the early postwar years the food produced in the British and American zones came to 975 calories per person daily, or less than two-thirds of the "normal" ration of 1550 calories prevailing from mid-1945 to mid-1948. The remaining third of the "normal" ration was imported.[67]

The early postwar food assistance to the Western zones of Germany can be subdivided into two phases. The first phase extended from mid-1945 to mid-1946, when the British and American military governments were engaged primarily in socalled disaster relief. This early aid helped to tide the country over the lean months until the harvest was reaped. In the fall of 1945 wheat imports were made under a joint Anglo-American arrangement, and with such strenuous efforts it was possible to keep the German food ration at the 1550 calorie level.[68] From June 1, 1945 to June 30, 1946, the British military government imported 1,245,900 tons of foodstuffs into the British zone, and only this aid prevented famine in the Ruhr.[69] During the same period 461,000 tons of food were sent into the American occupied zone, making the total for the year 1,706,900 tons. Such massive assistance to a former principal enemy was without parallel in recorded history.[70] Millions of Germans owe their lives to the early food imports of the Western Allies.[71]

However, it soon became obvious that ad hoc disaster relief would be insufficient to provide even the 1550 calories per day considered the absolute minimum needed to prevent widespread famine and unrest. The heavily industrialized British zone was particularly short of food. The Hague Convention required the victors to meet certain obligations toward the vanquished with respect to food, public order, and safety. The applicable provision reads as follows:

> The Authority of the legitimate power having in fact passed into the hands of the occupant, the latter shall take all the measures in his power to restore, and insure, as far as possible, public order and safety, while respecting, unless absolutely prevented, the laws in force in the country.[72]

Congress voted special funds in 1946 to prevent "disease and unrest" in occupied Germany. The "Government and Relief in Occupied Areas" appropriations stipulated that such funds might be used to finance only the imports of food, petroleum, and fertilizers. The use of GARIOA funds for the importation of raw materials, which were so vital to the recovery of West German industry, was explicitly forbidden.[73] The British counterpart of the American GARIOA funds was the U.K. contributions.

With the appropriation of special funds, the second phase of Allied food assistance began. On an average monthly basis, from the surrender to the currency reform in mid-June, 1948, foodstuffs were shipped into the British and American zones of occupation as shown in Table 8.

TABLE 8. Food Imported by U.S. and British Military Governments for German Civilian Use. (Monthly Average, in thousands of tons)

Imports	1945	1946	1947	1948 *
Breadgrains and Flour	38.9	161.6	328.7	301.3
Total Foodstuffs	50.1	262.9	361.2	510.5

*First six months.
Sources: U.S. Office of Military Government for Germany, *Monthly Report; Food and Agriculture,* No. 32 (1948), p. 21; Headquarters, Control Commission for Germany (British Element), *Monthly Statistical Bulletin,* Vol. III, No. 6 (1948), p. 7; *ibid.,* Vol. III, No. 7 (1948), p. 19.

In 1945 food imports were rather small, but in 1946 five times as much was brought in to keep the Germans alive. After the fusion of the two zones the United States paid virtually the entire bill, and in 1947 the monthly average of food imports came to a staggering 361,200 tons. Ninety percent of all these imports consisted of grain products, either wheat or flour. However, for the first quarter of 1947, over one-half of all grain imports consisted of corn, mostly of poor quality.[74]

Postwar German food imports included hardly any fat. It was estimated that only 14,000 tons of fat were imported during 1947, and the acute shortage was eased only after the beginning of the Marshall Plan in the second half of 1948.[75]

The cost of the mass-scale relief was borne by the governments of the United States and the United Kingdom. No reliable figures are available for 1945 and 1946. During the first year of occupation the British spent—according to their estimate—£80 million, or $320 million, to feed the former enemy,[76] while the American expenditures at the end of 1946 came close to $220 million. During 1947, when the Americans paid the lion's share, the costs came to $516 million.[77]

At the end of 1947, American expenses for providing relief supplies to Germany stood at $750 million [78] and by the end of March, 1948, the total amount spent was $918 million in grants and $92 million in credits for the upkeep of occupied Western Germany.[79] During the first three years of occupation, the American and British Governments together spent close to $1.5 billion for the relief shipments.[80]

Nevertheless, German rations remained considerably below minimum nutrition standards.

7. Food Rationing

German wartime rationing of foodstuffs was introduced on August 28, 1939. All civilians were divided into different rationing groups, depending upon age, nature of work, health status, and degree of self-sufficiency in food. Most farmers, of course, were self-suppliers, while most city people were not. The population was divided into the following groups: [81]

a) Normal consumers, comprising civilians over 18 years of age.

b) Babies 0–2 years of age.

c) Small children 3–5 years of age.

d) Children 6–13 years of age.

e) Teen-agers 14–18 years of age.

f) Heavy workers (hard laborers).

g) Very heavy workers (very hard laborers).

h) Night workers and workers of long hours on duty.

The rations differed from group to group but were uniform throughout Germany for each category. At the beginning of the war only the most important foodstuffs were rationed, and vegetables, potatoes, fruits, and fish remained unrationed. But rationing was gradually extended, and in 1944 hardly any important nonrationed foodstuffs were available. During the war a few minor changes took place in the rationing categories, but on the whole the above classification remained intact.

All men over 17 years of age and all women from 25 to 55 also received rationing cards for tobacco.

Although food rationing continued throughout Germany after the war, the formation of occupation zones destroyed its uniformity. During the first few months rations differed not only from zone to zone but from district to district. Uniform rations for the entire British zone of occupation were possible only after

TABLE 9. Rationed Foodstuffs Called Up for and Actually Obtained by a "Normal Consumer," 1945–1948. (In calories)

Rationing Period	Time	U.S. Zone Called Up Rations*	U.S. Zone Rations Actually Obtained	U.K. Zone† Called Up Rations	U.K. Zone Rations Actually Obtained	BEL Hamburg‡ Called Up Rations	BEL Hamburg Rations Actually Obtained	U.S.-U.K. combined Zone§ Called Up Rations	U.S.-U.K. Rations Actually Obtained	Schlange-Schöningen U.K. Zone Rations Actually Obtained Hamburg‖	Essen¶
	1945										
75	4/30–5/27	1050		1460							927
76	5/28–6/24	860		1470						1470	997
77	6/25–7/22	930		1404						1404	1126
78	7/23–8/19	980		1376						1376	1127
79	8/20–9/16	1100		1386						1386	1463
80	9/17–10/14	1160		1542						1542	1496
81	10/15–11/11	1260		1476						1476	1631
82	11/12–12/9	1540		1701						1701	1496
83	12/10–1/6/1946	1490		1699						1699	1548
	1946										
84	1/7–2/3	1550		1675						1675	1537
85	2/4–3/3	1540		1694						1694	1613
86	3/4–3/31	1540	1015	1133						1103	1056
87	4/1–4/28	1275	1040	1146						1042	1066
88	4/29–5/26	1280	1050	1155						1155	1079
89	5/27–6/23	1180	1050	1168						1137	1194
90	6/24–7/21	1235	1050	1216						1065	1002
91	7/22–8/18	1240	1135	1270						1239	1150
92	8/19–9/15	1240	1335	1478						1478	1378
93	9/16–10/13	1237	1410	1530						1530	1442
94	10/14–11/10	1550	1550	1566						1542	1245
95	11/11–12/8	1550	1550	1567						1547	1396
96	12/9–1/5/1947	1550	1540	1552		1542	1393			1529	1334

	1947								
97	1/6–2/2	1550	1540	1540	1252	1540	1449		1362
98	2/3–3/2	1550	1550	1564	1505	1564	1534		1517
99	3/3–3/30	1560	1330	1555	1410	1544	1566		1410
100	3/31–4/27	1550	1180	1552	1483	1537	1456	1552	1746
101	4/28–5/25	1550	1081	1553	1071	1554	1072	1120	1042
102	5/26–6/22	1555	1165	1186	1121	1186	1168	1192	1123
103	6/23–7/20	1555	1260	1142	1185	1130	1160	1218	1210
104	7/21–8/17	1550	1390	1387	1349	1256	1335	1388	1385
105	8/18–9/14	1555	1430	1431	1387	1431	1430	1426	1410
106	9/15–10/12	1555	1430	1256	1474	1244	1417	1432	1441
107	10/13–11/9	1550	1425	1425	1389	1389	1375	1426	1381
108	11/10–12/7	1555		1425	1279	1401	1358	1426	1322
109	12/8–1/4/1948	1425	1330	1425	1261			1426	1311

	1948				
110	1/5–2/1	1426	1311	1405	1424
111	2/2–2/29	1410		1411	
112	March	1339	1296	1398	
113	April	1563		1564	
114	May	1593		1593	
115	June	1575		1655	
116	July	1980		1995	

* U.S. Office of Military Government for Germany, *Monthly Report; Food and Agriculture*, Nos. 20, 22, 24, 26, 28, and the Statistical Annex, Nos. 11–17.

† Statistische Amt für die Britische Besatzungzone, *Berichte* Nos. 1–43 (1946–1948). The most reliable source on postwar rationing in these two zones of Germany.

‡ Freie und Hansestadt Hamburg, "Behörde für Ernährung und Landwirtschaft, *Jahresbericht 1947*" (unpublished report), p. 34; a very useful source.

§ Verwaltung für Ernährung, Land- und Forstwirtschaft, *Statistik der Land- und Ernährungswirtschaft, U.S.-Britisches Besatzungsgebiet Deutschlands, 1935–1947*, II, p. 26.

‖ H. Schlange-Schöningen, *Im Schatten des Hungers* (Hamburg: P. Parey Verlag, 1955), p. 306. The rations after the 81st rationing period are the average for the entire British zone.

¶ *Ibid.*, p. 307.

October 15, 1945.[82] A few months later, on January 7, 1946, a uniform ration card was also introduced in the American zone of occupation. With the economic fusion of the British and American zones on January 1, 1947, a uniform ration card was introduced for both zones.[83]

Only three types of ration cards for nonsuppliers were issued early in the occupation, but in 1946 the number of categories began to increase and the pattern of wartime classification re-emerged.[84]

The subject of postwar food rationing has been marred by incomplete reportage and biased assessment of the facts. A reasonably balanced view of the actual levels of rationing can be had by recourse to the large body of sources, such as military government reports, accounts of German economists, German government documents, German press reports, U.S. Congressional hearings, stenographic records of the German Economics Council, and books by former German officials.

Table 9 lists postwar rations for the "normal" consumer from the first postwar rationing period until the first month after the currency reform. It shows that although the official ration for the "normal" consumer was set at 1550 calories daily, the actual ration for almost three years fluctuated between 1000 and 1550 calories. The set ration remained only "paper calories" because frequently either the meat or fat coupons could not be honored in full.[85] It was only after the currency reform that the U.S. Military Governor was able to report that the "German people have enough to eat." [86]

To anyone who has never experienced gnawing hunger, the figure 1550 calories means little. Living on such a ration not just for a day or so but for years not only sapped the physical strength of the German population but affected its mental and moral responses. To appreciate what it means to live on 1550 calories a day, consider Table 10.

T A B L E 10. Typical Daily Food Ration of a German Adult, May, 1945–March, 1948.

Commodity	Calories per day	Ounces per day
Bread	890	12.7
Meat	25	.7
Fats	102	.5
Sugar	71	.6
Cereals *	258	2.5
Jam	22	.3
Cheese	3	.07
Potatoes	186	10.5
Total	1557	27.87
Skimmed Milk, when available	47	.2 Pt.
Total with milk	1604	. . . .

* Nährmittel.
Source: F. S. V. Donnison, *Civil Affairs and Military Government North-West Europe, 1944–1946* (London: HMSO, 1961), pp. 338–39.

There can be no question that the British and American relief shipments prevented mass starvation in the Western zones of Germany. The German people, nevertheless, were "desperately hungry." [87] The quantities of the various nutrients an average person's diet should contain differ from country to country and from race to race, but The National Research Council, for instance, has recommended 3000 calories daily [88] and the League of Nations called for a minimum of 2400 calories daily for a normal consumer.[89] The postwar rations in Germany amounted to hardly one-half of the recommended minimum level. The diet was also poor in composition; cereals and potatoes sometimes made up as much as 80 percent of the total, and proteins and fats were particularly deficient.[90]

Men of responsibility and authority admitted freely that the actual distributed rations "represented a fairly rapid starvation level." [91] U.S. military government authorities acknowledged that the 1550 calorie ration was "far below minimum standards" of nutrition.[92] Without additional food, one would eventually succumb to starvation.[93]

Under these conditions, the principal concern for a great majority of Germans was to secure additional food in one way or another. This was far more important than earning monetary incomes. It was estimated that from the defeat until the currency reform in mid-June of 1948, Germans in the British and American zones daily consumed an average of 500 calories of non-rationed foods. This was obtained either by bartering away possessions in the countryside, by raising food in garden plots, or by black market purchases.[94] Black market purchases of food were not as significant as they are sometimes made out to be. Many an Allied observer frequently mistook barter transactions for black market purchases. Most individuals could not afford to pay black market prices, which were often a hundred times the legal prices and more. Black market transactions were also generally considered shameful and the agents "immoral and asocial individuals." [95]

After the war the Allies maintained the Nazi labor conscription, which required every German citizen to register with the local labor office. Holding an approved job entitled one to claim a housing card and a ration card legally set at 1550 calories a day.[96] In conditions of acute food shortages, workers generally worked three or four days a week for money wages and devoted the rest of the time to securing food "extras." They exchanged their possessions for food at the farms,[97] and those with nothing to barter collected beechnuts, picked up grain ears on harvested fields, worked on garden plots, or simply stole.

The German vocabulary of the early postwar years was replete with words like *organisieren,* meaning to get something outside legal channels, or *kohlenklauben,* stealing coal wherever possible.[98] The considerable proportions of food and coal thefts are reflected in special statistics compiled by the U.S.

and U.K. military authorities. In the British zone, the amounts of food stolen from railways averaged 1,246 tons a month in 1946, 1,474 tons a month in 1947, and 626 tons a month in 1948.[99]

Field crops, orchards, even harvested fields were also subject to widespread depredations. The crime pattern of 1946–48 shows that food thefts were the most common offenses. In Hamburg, for instance, thefts of ration cards, production of duplicate ration cards, and issuance of unwarranted purchase permits for foodstuffs by city officials channeled hundreds of tons of food into illegal markets in 1947. Up to 100 percent of the meat and fat coupons returned to the food offices by some restaurants were false.[100] The German experience showed once again that the more desperately hungry men are the less law-abiding they become.[101]

From an individual's point of view such illegal, time-consuming food procuring was absolutely necessary, but economically it was highly wasteful. Human resources, instead of producing goods, were spent on the bare maintenance of lives. Such primitivization of economic activity made more people do more work, but output in industry and in agriculture remained low.

The postwar food shortage in Germany showed the level to which food rationing within the framework of direct controls may not be reduced. Rations insufficient to meet the basic nutritional requirements for human sustenance drove people to nonmonetary means of getting food. The result was the emergence of barter. Since the barter system is incompatible with the specialization and division of labor, the German gross national product fell drastically.

4

COAL AND STEEL PRODUCTION
1945–1948

J. M. Keynes remarked after World War I that "the German Empire has been built more truly on coal and iron than on blood and iron."[1] An authoritative U.S. source said in the same vein after World War II that ". . . lacking in virtually all other basic raw materials, Germany was much more dependent upon coal than most other industrial countries."[2] Coal was the backbone of all German industry, vital to her electric power, chemical, synthetic oil, and steel industries.[3]

After the end of hostilities in 1945 Silesia was incorporated into Poland and the Saar region went to France. The sequestration of these two coal producing areas meant a loss of roughly 18 percent of the 1938–39 coal output. The remaining coal deposits of Germany were situated in the British zone, mostly in the Ruhr Valley. The U.S. zone had only soft coal (*Pechkohle*), which is not used in industry.

1. Production of Coal

Low coal output was a conspicuous feature of the postsur-
render period. In absolute figures, Ruhr coal production was
137 million tons in 1938, but only 35.5 million tons in 1945,
53.9 million tons in 1946, 71.1 million tons in 1947, and 87
million tons in 1948.[4] The 1945 production was only 25 percent
of the 1938 output. By 1947 coal production was at 52 percent
of the 1938 level. In 1948, the year of the currency reform,
when German productivity rose rapidly, production climbed
only to 63 percent of 1938 output.

Five factors may account for this performance. First, immediately after the surrender the British military government
sequestered all collieries from the rest of the German economy
and regulated coal production and distribution directly for two
years through contacts with the old management organizations.
Second, an inadequate diet for coal miners affected production.
Third, heavy wartime damage to the German transportation
system and a shortage of railroad cars hampered shipments;
coal frequently piled up at the pits in spite of the demands of
the economy. Fourth, the various level-of-industry plans listed
many producers of coal mining equipment for dismantling.
Fifth, miners were in short supply, they were poorly housed,
and they lacked pit props.

NORTH GERMAN COAL CONTROL

The Morgenthau Plan in the fall of 1944 called for the flooding of all German coal mines after the Nazis' defeat. The Allies
were to assume responsibility for no German economic problems except those interfering with military operations. Critical
Western European coal shortages, however, proved stronger

than the wishful thinking of the Morgenthau-guided policy makers in Washington. To avoid a coal famine during the winter of 1945–46, the British urged that the remnants of the Morgenthau-White policies be scrapped and that the German coal industry be revived by all necessary means. The Potter-Hundley Coal Mission, which recommended this revival in the summer of 1945, also advocated the export to liberated countries of at least 10 million tons of coal during the second half of 1945 and an additional 15 million tons by the end of April, 1946, regardless of the consequences to German industry and population.[5]

The British-run North German Coal Control replaced the former Anglo-American Rhine Control in June, 1945. The British then launched an all-out drive to revive coal production in the Ruhr Valley. The agency requisitioned all coal produced under military authority and deprived German colliery owners of all responsibility for the production and distribution of coal. Production, distribution, and finance divisions of the agency, with headquarters in the Villa Huegel, near Essen, became responsible for spurring coal production and for distributing the output in accordance with the allocations of the Allied Control Council.[6] In September, 1945, the British nominally dissolved the *Rheinisch-Westfälisches Kohlen-Syndikat*, the well-known German sales organization for coal, and replaced it with a newly created North German Coal Distribution Office.[7]

The critical need for coal necessitated the virtual reactivation of the German coal syndicates. All the British could do was to remove the most notorious Nazis from the leading positions and change the name of the sales organization. Despite minute British control, direct responsibility for mine operations remained in German hands. Ownership also remained German, for the time being.

But in December, 1945, the British military authorities ordered the expropriation of all collieries in the British zone without compensation.[8] The British supposedly acted as temporary trustees of the property for the German people.[9] All Nazi-implicated managers and engineers were removed at the same time.[10] Germans now had no voice either in production or distribution—they could only mine the coal.

After the economic fusion of the American and British Zones in 1947 some authority and responsibility in the coal mining industry was given back to the Germans. A new German coal organization, *Deutsche Kohlenbergbau-Leitung*,[11] was nominally made responsible the following fall for the operation and management of the bizonal industry. However, the Bipartite Coal Control Office retained final authority over such matters as production, loading, and distribution. For this reason the German agency remained an instrument of Anglo-American policy for some time.

MINERS' FOOD RATION
AND THE COAL OUTPUT

In the spring of 1945, the Western Allies knew that coal production in the Ruhr would have to be maximized to avoid a coal famine in Western Europe. The chief obstacle was the shortage of food. The Ruhr Valley, the largest industrial area in Europe, was heavily dependent on food imports. The British zone's agriculture was unable to provide even the minimum diet of sustenance, and without food imports the prospect for coal production looked grim.

Coal output and miners' rations were inextricably intertwined. The counterpart of higher food rations was higher coal output. The coal miners' food ration varied as follows:[12] July, 1945–March 4, 1946, 3,400 calories daily; March 4, 1946–June, 1946, 2,900 calories daily; June, 1946–October, 1946, 3,400 calories daily; October, 1946–March, 1947, 4,000 calories daily; March, 1947–July, 1947, 3,600 calories daily;

and July, 1947, to the currency reform in mid-June, 1948, 4,000 calories daily.

Although the miners' ration was almost adequate to meet the basic nutritional requirements of the occupation, their dependents had to linger on the 1550 calorie ration. For months even this level of nutrition could not be met, and frequently miners' dependents existed on 1,000 calories a day. Fat and potato shortages made the situation particularly acute.[13] Under these circumstances, miners shared their rations with their wives and children. This meant that miners lived on a low diet. It was not unusual to find signs of considerable malnutrition,[14] and the miners reacted indignantly when their rations were cut. After the first 500-calorie cut in March, 1946, "coal output in the Ruhr fell sharply." [15] The miners' ration was restored in June, 1946, and coal production went up. In January, 1947, a so-called point system was introduced to reduce absenteeism [16] —the better the attendance, the better the availability of consumers' goods and rationed food. Although absenteeism fell, productivity remained low; the crucial weakness of the early point system was that it stressed attendance and not performance. Even so, the coal output of the Ruhr rose slowly until March, 1947, when the miners' ration was again cut to 3,600 calories. The miners' reaction to this cut was violent, and in the following month production dropped more than a million tons.

In April, May, and June, 1947, the normal consumer in the Ruhr actually received no more than 800 calories.[17] In early May the daily calories actually issued came to 800 in Hamburg, 770 in Hannover and 740 in Essen.[18] Protest strikes broke out all over the valley, but they remained orderly, disciplined and nonviolent. In Hamburg, for instance, 150,000 workers demonstrated and warned that if rations remained at such low levels violence was likely. General Clay and Sir Sholto Douglas replied with warnings of their own, hinting that demonstrations could not help to relieve food shortages, and Sumner Sewell, U.S. Military Governor of Württemberg-Baden, stated that strikes and demonstrations might result in a loss of relief supplies.[19] British and American officials attributed the food crisis to inadequate farm collections and black marketing of food; it was still popular to apply the "you can do it" or "blame the Germans" concept.[20] Indeed, German farmers cannot be absolved, because during 1946 hundreds of thousands of pigs, sheep, and cattle simply disappeared.[21] But also it should be kept in mind that the British and American zones had to feed 10 million more mouths in 1947 than in 1939.

In July, 1947, miners' rations went up again and various incentive schemes were put into effect. These programs promised additional food and consumer goods if the miners' productivity increased and if the production targets were met.[22] But the U.S. Military Governor reported that miners continued to be absent from the coal mines.[23] Potatoes remained scarce, and the miners went to the fields to dig a few for the coming winter. Although coal production rose, productivity remained low. For instance, the average daily output per miner in 1938 was 1.5 tons,[24] but in 1946 and 1947 the average output was .86 tons and .88 tons per day, respectively.[25] Productivity went up sharply only after the currency reform, when over-all economic conditions improved considerably.

DISRUPTED TRANSPORTATION SYSTEM

The U.S. Strategic Bombing Survey reported that the destruction of the German railways in 1944 and 1945 "was the major factor contributing to the rapid collapse of the German coal economy."[26] The Allied bombing damage to German tracks, bridges, and switches was particularly heavy. It is estimated that in May, 1945, in the Western Zones of Germany, 2,300 railroad bridges remained destroyed, 12,800 switches were not operating, 1,600 signal booths did not function, and 5,000 main signals did not flash.[27] By the late fall of 1945 the Ruhr Valley had re-established the most important haul lines.[28] But blocked waterways and lack of barges and tugs crippled water transportation, which imposed additional strains on the German railroads. In 1946, 80 percent of all coal was transported by rail, a considerably greater proportion than in 1938. The Ruhr's hard-coal industry had at its disposal daily around 11,500 cars of 10 tons each,[29] almost 3,500 cars less than required, but at least whatever coal was mined in this period was also moved.

The British knew, of course, that the Potsdam Agreement imposed stringent production ceilings on important segments of German industry, but they still hoped to win the coal battle.[30] However, in the fall of 1946 it became quite evident that the over-all stagnation of German industry was likely to block further recovery of coal production. For one thing, the lack of raw materials, spare parts, and facilities hampered railroad repair shops.[31] Lack of repairs and upkeep, in turn, resulted in a serious reduction of serviceable rolling stock. The pool of nonserviceable locomotives and cars grew rapidly; in May, 1947, 30 percent of the entire service-car stock was out of commission, compared with a normal figure of 4 percent.[32] In early 1947, 25 percent of all locomotives were also in disrepair.[33] The entire transportation system was virtually paralyzed by the unusually hard winter of 1946–47, but even after the cold weather passed transportation remained a major bottleneck.

The principal reason for continued transportation difficulties was the Allied industrial disarmament policy. Stagnation in other sectors of the economy spread and eventually hobbled the transportation system. In 1947 the Western German economy was retrogressing rapidly. In such a milieu, the Executive Director of the Bizonal Economic Department felt that, compared to 1947, 1945 still had been "golden times." [34]

A general survey of the German economy in mid-1947 stated

that no additional coal would be available without better transportation.[35] In 1947, on the average, the hard coal industry of the Ruhr had fewer cars at its disposal than in 1946.[36] The shortage of locomotives and railroad cars was aggravated by the refusal of the liberated countries, France especially, to return cars that went to them with coal exports. After long disputes, only personal intervention by General Clay finally put an effective end to such practices.[37]

Mined coal now remained unmoved at the coal pits, causing industries to curtail operations or close. The miners were hurt psychologically because no matter how much coal they mined it remained at the pits.

COAL PRODUCTION AND ITS RELATIONSHIP
TO INDUSTRIAL DISARMAMENT

The policy of industrial disarmament, besides crippling coal transportation, affected the mines directly. The policy called not for the mines' destruction but for a considerable stimulation of the industry for greater exports.[38] But this effort was partially thwarted by what may be called the sector planning of the British military authorities.

The emphasis was on the speediest possible increase in coal production, while the rest of the economy remained subject to the strictures of the Potsdam Agreement.[39] While the wartime damage underground was small, the damage to the mines' surface power-generating facilities and pumps was heavy.[40] Replacement of worn-out mining equipment generally had been neglected, and without replacements frequent breakdowns were inevitable. Although the lack of pneumatic hammers and their spare parts, driving belts, cables, and hundreds of other items hampered coal production, ninety-seven firms producing coal mining equipment—most of whom had supplied little or nothing to Hitler's armies—remained on the dismantling list.[41]

The shortage of pit props also hampered postwar coal mining operations. Before the war, as much as 55 percent of the Ruhr's pit-prop needs came from the Soviet zone and the provinces ceded to Poland. Much of the rest came from the U.S.-occupied area. At the time of surrender, the Allies found no reserve of pit props in the Ruhr. Since the British zone could not meet all the pit-prop requirements from its own sources, and since requests to the Soviets yielded no results, the solution of this problem hinged upon pit-prop supplies from the U.S. zone.[42]

By the end of the summer of 1945 the critical immediate shortages of pit props were overcome, but the supply situation for the future was not bright. The British and Americans knew that unless more coal could be mined a coal famine in Western Europe would be inevitable. An assured supply of pit props was indispensable. Through joint efforts the British and Americans managed to keep the mines operating, but pit-prop supplies remained inadequate for years.

A lack of timber imports and the Allied exports of German timber were two principal reasons for the shortage of pit props. Timber exports from the U.S.-occupied zone were particularly heavy. American military government sources admitted that such timber exports were necessary for the "ultimate destruction of the war potential of German forests." [43] Clear felling was widely practiced, and an extensive deforestation resulted which could "be replaced only by long forestry development over perhaps a century." [44]

It was estimated that during the winter of 1946–47 less than 50 percent of the pit-prop requirements was met.[45] In November, 1947, the deliveries came to 73 percent of the requirements, the deficiencies being met from stocks.[46] In January, 1948, pit-prop deliveries continued well below requirements and the general position was "still extremely grave." [47]

HOUSING AND LABOR SUPPLY

Housing was another major factor which kept in check the postwar coal production in the Ruhr. Wartime bombing caused heavy destruction of miners' homes. A survey showed that only 58,890 of 315,858 miners' apartments had not been damaged.[48] Out of 149,267 company-owned apartments, 82 percent were either destroyed or damaged.[49]

During the first eighteen months of occupation, hardly any progress was made in repairing the homes of the miners. Lack of building materials and manpower and lack of British interest in any definite miners' home repair program were the major reasons. The bombed-out miners lived in emergency quarters, chiefly barracks. Substandard housing impinged negatively upon miners' productivity. In the summer of 1947, Robert Moses, the well-known Park Commissioner of New York, made a special inquiry into the housing conditions of the Ruhr miners and was appalled at what he found. If before the war German miners lived better than any other miners in the world, after the war they lived worse.[50] He contended that unless there was an immediate home-building program for miners, productivity would remain low. The German coal-mining management also pressed time and again for such a program, but all such pleas fell on deaf ears.[51]

A shortage of miners was another bottleneck. In May, 1945, after foreign workers and former prisoners of war had returned to their own countries, employment in the hard-coal mining industry in the British zone stood at 203,000, only 60 percent of 1938 employment.[52]

The British military government decided to recruit miners on a compulsory basis. The British Manpower Division, together with the German labor offices, selected young German men and sent them under guard to the Ruhr,[53] and employment in the industry stood at 320,000 in December, 1946.[54]

Of the increase, 53,000 were former coal miners returned from prisoner-of-war camps and the rest were "green" labor. During a few months of 1946 up to 80 percent of the "green" labor force deserted the mines.[55] The desertion rate during 1946 was 64 percent of recruitment.[56] Employment rose with the introduction of the various incentive schemes in 1947 and in December, 1947, stood at 391,000. Higher pay, more consumer goods, and greater care in selecting new miners reduced the desertion rate to 44 percent in 1947.[57] It was particularly important to cut the rate because most deserters disappeared with the issued miners' gear, such as clothing, boots, and tools.[58]

Ruhr mining employment now was slowly reaching the saturation point. Greater employment would be possible only with more and better machines. Coal output rose less rapidly than employment because productivity remained low. It was estimated that in September, 1947, the output per miner was 52 percent of the 1936 level.[59]

2. Distribution of Coal

COAL EXPORTS

During the first eighteen months of occupation, American policy held that German coal must be exported to liberated countries "even at the cost of delaying recovery in Germany." [60] Twenty-five years before, Keynes admonished the peacemakers at Versailles that if Germany was forced to export coal she could not continue as an industrial nation. He warned that Germany without industry would undergo "starvation en masse." [61] But mankind seems to have a remarkable propensity for disregarding the lessons of the past. After World War II, the Western Allies were bent on safeguarding Europe by depriving Germany of a considerable portion of her heavy industries. With less industry in Germany, it was believed, more coal would be available for other countries.

Once Germany had surrendered, the Allies found substantial coal stocks in the Ruhr, estimated at from 5 to 6 million tons.[62] The Fuel Committee of the Allied Control Council in Berlin, with the European Coal Organization, was in charge of meeting the most urgent coal needs of the liberated countries.[63]

The postwar coal shortage was particularly acute because Britain did not export coal until the end of 1947. Germany was called upon to make up part of the deficit. The European Coal Commission made regular recommendations concerning the division of German coal exports, and the Fuel Committee of the Allied Control Council accepted them without question. By the end of 1946, practically all the Ruhr coal stocks were gone. In the prevailing climate of opinion German coal needs were neglected, and nobody knew what they were or what they were likely to be.

The Potter-Hyndley report had recommended stepped-up coal exports from Germany.[64] There is some evidence that, at times so much Ruhr coal was rolling into Belgium and Denmark, these countries had "no space to store it." [65] A British traveler in Belgium was reported to have seen "huge stocks of coal at practically all stations, piled high and wide." [66]

The first major policy change came after the abortive Moscow Conference on Germany in March, 1947, when the British, American and French governments agreed on a formula for fixing the proportion of German coal exports. Beginning with July 1, 1947, exports of American and British zones were to be fixed in terms of a percentage of marketable coal produced, starting with 21 percent when the production reached 280,000 tons a day and rising to 25 percent when it reached 370,000 tons a day.[67]

TABLE II. Coal Exports of the British Zone of Germany. (In millions of tons)

Year	Output	Exports	% of output	% of marketable output *
1936	158	28	18	. . . .
1946	53.9	10	20.4	24
1947	71.1	9.3	14.6	18.3
1948	87.0	16.3	21	24.4

* After allowance for coal consumed at collieries and issued to miners.
Sources: 1936, Statistisches Reichsamt, *Statistisches Jahrbuch für das Deutsche Reich* (Berlin, P. Schmidt, 1937), p. 145; Deutsche Kohlenbergbau-Leitung, *Zahlen zur Kohlenwirtschaft*, No. 3 (April, 1948), p. 14; No. 7 (April, 1949), p. 14.

Table 11, which shows the coal production and export data, omits 1945, for which little reliable information is available. Calculations based on U.S. military government reports show exports of 4.4 million tons, about 12 percent of the coal mined for the rest of 1945, but this figure seems low because it is known that from May, 1945, through the summer of 1946 a high proportion of the coal mined was exported.[68]

The figures for 1946 would have been higher if the British military government had not yielded to German pleas and cut coal exports by 350,000 tons a month in October, 1946. It was expected that lower coal exports would help to revive German industrial production which, in turn, would spur both output and the industrial recovery of other Western European countries. In April, 1947, coal exports were again stepped up, primarily to meet the coal needs of France, but for the year as a whole coal exports were smaller than in the previous year.[69]

In 1948, especially in the second half after the monetary reform restored normal economic incentives, coal production and exports rose considerably. Over-all exports from the bizonal area, as compared with prewar years, were not excessively large.

Exports in 1947 came barely to one-third of the 1936 level, and the frequently heard German charge that the "British took away our coal" has little foundation.[70]

Coal was one of thirteen commodities whose prices were regulated by the Allied Control Council.[71] The coal price was set at RM 15 per ton, about the same level as during the war. Since this had not covered the costs of production, the Reich government had paid subsidies to producers. After the war, in the absence of any new ruling on the continuation of subsidies, coal mines in the Ruhr were hard pressed for cash. They had to obtain short-term loans from banks to meet payrolls and other costs. Because of low output, rising costs of pit props, and higher wages, costs of production rose to RM 30 a ton.[72] The official price was just about enough to cover half of this. After the formation of the North German Coal Control, mines were given subsidies to meet operating costs. However, the debts incurred with commercial banks were never repaid,[73] and no funds were provided for repairing war damage. It was estimated that from the surrender to November, 1947, RM 1.8 billion were paid to hard-coal producers in the two zones.[74] The taxpayer, of course, footed the bill.

From May, 1945, to September, 1947, the Western Allies exported German coal at $10.50 a ton, while the world price was $25 to $30 a ton.[75] In September, 1947, the export price was raised to $15 a ton, but this price was still $5 to $7 less than the price of American and Polish coal. Estimating that approximately 25 million tons of coal were exported from May, 1945 to the end of 1947, the net loss to the German economy from this source alone was almost $200 million.

After World War I Germany used to barter her coal for Danish butter, Swiss milk, and Norwegian fats.[76] But after World War II German coal exports were determined by the Western Allies and no deals could be arranged. There were many offers because Western European countries desperately needed German coal and steel. The Italians could not sell the vegetables they had previously sold in Germany. The Dutch wanted to sell vegetables for German machinery and coal, but the Allies refused to consider the offers and the Dutch had to destroy considerable portions of their crop. Denmark offered 150 tons of lard a month; Turkey wanted to sell hazelnuts; Norway was ready to sell fish and fish oil; Sweden even offered considerable quantities of fats to alleviate shortages in the British zone in exchange for the toys of Nuremberg. But again nothing happened.[77]

INTERNAL COAL CONSUMPTION

Table 12 offers a view of the distribution of the coal mined in the immediate postwar years. Among its notable features are the figures for colliery consumption and miners' allowances. In 1938, the coal mines of the Ruhr consumed roughly 8 percent of the amount mined. But they consumed 21.26 percent in 1946 and 17.84 percent in 1947, because of insufficient utilization of mines and poor operating efficiency of the machinery and equipment.[78] Miners' allowances rose from 1.5 percent in 1938 to almost 4 percent in 1946, primarily because of somewhat smaller employment while productivity remained at roughly 50 percent of prewar levels.

The table shows that the amount of coal allocated to German industry in 1946 equaled exports and consumption by the occupation forces and the German transportation system. In 1947 industry's consumption rose well above the other categories' total.

Civilians' homes fared less well. Before the war, households and small businesses consumed about 20 percent of German coal output. No hard coal or briquettes were allocated in the fall of 1945 for civilian heating or cooking. North German Coal Control permitted the issuance of 100 kilograms of inferior coal

TABLE 12. German Coal Consumption, 1946 and 1947. (In millions of tons)

ITEM	1946	1947
Total Output	53.9	71.1
Coking & briquetting	2.6	4.0
Miner's allowances	2.0	2.3
Consumed at collieries	11.2	12.2
Other Deductions	0.5	0.9
Available for Distribution	37.7	51.7
Actual Distribution	42.0	50.8
Railroad & Water Transportation	8.6	10.6
Military	1.4	2.5
German Industry	20.9	27.2
Domestic Fuel	1.1	1.3
Exports	10.0	9.3
Change in Stocks	−4.3	+1.1

Source: Deutsche Kohlenbergbau-Leitung, *Zahlen zur Kohlenwirtschaft,* No. 3 (April, 1948), p. 14.

per household per month,[79] but this amount was not sufficient. To supplement this ration the Germans received wood in various quantities and qualities—each person in Frankfurt was allocated 300 kilograms of wood in the first postwar winter.[80] This wood was generally used for the preparation of meals, and nothing was available for heating homes. Fortunately the winter of 1945–46 was exceptionally mild.

As the second postwar winter approached the Western Allies maintained this policy. German authorities in the British zone outlined the so-called "Eutiner Plan" of September 20, 1946, which called for some minimum allocation of coal, briquettes, and inferior coal for household heating purposes, but the Allies insisted that wood, gas, and inferior coal should suffice. Then came the winter of unusual severity, and under heavy pressure the Allied Control Council allocated 25 kilograms of coal per household in January, 1947 and raised the ration to 37.5 kilograms per household in February and March.[81]

In March, 1947, the bipartite economic control groups made the first allocation of coal for German household heating purposes. Every person was to receive 300 kilograms of briquettes per year, and the total amount to be distributed came to 1.5 million tons of hard coal and 3 million tons of brown-coal briquettes.[82] These amounts were actually issued, but they were far from sufficient to meet the minimum requirements for warmth. In the second postwar winter, the average German household in the two Western zones received 260 kilograms of briquettes or coal.[83] During the last year of the war every German household received about 500 kilograms of coal for heating.

The inability to obtain coal legally drove the Germans to illegal means. Coal dealers' stocks, moving or standing coal trains, and coal piles of occupation troops became subject to widespread depredations. German business establishments also distributed substantial portions of their officially allocated coal to workers [84] because they knew that hungry and freezing workers were unfit for work.[85]

3. The Postwar Steel Industry

All Allied blueprints for the industrial disarmament of Germany aimed at a considerable reduction of her heavy industry, especially iron and steel. The first and second level-of-industry plans imposed such low ceilings on Germany's steel and iron output that other industrial production could never attain even the permissible levels.[86] The steel production cut was so substantial that it brought the bizonal economy to rock bottom early in 1948.[87] The shortage of steel was the major bottleneck of industrial production.

The British zone had 70 percent of Germany's steel and iron industry. The region in 1938 produced 14.4 million tons of raw iron, 16.4 million tons of steel, and 10.5 million tons of rolled steel.[88] During the war some of this capacity was destroyed or damaged, but considerable capacity remained intact. With a minimum of repairs and with an adequate supply of Swedish iron ore a steel output of 6 million tons a year was possible. But the actual output of raw iron, steel, and rolled steel during the first three postwar years lingered at around 25 percent of 1938 levels.

NORTH GERMAN STEEL AND IRON CONTROL

The poor production performance of the postwar German steel industry was conditioned by the fact that the German administrative bodies had little or no responsibility. The British sequestered the steel industry from the rest of the economy and regulated it directly.

In the fall of 1945 the Allied Control Council was greatly concerned with the dissolution of German cartels, which was deemed necessary to reduce the German war potential in steel, chemical and machinery making. With this in mind the British put the entire iron and steel industry under the direct control of the military government's Metallurgy Branch. Subordinate to it was the newly established, German-administered Steel and Iron Office (*Verwaltungsamt für Stahl und Eisen*), with headquarters in Düsseldorf, which supervised fourteen branches of the industry and was responsible for supplying plants with coal, iron ore, scrap, alloys, manpower, and other requirements.[89] The Steel and Iron Office could not form policy; it could only implement British policy.

With the formation of the first German administrative agencies in the fall of 1946, the Steel and Iron Office was incorporated into the Central Economics Office (*Zentralamt für Wirtschaft*) in Minden.[90] The Steel and Iron Office was given greater responsibility for the industry's day-to-day operations but could not issue operating permits, determine prices and exports, or deal with personnel matters. These problems were still under the sole jurisdiction of the British military government. After the unification of the British and American zones the Central Economics Office was dissolved and the Steel and Iron Office was incorporated into the bizonal Economics Office (*Verwaltungsamt für Wirtschaft*).[91]

In addition to the sequestration, a series of purely political experiments were undertaken in the iron and steel industry. Proceedings to break up cartels in the industry were initiated.[92] In December, 1945, all coal mines and coke-making facilities were separated from steel and iron producing concerns.[93] On August 20, 1946, the British seized all steel and iron factories [94] and put them under the supervision of the North German Iron and Steel Control.[95] This agency, a trusteeship headed by Heinrich Dinkelbach with headquarters in Düsseldorf, held the basic objective of breaking steel and iron cartels into smaller units.[96] In the spring of 1947 "Operation Severance" was launched to establish new steel and iron producing firms with a starting capital of RM 100,000. On March 1, 1947, four of these companies were in existence, and by April 1, 1948, there were twenty-five.[97]

The financial consequences of this experimentation were far-reaching and costly. During 1946, the German steel industry in the British zone lost RM 175 million; in 1947, the loss was over RM 200 million.[98] These companies were paid subsidies of RM 66 per ton of iron and RM 23 per ton of steel to keep them going.[99]

Low-capacity operation was one costly factor. Even more costly was the lack of Swedish iron ore, which was barred by the Allies. The use of low-grade German ore resulted in a highly uneconomical use of coal. Production of a ton of raw iron took about 1.2 tons of coal with Swedish ore but about five tons of coal with German ore.[100] To produce a ton of steel required almost twice as much coke with local ore.

As long as the Allies continued to maintain wartime prices for steel the entire industry suffered losses. On April 1, 1948, steel prices were raised and the subsidy was discontinued. Steel production remained unsatisfactory despite the price hike, and the Germans still had hardly any voice in management. The Allied postwar political experimentation with the German steel industry was drawing to a close, and the steel famine in Western Europe clearly sobered some of the most enthusiastic advocates of "decartelization." The economic consequences of the measure were disastrous.[101]

IRON ORE AND SCRAP SUPPLY

Even in August, 1939, during the last-minute preparations for the war with Poland, the German steel industry depended on foreign sources for 65 percent of its iron ore.[102] Practically all ore imports came from Sweden, and the source was not cut off until the fall of 1944, when the Swedes refused to make further shipments.[103] No more ore came from Sweden until almost three years after the fighting had ended.

The first level of industry plan of 1946 limited Germany's steel production to 5.8 million tons a year. The revised plan of 1947 for the bizonal area raised the permissible level to 10.7 million tons.[104] But with only local supplies of ore and other difficulties the bizonal industry could produce only 3 million tons of steel in 1948,[105] although the planned production had been 4.8 million tons.

To step up steel output, the Anglo-American military authorities decided to permit ore imports from Sweden. For 1948, 2.5

million tons of high-grade iron ore were necessary. After a serious struggle with the British, who wanted Germans to buy Swedish ore by way of London, direct purchases were arranged and the first shipload of ore docked at Rotterdam February 4, 1948.[106] This step was of considerable importance for the restoration of more efficient ways of producing steel.

Scrap iron was the only ingredient of steel production which was not in short supply after the war. If the bizonal steel industry had been permitted to operate at capacity, high output would have been possible with the available scrap supply. The steel industry in the United Kingdom and the rest of Western Europe was booming and the demand for scrap from all sources was insatiable. Statutory stagnation of German industry made Germany a particularly attractive source of scrap supply. For the United Kingdom, the heavily industrialized British-occupied zone of Germany became "the only source of scrap supply" in the early postwar period.[107]

The British obtained a substantial amount from three sources: booty, reparations, and commercial channels. Booty scrap consisted of all warlike material as determined and collected by the Disposal Group of the British Control Commission. Reparations scrap came from machines and machine tools which the Germans had to surrender to the Inter-Allied Reparations Agency in Brussels. If no nation wanted a particular piece of equipment for re-use it was taken over by the British as reparations scrap. The amounts of booty and reparations scrap are not known exactly, but they were quite substantial; 3 million tons would be a fairly close estimate.[108]

Three British government agencies purchased and shipped scrap by commercial channels. The Commerce Division of the British Control Commission, acting as an agent for the Ministry of Supply, and the Iron and Steel Disposals, Ltd., were endowed with considerable authority in the German scrap market and could practically requisition the available stocks for worthless Reichsmarks. During the early period of occupation they obtained sizable amounts of scrap in this way. The third agency, the Scrap Export Agency, was primarily concerned with the transportation of scrap to the United Kingdom.[109]

From mid-1946 to mid-1947, 450,000 tons of commercial scrap were sold to the British at £3 a ton, while the American price fluctuated between £7 and £11 a ton.[110] In the last quarter of 1947 the British demanded an additional million tons of commercial scrap. They estimated that, because of the low level of German steel production, roughly 5 million tons would easily be available for export. However, in view of the approaching European Recovery Program, the Germans successfully resisted British demands.

The very crux of the Marshall Plan was to revive the existing German steel capacity and put it back into operation with all possible speed. An indispensable part of the new and more positive economic policy of the Western Allies toward Germany was currency reform. But anticipation of such a reform made the scrap dealers reluctant to part with their stocks. Everybody knew that any currency reform would scale down the existing monetary wealth, while real wealth would not be immediately affected. A considerable flight from money into real goods took place, and the West German steel industry experienced difficulty in obtaining sufficient scrap to maintain an output of even 5 million tons a year.[111]

Under pressure, the Germans agreed in March, 1948 to export 100,000 tons at a price of £ 6/10 a ton.[112] In terms of dollars the British paid $26 a ton, while the current world price ranged from $40 to $43 a ton. Such transactions were costly both in terms of foreign exchange foregone and in terms of steel available for domestic consumption.

INDUSTRIAL DISARMAMENT
AND STEEL PRODUCTION

The Allied policy of industrial disarmament impinged directly upon steel production. Insufficient allocations of coal, lack of high-grade iron ore, and insufficient transportation were some of the difficulties which affected the steel industry directly.

During the first two postwar years German administrative agencies allocated the available coal to as many industries as possible so as to keep all going on a limited scale.[113] Only after mid-1947 were priorities assigned that gave the steel industry more coal. However, the Allied coal allocations remained insufficient to attain even the permissible steel output of 10.7 million tons a year. The bizonal steel industry consumed 4,417,997 tons of coal and coke in 1946, 4,631,678 tons in 1947, 7,916,325 tons in 1948, and 10,045,094 tons in 1949.[114] In 1949, the first year when the Allied economic chains were cast away, coal consumption rose more than 40 percent above the previous year.

The yearly reports of the *Verwaltungsamt für Stahl und Eisen* for 1946 and 1947 throw much light on the adverse effects of the Allied industrial disarmament policy on the German steel industry. Such indispensable supplies as alloys, stones, carbide, electric bulbs, timber, and protective clothing were available at first from wartime stocks only. By the end of 1946 most stocks were gone, and it was estimated that the industry in 1947 obtained about 20 percent of all required complementary items for steel production.[115] Under such circumstances, as shown by Table 13, production was low.

Immediately after the surrender, steel and iron output wavered at around 20 percent of the prewar level.[116] Only after the inauguration of the Marshall Plan was the German steel industry permitted to take its traditional role in the international division of labor in Western Europe.

TABLE 13. Iron and Steel Production in the Bizonal Areas, 1946–1949. (In thousands of tons)

Year	Pig Iron	Steel	Rolled Steel
1946	2,084	2,496	1,970
1947	2,264	3,000	2,161
1948	4,663	5,466	3,721
1949	7,140	9,025	6,339

Source: Amt für Stahl und Eisen, *Statistisches Vierteljahresheft,* January-March, 1950, p. 6.

With industrial output low, exports of machinery, steel, and chemicals were partially replaced by the Allied-sanctioned exports of raw materials. Of the total exports from the bizonal area of Germany, 75 percent was coal and 15 percent other raw materials in 1946, and 55 percent was coal, 24 percent other raw materials in 1947.[117]

These policies transformed Germany into a raw material exporting country, her economic status more than a hundred years before. Almost fantastic scarcities of raw materials and fuel resulted. German businesses, however, did not stop operating. They turned to illicit sources of supply.

5

POSTWAR INDUSTRY IN
THE BIZONAL AREA:
AN OVER-ALL VIEW

Scarcities of food, raw materials, and coal threatened the existence of business as well as men. German businesses could not operate on the meager official allocations of coal and raw materials. To keep the firms going at all, German businessmen turned to the black market, where prices were a hundred times the legal prices, and barter. A number of institutional factors as well as almost unbelievable shortages caused industrial stagnation in the bizonal area. Among these were uncertainty arising from the threat of reparations removals, the expectation of currency reform, and the postwar price freeze. This chapter will examine these factors.

1. *Industrial Output, 1945–1948*

The level of industrial production is a good indicator of the prevailing economic situation in an economy. Table 14 shows

TABLE 14. Index of Industrial Production, Bizonal Area of Germany. (1936 = 100)

Month	All Industrial Groups *	Coal	Iron and Steel	Vehicles	Mining Excluding Coal	Building Materials	Sawmills	Chemicals	Rubber Products	Paper and Pulp	Leather	Textiles	Electricity
1946													
January	26	47	13	15	21	27	75	30	29	20	27	15	73
February	27	48	15	14	21	26	76	34	21	18	28	14	71
March	30	45	17	14	33	27	87	38	29	19	30	15	78
April	30	46	16	16	42	32	87	40	30	22	30	16	70
May	32	47	21	17	50	38	100	43	32	24	30	17	72
June	33	49	21	15	53	36	101	46	32	24	29	19	75
July	36	50	26	17	63	43	110	49	38	28	34	21	76
August	37	50	28	19	70	47	107	48	38	38	34	20	81
September	37	52	26	22	72	42	92	45	39	27	36	22	81
October	38	52	21	21	76	42	97	47	44	28	37	23	90
November	38	55	26	17	79	43	91	47	43	25	35	22	90
December	32	55	27	14	61	32	83	43	35	22	27	20	89
Monthly av.	33	50	21	17	53	36	92	42	34	25	32	19	79
1947													
January	29	58	20	12	44	24	70	32	18	21	28	18	86
February	28	62	18	10	27	24	68	26	23	18	25	19	80
March	33	64	22	11	35	25	58	33	31	19	33	24	89
April	37	58	24	20	64	33	88	47	44	26	36	28	88

May	35			22	72	40	96	50	42	28	36	29	89
June	39	61	24	21	71	42	94	44	43	30	37	29	86
July	42	63	26	24	82	44	98	47	46	32	34	31	88
August	42	65	27	24	83	47	99	49	41	32	31	31	88
September	41	66	27	23	85	46	99	44	45	31	31	32	86
October	43	68	30	19	83	45	98	44	47	32	37	36	91
November	44	72	30	23	85	44	94	44	48	32	32	35	94
December	43	72	29	20	86	41	83	51	48	33	31	32	99
Monthly av.	38	64	25	19	68	38	87	43	40	28	33	29	89
1948													
January	44	72	30	23	92	38	78	54	47	35	33	37	100
February	45	70	29	26	88	35	65	54	56	37	36	40	99
March	48	77	32	29	99	45	66	59	58	37	42	44	103
April	50	76	34	31	110	50	87	55	64	37	40	48	102
May	45	66	30	29	93	46	92	50	52	35	31	41	95
June	50	79	35	32	107	51	82	50	50	38	25	47	97

* In the absence of truly bizonal data, the above production index was calculated by weighing together the published production indices for the British and American zones. It is a weighted average of the two zonal indices, where the individual industry groups were adjusted to achieve comparability between the two zones.

Sources: Control Commission for Germany (British Element), *Monthly Statistical Bulletin*, No. 3 (July, 1948), pp. 60-61, and U.S. Office of Military Government, *Monthly Report*, No. 38 (August, 1948), p. 98.

that in 1946 the bizonal area's monthly average of industrial production was one-third the 1936 level; in 1947 the average was 38 percent.

The data show divergent trends among the various segments of industry. The index of coal production rose slowly but steadily from the beginning of the occupation; the brief dips were brought about primarily by the recurrent food shortages in the Ruhr Valley, as discussed in Chapter IV. Production of the steel and iron industry, also discussed in Chapter IV, was most unsatisfactory. The shortage of steel and other industrial supplies was clearly reflected in the low level of operations of the automobile industry. The chemical and rubber producing industries operated at around 40 percent of the 1936 levels, well above the performance of the paper, leather, and textile industries. The production performance of the extractive industries, such as iron-ore mining, and of the building materials group was considerably higher than in industries that depended on the supplies of other industries.

THE ALLIED REPARATIONS PROGRAM AND UNCERTAINTY

During the first three years of occupation, plant removals for reparations from the Anglo-American zones were much smaller than had been expected and announced. An American writer on the subject has stated that in this period "physical dismantling and deliveries [of industrial plants] had minuscule proportions."[1] With the onset of the cold war between East and West, the British and American governments started to revise some of their wartime views on the permissible level of German industry. The inter-Allied negotiations on reparations and the future of German industry were long and indecisive. The German business community knew that many plants would be removed or destroyed, but nobody knew which plants. Businessmen simply marked time. Although during the first two years of occupation considerable effort went into the restoration of plants and equipment,[2] entrepreneurial initiative was lamed and incentives were blunted.[3]

The first Allied "Plan for Reparations and the Level of German Post-War Economy" of March 26, 1946, called for the removal of about 1600 plants from the American and British zones of occupation.[4] The restoration of German economic unity was necessary for quadripartite acceptance of the plan. But the hoped-for economic unity remained unfulfilled, and the country continued to be divided into four almost watertight zones of occupation. This led to a major stall of the Allied reparations program. In May, 1946, the U.S. Military Governor suspended all reparations pending restoration of economic unity[5] and the British followed suit.

Since some hope for the economic unification of the four zones remained, the Americans and British continued to process and to evaluate German plants for eventual reparations in accordance with the first level of industry plan. Table 15, showing the chronological development of the number of plants on the reparations list, reveals indecisive variations. At the end of 1946 the Inter-Allied Reparation Agency had been able to allocate only thirty-three plants for distribution from the two zones.[6]

TABLE 15. Number of Plants Approved for Reparations from U.S. and U.K. Zones.

Date	U.S. Zone	U.K. Zone
April 30, 1946	161	266
June 30, 1946	149	451
September 30, 1946	157	444
March 31, 1947	158	477
September 30, 1947	173	481
December 30, 1947	187	496

Source: U.S. Office of Military Government, *Monthly Report: Reparations and Restitution,* Nos. 9, 12, 15, 21, 27, 30.

Despite wartime destruction the German industrial potential was considerably greater than the Allies were initially willing to permit. The climate of opinion in the Allied countries held that the available German industrial potential was vastly above the future requirements of the economy and that a limited reparations program from the three Western zones could be initiated.

The Inter-Allied Reparation Agency exerted great pressure on the American and British military governments for the immediate release of some capital equipment. The agency's spokesmen argued that making German industrial machinery available to the victors would speed up economic recovery in the liberated countries. As the pressures mounted, the British and Americans agreed to make an allocation of general-purpose machine tools for the Reparation Agency. In November, 1946, some fifty-one plants in the three Western zones, valued at RM 42 million, were released for distribution.[7]

At the same time the British promised to make available machinery and equipment valued at RM 75 million from their zone alone and initiated the Emergency Delivery Scheme the following month. Under the terms of this program, machine tools and other equipment were not to be taken from the plants which, because of bomb damage, had not been declared available for reparations as working units. The machines removed should be surplus—that is, they should not be unique and their removal should not reduce seriously the productive capacity of the plants from which they were to be taken.[8]

The execution of the program differed considerably from this aim. In terms of day-to-day operations, the Inter-Allied Reparation Agency initially requested specific types of machinery and equipment from the lists of plants approved by the Economic Subcommittee of the Allied Control Council. But British military government officials commonly selected the requested equipment not from the damaged plants but from plants that were not on the reparations list at all. In all such cases the most modern available equipment was selected. It was not unusual after the removal of one special-purpose machine for the output of a factory to decline as much as 50 percent.[9] In other cases the removal of special-purpose equipment lowered the quality of products. Since most of the machinery removed went to Great Britain, the German business community gained the impression that one of the main purposes of the program was the crippling of German industry to eliminate a potential British competitor.[10] By the end of September, 1947, some 4,082 machines, of which 98 were highly specialized items, had been removed from the British zone.[11] Thus while the removal of whole plants was indeed of "minuscule proportions," the removal of special purpose machinery was substantial and considerably retarded industrial output.

The British terminated the program with the publication of the bizonal level of industry plan. Under the program, the Inter-Allied Reparation Agency had obtained general-purpose machinery valued at RM 24 million in 1938 prices.

After the acceptance of the new level of industry plan a great number of the plants scheduled for dismantling were made available to the Inter-Allied Reparation Agency. By the end of 1947, 197 plants valued at RM 206 million in 1938 prices had been allocated for transfer to liberated countries.[12]

Thus, during the first two years of occupation actual plant removals in the American and British zones were relatively few.[13] However, the existence of the reparation and restitution programs, the British machinery removal, and an often high-handed interpretation of the reparation and restitution programs by Allied personnel subjected the entire German business community to fear and uncertainty. By the end of 1947, German industry demanded an immediate end of the restitution program and charged that under the pretext of restitution it had been thoroughly and systematically exploited by some unscrupulous members of the military governments.[14]

During the first six months of 1948 no plants were dismantled in the American and British zones. It should have seemed obvious that the continuation of plant removals would work at cross purposes with the European Recovery Program, but politics proved stronger than purely economic considerations and the dismantling of German plants was resumed. In the second half of 1948, 157 plants were dismantled, 118 of which were engineering plants. The removal of German industrial facilities continued,[15] until the reparations program officially came to an end in 1951. In all 667 plants with an estimated 1938 value of RM 708.5 million were removed from the Western zones of Germany.[16]

Though in quantitative terms the reparations extracted from the bizonal area of Germany were small, German industry was also subjected to screening teams of Allied economic experts empowered to examine all patents and drawings and to learn all business secrets. The value of this material has been estimated at 12 to 30 billion marks.[17]

Such appropriation of business secrets reduced producers' initiative. This and the widespread uncertainty over potential dismantling were more important factors than the dismantling itself in the industrial stagnation prior to the economic and currency reform of 1948.

THE EXPECTATION OF THE CURRENCY REFORM

The unsettled currency situation was another phenomenon which intensified the economic stagnation of the American and British zones of occupation. This section will discuss the "flight out of the Reichsmark" and the process of splitting the economy by the hoarding-oriented German business community.

From 1936 to the end of the war, the Reich debt grew from about RM 30 billion to RM 400 billion, excluding war-induced claims, which came to another RM 400 billion. During the same period, currency in circulation increased from RM 5 billion to RM 50 billion, and bank deposits expanded from RM 30 billion to about RM 150 billion.[18] In contrast to the spectacular increase in monetary wealth, the German real wealth had shrunk from about RM 500–600 billion in 1939 to RM 300 billion in 1946, in terms of 1939 values.[19]

Under the existing postwar conditions, three principal alternatives or combinations thereof were available in the face of the inflationary potential:

a) Remove all controls on prices and wages and throw the gates open for the price mechanism to re-establish the equilibrium.

b) Reduce the wartime monetary wealth by a currency reform.

c) Retain the existing direct controls and work off the excess demand gradually by increasing the supply of goods and services.

For a number of reasons, the first alternative was unacceptable to the Western Allies. In an open inflation forced savings generally become available for capital formation. For example, the German hyperinflation after World War I was instrumental in the extensive modernization and expansion of German heavy industry. But the hyperinflation broke the back of the German middle class. Savings disappeared in the monetary chaos and with it the source of independent incomes. The economic uprooting, or "proletarianization," of the middle class contributed greatly to the rise of Nazism.[20] The Allies believed the avoidance of another monetary chaos was necessary to prepare the defeated Germans for democracy.

To nip the inflationary potential in the bud, the Potsdam Agreement and JCS 1067, the United States directive, called for the control of wages and prices and the rationing of all essential goods.[21] The Allied Control Council Law No. 1 retained the Nazi economic controls. But this did not mean that the Allies subscribed to the aims of the third alternative mentioned above. Norway, for instance, after World War II kept the system of price and wage controls, rationing, allocations, import controls, and even direct allocation of labor to speed economic recovery.[22] But the principal objective of the Allied occupation of Germany was industrial disarmament, and it was out of the question to use direct controls for the restoration of industry. Controls were to avert capital accumulation in the form of industrial plant and equipment out of the forced savings created in an open inflation. And since industrial disarmament implied a considerable reduction in industrial output, the stagnation of the bizonal economy under postwar controls lends considerable support to the view that the controls were used to bring about the weakening of the German economy.[23]

But the controls themselves could not reduce the excess monetary liquidity. The scaling down of swollen bank deposits and of currency in circulation was indispensable to the restoration of some balance between the permitted level of industrial activity and the aggregate demand. In the Soviet zone of occupation all bank deposits were blocked immediately after the occupation began, while the currency in circulation was untouched. This measure eliminated considerable portions of the existing monetary wealth in the Soviet zone, thus flattening the monetary "overhang." No comparable steps were taken in the American and British zones of occupation, and it became obvious that a monetary reform to eliminate excess liquidity was inevitable.[24]

During the first two postwar years the four Allies negotiated without success for a currency reform for Germany as a whole.

Since the occupation powers could not come to terms on either German economic unity or currency reform, the monetary and financial policies of the four zones of occupation were determined by the respective directives of the Allied military governments. In the U.S. zone, for instance, JCS 1067 forbade the Military Governor "to take any steps designed to strengthen German financial structure." Under these circumstances a separate currency reform for the U.S. zone was ruled out and the existing inflationary potential had to be checked by controls.

The exact amount of Reichsmarks in circulation, including demand deposits, has never been known. As of September 30, 1946, the total money supply in the U.S. zone of occupation was estimated at RM 53.1 billion.[25] For the three Western zones prior to the currency reform, the Reichsmark money supply came to roughly RM 135 billion.[26]

Hoarding

During the war, factor earnings were high and business profits good. Since the controls severely restricted the propensity to consume and the propensity to invest, substantial savings came into being. The patriotic appeal during the war was strong, and the Nazi government's promise to convert wartime savings fully into goods after the victory was taken seriously by the public. The Reichsmark remained the store of value practically throughout the war and no perceptible flight into goods took place.

The unconditional surrender of the German armies destroyed all hope for full convertibility of wartime savings into goods. The protracted Allied negotiations on currency reform destroyed the Reichsmark as a store of value, although it remained a "unit of account." It was rumored that up to 90 percent of the existing money supply would be destroyed by the monetary conversion. Fear that existing monetary claims would be drastically scaled down resulted in a flight by individuals and business from the Reichsmark into material values.[27]

With the onset of 1946, the hoarding of goods became an accepted feature of the economic landscape of the bizonal area. The U.S. Military Governor reported month after month that companies were keeping unusually large inventories of raw materials and finished products because of the uncertain currency situation.[28] Various German chambers of industry and trade also reported that the widely expected currency reform was the principal reason for hoarding. To preserve the working capital of the firm, everybody kept as much in the form of goods as possible and a reluctance to sell was widespread.[29]

As Allied talks lagged and the American and British attitudes toward Germany turned more constructive, anticipation grew of a separate currency reform for the Western zones of occupation. During the extensive hearings on the European Recovery Program virtually all testimony called for financial reform. W. Averell Harriman, for instance, indicated that the bizonal economy could not recover from stagnation as long as the Reichsmark currency remained "a dream world." [30]

Under the unsettled currency situation, the German business community pleaded forcefully and eloquently that hoarding of consumer goods at that time was indispensable to the success of any future currency reform. Many high German administrators, including Ludwig Erhard, openly encouraged hoarding. In fact, the hoarding of goods did increase the appearance of success of the currency reform, since it had the effect of heightening the inflationary pressures in the precurrency reform period, while the goods were held off the market, and released a supply of goods when the new money arrived. Thus the hoarding emphasized the apparent swing in the economy from the period of repressed inflation to the period of monetary stability.

It is difficult to quantify the extent of hoarding out of current production during 1947 and the first half of 1948, but it is safe to say that 50 percent of the output either went into the hoards or was used for barter purposes, while the other 50 percent was produced for the legal market.[31] Consumers entitled to "incentive" goods, such as the coal miners and the employees of the German railways, consumed almost the entire legally available output of consumer goods, leaving nothing for the normal consumer.[32]

It was rumored that currency reform would convert coins at better terms than the note currency and bank deposits, and there was a mad rush into coins. It was reported that one street-car conductor in Stuttgart had a greater hoard of coins "than that in the possession of any single Stuttgart bank." [33]

With material values preferred to monetary values, the cigarette emerged as currency. Cigarettes frequently bought goods the Reichsmark could not. The cigarette was never declared legal tender, but it was widely accepted and used,[34] and people preferred them to Reichsmarks. The cigarette became "good money," while the Reichsmark was treated as "bad money." This preference reversed Gresham's principle and the so-called good money, the cigarette, drove out, to some extent, the bad. The history of past monetary upheavals has referred to this phenomenon time and again.[35]

The German hyperinflation in the early 1920's resulted in a continuous depreciation of the mark. In the last stages the mark was repudiated as a store of value, as a unit of account, and as a medium of exchange. Direct controls after World War II repressed the inflationary potential. The Reichsmark preserved a stable purchasing power for the legal food ration, rent, gas, electricity, taxes, and fares. The Reichsmark remained a unit of account and a medium of exchange, although it bought virtually nothing more than the highly inadequate food ration. But distrust of its future value led, especially during the last

half of the year prior to the currency reform, to flagrant hoarding of goods.[36]

Another institutional factor which stimulated the hoarding
of goods was the early postwar method of raw material control
and distribution. American insistence on broad administrative
centralization destroyed the Nazi-era unity of direction and
execution, and the reinstated wartime controls became a farce.
It soon became obvious that the greater the decentralization,
the more flagrant the evasion.[37]

In the British zone the extent of administrative decentralization was considerably smaller. At the top, the existing system
of economic control was firmly in the hands of the Economics
Division. German administrative agencies served merely as the
executive agencies on the lower and lowest levels of administration. For instance, coal and steel production, as we have
seen, was in British hands, and the tasks of German administrators were limited to the distribution of coal and steel to the
principal sectors of the economy. After the fusion of the American and British zones German administrators were given executive functions, but the change was slow and cumbersome. A
reasonably uniform procedure for the allocation and distribution of raw materials, semifabricates, and consumer goods
throughout the bizonal area was not established until mid-
1947.[38]

From the surrender till then, the allocation of raw materials
and semifabricates was separated from the distribution to consumers of finished products. At first, the allocation of coal,
steel, timber, and semifabricates was based on the "production
oriented" planning.[39] Under this system all major producers in
the principal sectors of the economy were given quota rights

(*Kontingentträger*) for raw materials and fuels. The designation of a firm as *Kontingentträger* implied the right to regular allocations of steel, coal, and industrial supplies. The shipbuilding and machinery-making industries, for instance, received small but regular allocations of raw materials. The quarterly allocations to all firms holding quota rights were more or less automatic. But the amounts allocated were grossly deficient for continuous production, and firms had to secure many legally unobtainable supplies through "compensation" channels —barter—to keep going.

The principal drawback of the "production oriented" distribution system was that the allocations *were not linked with either definite production or sales performances*. The firms' managements could use the allocated raw materials any way they deemed necessary, and in the rapidly spreading milieu of hoarding the producers found this method of distribution highly convenient. Manufacturers with quota rights received raw materials, produced finished or semifinished articles, and put most of them into inventory in anticipation of the currency reform. A sale of a fraction of their output in the black market was an easy way to replenish their cash. Government agencies had no effective way of compelling producers to part with their huge hoards of manufactured goods.[40]

A new method of raw material distribution was needed. One proposal called for the elimination of quota rights and the institution of "utilization oriented" allocation of raw materials.[41] Under this system the mining, transportation, agriculture, and other major sectors of the economy would receive fixed quotas of supplies and raw materials. Whether the steel quota of agriculture, for instance, would be used for the production of the nails, chains, pails, or tractors would be decided by the farming community. Rising and falling demand would signal what products were needed. Allocations of industrial supplies would be based on sales performance, not on quota rights. All products would be sold only on the basis of the purchase permits and the greater the sales and the more purchase permits a manufacturer had the more raw materials he could demand.[42] Because no raw materials would be allocated without purchase permits, a hoarding firm would not be able to obtain raw materials and coal.

This proposal went into effect in the second half of 1947, but hoarding of goods continued to spread and the economic situation deteriorated until the day of the currency reform. The German business community sensed that the reform would take place and that large stocks of finished goods and raw materials would safeguard the working capital of the firms.[43]

Allied officials knew of the hoarding, but the slowly changing climate of opinion tied their hands. The German business community exploited the situation for its own benefit.[44] Under the prevailing administrative near-chaos the interests of the business community ran counter to the wishes of the consuming public, and in the absence of a strong hand it was impossible to cope with the hoarding conspiracy of business.[45]

The Compensation Trade

The general distrust of the Reichsmark by the German business community gave rise to another institution—the compensation trade, a kind of barter system. The black market and the compensation trade were by no means synonymous. Compensation deals generally involved an exchange of goods at fixed prices, but the legal prices paid were of secondary importance. The main purpose of compensation deals was to obtain raw materials, semifabricates, or finished products in exchange for other goods. To make such transactions look legal and acceptable to the tax authorities they were booked as regular sales at fixed prices.[46]

Suppose that a shoe producer in Northern Germany needs bricks to repair his bombed-out plant. A request for an allocation of bricks at the local economics office has been turned down, presumably because no bricks are available for distribution. The shoe producer knows that the manager of the local brickyard has bricks and cannot get the typewriters and electrical switches he needs through legal channels. The two producers meet and agree on a swap deal. The shoe producer knows that electrical switches can easily be obtained for shoes from a firm in Southern Germany and dispatches a "compensator" there at once. Another "compensator" goes to Erfurt in the Soviet zone, where typewriters can be exchanged for shoes. After the two "compensators" return with the typewriters and electrical switches the deal is concluded and everyone has what he wanted. The accounting department records the transaction as a regular sale at the fixed prices.

The amount of time and effort spent on such transactions was almost unbelievable.[47] The spreading compensation activity resulted in a considerable "primitivization" of economic activity, since barter is incompatible with the specialization and cooperation of an industrial community. Division of labor and the roundabout method of industrial production are based on the existence of a functioning monetary economy, where there is a unit of account, medium of exchange, and store of value. In the period before the currency reform more people did more work, but the output remained low.

The Allied-imposed embargo on imports of raw materials into the American and British zones, which lasted until 1948, was partly responsible for this deterioration. After the surrender German industry had ample stocks of raw materials and semifabricates on hand. Industrial pipelines were also reasonably well filled, and the greatest portion of German manufacturing capacity survived the war intact, despite the massive bombing raids by the Allied planes.[48] German industry lived off its wartime stocks because of the embargo. By mid-1947, empty stock rooms and dry industrial pipe lines augured ill for the economy. And with the approach of the currency reform considerable amounts of the still-available raw materials and semifabricates were unquestionably hoarded.

Scarcities of raw materials and industrial supplies grew acutely. The official allocations of raw materials in 1946 and in 1947 came roughly to 20 percent of the requirements, but in most cases even less was actually distributed.[49] By turning to compensation trade as a source of regular supplies,[50] German producers were able to operate and to keep their working capital intact as well. It was estimated that in 1947 as much as 50 percent of the entire output of the bizonal economy was traded in compensation deals.[51]

Before the currency reform the War Economic Ordinance of 1942 was still the existing law.[52] It prohibited all compensation activity and provided severe punishment for violators. Under the Allies all *Land* Economic Offices acknowledged that *in principle* compensation trade was still prohibited, but nevertheless limited compensation activity was tolerated by all German administrative organs. Erhard, for instance, then Bavarian Minister of Economics, allowed controlled compensations to maintain production.[53] German firms were generally allowed to use up to 15 percent of their output for such deals. All producers' applications for "compensation quotas" had to be approved by the economic offices, but all compensation was supposed to be recorded. Retailers and wholesalers were explicitly forbidden to engage in compensation activity, and no foodstuffs were allowed to be traded in this way.[54]

A bid by the German Economics Council for the legalization of the compensation trade was turned down by the U.S.-U.K.

Control Group—throughout 1947 the industrial disarmament of Germany was still a basic objective. The Allied answer to the German request was Control Council Law No. 50 of March, 1947, which was specifically designed to combat the compensation trade.[55]

By this time compensation activity was so extensive that Law No. 50 turned out to be grossly inadequate to cope with the situation. The law called for severe penalties for the offenders, but in the postwar period even the most flagrant violations of economic legislation were not subject to capital punishment, as had been the case under the Nazis. The system existing before the Nazi take-over in 1933 was in effect.[56] German officials argued repeatedly that only by making "economic misbehavior" subject to the death penalty again would it be possible to cope with the situation. Dr. Schlange-Schöningen, the Director of the Bizonal Food and Agricultural Administration, said that the worst aspect of the gray market, i.e., compensation trade, would be checked if a few people were hanged.[57] The Western powers, however, did not heed Schlange-Schöningen's plea. Meanwhile the spreading barter was slowly but steadily destroying like a cancer the entire system of postwar economic control.[58]

The compensation trade stood its first court test in the Spinnfaser A. G. trial in the fall of 1947.[59] The accusation was not directed against the compensation activity itself but against its excesses. The testimony showed that the use of "compensation quotas" to obtain raw materials and industrial supplies needed to maintain production was permitted. In view of the expected currency reform the Spinnfaser company had employed its "compensation quotas" to build up inventories.[60]

The outcome of the trial was inconclusive. The judgment stated that German administrative agencies might not approve the use of "compensation quotas" for barter purposes. Nevertheless, the court added, in the given postwar conditions compensation trade had become a necessity and hence approved barter should be tolerated to keep industry operating.

After the trial, Württemberg-Baden and Bavaria withdrew their existing ordinances permitting firms to set aside part of their output for compensation purposes. Hesse, however, continued a similar measure.[61] In November, 1947, Bavaria reintroduced industrial quotas for compensation, but out of fear of higher authorities the directive was oral, not written. Thereafter U.S. and U.K. occupation officials tolerated officially approved barter as a *sine qua non* for the maintenance of minimum industrial operations.

The system of controlled barter led to flagrant abuses. Officially, only 10 percent of a company's output could be used for legally unobtainable supplies and the other 90 percent had to be sold at legal prices. But it is estimated that sometimes as much as 90 percent of all goods produced went either into the rapidly growing inventories or compensation.[62] This figure is probably much too high, but the hoards of consumer goods were quite substantial.[63]

The existence of the barter trade, the black market, and the legal trading activity at fixed prices split the postwar German economy into legal and illegal sectors. In the legal sphere goods were bought and sold at legal prices either against the rationing coupons or purchase permits; in the illegal sector goods were obtained either in the black market or through the compensation trade. Due to the absence of a store of value, an increasing portion of the output circulated in the illegal sphere, mostly the compensation sector.[64] As the currency reform drew closer, an ever-growing proportion of the German industrial output entered the illegal channels, leaving little for the legal market.

In his memoirs, General Clay admitted that the illegal activities of the German business community and German administrators hampered the work of the Allied authorities to such an extent that the existing economic controls became almost meaningless.[65] In this context, General Clay forgot to add that in 1947 American and British occupation authorities were still engaged in the industrial disarmament of Germany, a policy which aimed at a considerable strangulation of the German economy, but his admission of the utter failure of this early policy is of utmost significance.

THE STABILITY OF LEGAL PRICES

The market's split did not destroy the stability of the price and wage levels because compensation activity took place at legal prices and the black market accounted for no more than 10 percent of the entire trade volume.[66] However, the legal prices of the various commodities did not by any means remain frozen. Divergent price trends soon developed for different commodity groups, and this development negatively affected the production of many articles.

The Price Control of the 13 Basic Commodities by the Allied Control Council

In May, 1946, the Allied Control Council assumed the responsibility for the prices of thirteen basic commodities, such as iron, steel, coal, basic chemicals, foodstuffs, wool and hides, electrical power, and gas.[67] The quadripartite price control implied that any price adjustments for these commodities were subject to the unanimity rule of the Allied Control Council. Prices of all other commodities were put under the jurisdiction of the respective *Land* economic offices, which, in turn, were under the general supervision of the four military governments.

The disagreements in the Allied Control Council were not limited to political issues. Bickering over prices of the basic commodities was another pastime of that body.[68] Only after it became obvious that the wartime alliance was rapidly breaking apart did the Western Allies raise coal and steel prices on their own. But while hopes for Allied co-operation remained, prices were not changed. If the resulting price stability is taken as a yardstick, Allied price control was an unqualified success. Nevertheless, this very stability was responsible for a decline of German production and a drastic change in the composition of output.

Divergent Price Patterns

In general, the Allied price policy called for the continuation of "the pre-defeat system of German price levels" [69] for the postwar period. At the time this decision was made it was anticipated that Germany would be administered as an economic unit and that a tight, central control would keep the existing inflationary potential in check. Allied inability to administer Germany as an economic unit and the emergence of different political systems made it virtually impossible to preserve the Nazi system of price fixing. The situation was especially aggravated by the zonal split, shortages of fuel and power, lack of raw materials, low productivity of men due to malnutrition, lower output per machine due to obsolescence and lack of repairs, damages to industrial plants, and over-all stagnation of West German industry. These factors brought about sharp increases in production costs; [70] legal prices were often much lower than the costs of production and losses were inevitable.

The Allied price policy was contradictory. On the one hand,

the American military government admitted that "economic conditions must be fitted into legal price structure." [71] But the Americans were also committed to keeping price increases at a minimum to maintain the stability of wages.

For the basic commodities a policy of virtual price freeze was adopted, and most producers of such items incurred losses. The yearly reports of the various German chambers of trade and commerce reported repeatedly that most firms were heading for bankruptcy unless prices were raised. [72]

A 1947 industrial survey of forty-four representative firms by the American military government also showed that "the majority of firms showed manufacturing costs which indicated a loss." [73] For instance, in the spinning and knitting mills production costs were found to be 50 percent higher than the legal sales price. [74] In the case of chemical plants, production costs exceeded prices by as much as 80 percent. [75]

As long as the British and Americans carried out the industrial disarmament of Germany, production losses in the basic industries were useful. Whether the reduction of German plant and equipment was brought about by dismantling, destruction, decay from lack of repairs, or bankruptcy was immaterial. The German business community knew this and many ingenious ways to save firms from bankruptcy were devised. Since it was impossible to obtain upward revisions of prices for any of the reserved commodities, German business turned to the manufacture of "new," formerly unknown goods.

It was only after the British and Americans realized that German economic prosperity was indispensable for the well-being of other Western European nations that the entire system of price and wage regulations was revised. Growing apprehensions about the Morgenthau-inspired wisdom of keeping Germany economically weak hastened the Western Allies to initiate the long overdue price adjustments. Since price fixing primarily served non-economic objectives, the change of Allied objectives in Germany required a new economic policy as well.[76] In the spring of 1948, the Director of the Bipartite U.S.-U.K. Control Office ordered that "there must be a correction of the maladjustments within the internal price structure so that, within industry as a whole, prices will cover production costs." [77] Many prices went up, but not all. From 1945 to mid-1948, the rate of price changes was different for various groups of commodities and divergent price trends emerged, as set forth in Table 16.

From 1938 to the end of 1944, the prices of steel and steel products showed a remarkable stability. The price of steel slabs rose 4.5 percent and the price of rolled wire 8.2 percent. In the postwar period the wartime prices for steel slabs, rolled wire and thick plate remained unchanged up to April 1, 1948. The recorded price for thin plate of RM 18.40 in the postwar period does not represent an exception; the 1944 price does not show the RM 4 subsidy paid, the postwar price does.

As shown in chapter IV, the steel industry in the British-occupied Ruhr Valley operated at roughly 20 percent of the 1936 level. With such low volume, costs of production exceeded prices considerably. The situation was also aggravated by the Allied "deconcentration" measures for industry—many formerly integrated steel plants were cut up into a number of separate units and production costs soared. To keep the steel industry going the British military government paid a subsidy ranging from RM 50 to RM 60 per ton of steel produced.[78] After it was decided to include West Germany in the European Recovery Program the policy of subsidized ruin could not go on. The U.S. and U.K. authorities raised steel prices after ending extensive deindustrialization. Once West Germans were permitted to retain the major portion of the steel industry, it was necessary that production losses be eliminated as quickly as possible. The increase in steel prices as well as permission to retain the steel industry were purely political decisions, but

Prices of Selected Commodities in the American and British Zones: Selected Periods, 1938–1948. (In Reichsmarks per 100 kilograms except where noted)

Commodity	1938	End of 1944	Dec. 26, 1946	Jan. 1, 1947	Early 1948 *
Ferrous Products					
Steel slabs	11.00	11.50	11.50	11.50	21.25
Rolled wire	11.76	12.73	12.73	12.73	21.90
Thick plate	12.73	13.23	13.23	13.23	23.40
Thin plate	13.90	14.40	18.40	18.40	30.00
Non-Ferrous Products					
Copper	58.85	75.00	102.50	102.50	153.50
Lead	19.80	22.00	67.50	90.00	90.00
Zinc	18.27	22.00	67.50	90.00	90.00
Aluminum	133.00	127.00	127.00	127.00	127.00
Agricultural Staples					
Wool	910.00	910.00	910.00	910.00	910.00
Cow-Hides	86.00	86.00	86.00	86.00	86.00
Flax	12.00	19.25	19.25	19.25	19.25
Building Materials					
Cement	3.60	3.60			4.91
Paper	21.59	23.75			39.00
Bricks					
(1,000 pieces)	33.00	30.00			56.00
Consumer Goods †					
Cupboard					
(wardrobe)	95.00				158.00
Light bulb	1.00				1.25
Cooking pot ‡	2.50				4.35
Dinner ware §	0.30				1.10
Men's shoes ‖	12.00				22.00
Men's shirts ¶	3.40				4.50

* June 15 for consumer goods, April 1 for all others.
† In Bremen.
‡ With cover, 24 cm. diameter.
§ Plate, china, 24 cm. diameter.
‖ Leather work shoes.
¶ Cotton work shirts.
Sources: Statistisches Amt des Vereinigten Wirtschaftsgebietes, *Statistische Berichte: Die Indexziffer der Grundstoffpreise im Vereinigten Wirtschaftsgebiet im Dezember 1949*, p. 3; Statistisches Amt des Vereinigten Wirtschaftsgebietes, *Statistische Berichte: Die Grundstoffpreise 1938, 1944 und seit der Währungsreform und die Berechnung einer Indexziffer der Grundstoffpreise*, No. 28 (1948), pp. 2–5; Statistisches Amt des Vereinigten Wirtschaftsgebietes, *Statistische Berichte: Die Einzelhandelspreise am 15.11.1948*, pp. 17–28.

these steps initiated the first measures designed to create order out of chaos and stagnation.

Since no unanimous four-power agreement was necessary for the adjustment of prices of non-ferrous metals, considerable upward movement of such prices took place. From the end of 1944 to January 1, 1947, the price of copper rose by 36 percent and the price of zinc more than quadrupled. The price of aluminum remained unchanged because the production of aluminum was at first prohibited as a security measure.

Agricultural prices remained unchanged throughout the period. However, prices of building materials, such as paper, bricks, and cement, rose considerably, an average of more than 60 percent.

The most pronounced price changes occurred in consumer goods. Although the data are incomplete and discontinuous and price series for many articles do not exist, it is possible to make some inference about price trends. How could prices of consumer goods rise when they were subject to the price fixing legislation of 1936? A partial answer to this seeming riddle lies in the manufacture of "new" products, which were allowed higher official prices. Moreover, since allowances and adjustments were granted for cost increases, the decline in the overall efficiency of German production also contributed to the upward drift in controlled prices.

Table 16 shows that over a ten-year period during which prices were controlled the price of cupboards rose 66 percent, pots 74 percent, men's shoes 83 percent, men's work shirts 32 percent, light bulbs 25 percent, and china plates nearly 400 percent. The over-all advance in prices, however, was much smaller during the war than in the postwar period. A special study of wholesale prices in the bizonal area showed that from the end of the war to May, 1947, the prices of consumer goods had risen by 97 percent while prices of industrial raw materials were only 22 percent higher. From 1936 to the end of 1944 consumer goods went up 14 percent and industrial raw materials 13 percent.[79]

Misdirection of Resources

One way out of the postwar loss squeeze was the production of "new" commodities, formerly unproduced items frequently luxurious or semiluxurious in nature. Since prices were generally fixed on the basis of costs, higher production costs sufficed to secure higher prices. In the postwar period there was a flood of "new" products. From the surrender to the currency reform more than 5,000 price increases were granted, mostly for the production of "new" goods.[80]

Ash trays, fancy lamps, dolls, chandeliers, and other low utility items poured forth while the production of cups, pails, pots, plates, and other daily necessities stagnated.[81] For example, a firm that formerly produced 75,000 electrical switches a month began manufacturing previously non-existent bakelite ash trays for which it had obtained a profitable price from the price-fixing authorities.[82]

The over-all effect on German business of the Allied adoption of Nazi-era price legislation was that the incentive to produce was in almost "directly inverse proportions to the social utility of the product." [83] The more useless a proposed product the greater the probability that it had not been available before the war and the easier it would be to obtain a profitable price. As a result, Western zones of occupation prior to the currency reform had what one Swiss economist facetiously called a "hair oil-ash tray-herb tea economy." [84]

The black market, of course, was another outlet. Generally speaking, black marketing was considered "shameful" and "immoral," and the German business community—with exceptions, of course—did not wish to be involved in it.[85] The flood of "new" commodities seems to support this contention.

By way of digression, the production of new but almost useless goods gives some food for thought on the Schumpeterian innovator, his behavior, and his motivations. Schumpeter's analysis turns on the entrepreneurial action, innovations, and the credit mechanism. Successful introduction of an "innovation" implies the breaking of the initial consumers' resistance.[86] But in the period under discussion consumer resistance was an unknown entity.[87] The expected currency reform prompted people to buy up anything in reach. In Schumpeter's analysis, the creation of a socially useful commodity or service is an indispensable condition for profit. The interaction between the innovators and consuming public represents a community of interests. But in postwar Germany, due to the previously described institutional and political factors, "The self-interest of individuals and of firms was strictly opposed to the common interest." [88]

Under the postwar system of economic control, the anticipation that savings would be of little value after the currency reform resulted in the "atomization" of the German economy and society. The German business community was primarily concerned with the preservation of the firms' working capital, and the hoarding of goods and raw materials was the best way to achieve that end. Since the production of price-fixed items resulted in losses, Germans turned to the production of semiluxurious, frequently useless goods, while useful goods paradoxically were scarce beyond comprehension. Such misdirection of resources clearly indicated that German economy was heading toward chaos. Only a fresh start could put it into proper working order.

6

THE CONTROL OF

MANPOWER AND WAGES

The Allies after World War II feared that hyperinflation such as followed World War I might promote the emergence of another totalitarian doctrine and thus "strike at the heart of Allied hopes for a democratic Germany." [1] From the post-World War I experience the Allies knew that the reduction of German industrial potential would be impossible without direct controls. The German hyperinflation had unquestionably ruined receivers of fixed income, salaried workers, and small businessmen. But thanks to the high level of economic activity the demand for investment goods had remained brisk. The flight out of the mark into real values was particularly heavy, and the expansion of basic German industries continued unabated until the stabilization of the mark. At the end of the hyperinflation Germany possessed greater capacity in heavy industries than in 1913. [2] Some American economic planning experts felt that the German monetary chaos after World War I had been the work of the government of the Weimar republic, the major industrialists and the underground General Staff.[3] By pleading poverty and social chaos, the German government could assert that it was unable to pay reparations while the industrialists were building greater empires than ever. To prevent such a course of events after World War II, and to bring about the envisaged industrial disarmament of Germany, the Western Allies used direct controls.

1. Control Over Labor and Repressed Inflation

A shortage of labor is one of the salient features of a fully employed economy. Without control over wages, salaries, and non-wage incomes, all costs and disposable incomes are bound to go up. A rise in money incomes in general and a persistent rise in personal incomes in particular are likely to set off a wage-price spiral. To avoid such a possibility some degree of control over incomes and costs is indispensable. Direct controls are the most effective means of limiting wage increases. Wage controls can be exercised either in terms of a general freeze or in terms of an alliance where the government, labor unions, and employers attempt to maintain existing wage levels. Under this policy, labor unions promise to abstain from wage demands if the government will give assurance that prices of foodstuffs and essential consumer goods will not rise.[4]

But control of wages and salaries is not enough to meet the government's production goals and to assure an adequate labor supply. Generally the government also needs some control over the allocation of labor among the various claimants. A mild form of this type of control merely attempts to reduce the mobility of labor. For instance, after the war the British Control of Engagements Order stipulated that workers in the farming and coal-mining industries could not take jobs in other industries without the approval of the government. But the Order was used sparingly and the government did not succeed in directing a sufficient amount of manpower into the favored industries.[5]

The most effective way to reduce labor mobility is outright labor conscription, which was widely practiced by the Soviet and Nazi governments during the war. After the defeat of Nazi Germany labor conscription was retained by the Allied Control Council.

Under all forms of repressed inflation, most of the essential foodstuffs and consumer goods are rationed. Legal expenditures are determined by rationing coupons and not by money incomes. Since consumption is limited, legal money incomes exceed legal money expenditures and some saving takes place perforce. Under these circumstances the labor supply curve of all income groups is less elastic than under a free market economy. Or to put it differently, all income groups tend to offer less additional labor for monetary inducements; real goods are more important than money wages.

Of course, the degree of inelasticity varies among income groups. The lower income groups are least reluctant to exchange additional labor for additional income because ordinary living expenses take up most of their wages in any case. But for the higher income groups additional work means more savings, because under rationing the added income is deprived of legal purchasing power. Reluctance to work for money wages, hoarding of labor by employers, falling productivity of labor, and a shortage of labor invariably become the striking features of such an economy.

Looking again at Norway's postwar use of direct controls, that government's aim, in general, was to step up the rate of capital formation by limiting expenditures for private consumption. The immediate objectives were rapid reconstruction, maintenance of full employment, and the gradual elimination of the inflationary potential.[6] The principal controls were rationing of goods, licensing of imports, control of investment activity, and skillful use of fiscal tools. To accelerate the formation of capital, private consumption was to remain somewhat below the 1939 level for the first five postwar years. The existing inflationary pressures were to be worked off not through a drastic currency reform but by increased production and considerable import surpluses. Thus the Norwegian government used direct controls deliberately and systematically to bring about the eventual disappearance of inflationary pressures at a higher level of real output.

The situation in occupied Germany was altogether different. Because industrial disarmament was one of the main objectives of the occupation, it was out of the question to use direct controls to step up industrial output and raise productivity to work off the inflationary potential gradually. In operational terms, industrial disarmament—outright destruction of industrial facilities, the imposition of production ceilings, and the delivery of machinery as reparations—necessarily involved a reduction in the output of all goods and services. The victors were interested in keeping stable wages and prices merely to prevent an open inflation.

A severe repression of demand was one way to stem the German inflationary potential. But since the policy of industrial disarmament throttled industrial activity, inflationary pressures mounted. Wartime monetary wealth could not be worked off merely by freezing prices and wages, and scaling down the monetary wealth through a currency reform was inevitable. This possibility haunted all Germans for the first three years of occupation and generated a set of attitudes which greatly upset the over-all operations of the German economy.

2. The Nazi System of Labor Control

Under the Nazis, control over the labor force before 1936 was exercised primarily in terms of restrictions on labor mobility. Direct labor conscription did not exist until 1938.

The vigorous Nazi drive to eliminate unemployment led to bottlenecks in specific skills as early as 1934. As a result, skilled metalworkers were forbidden to take employment outside their district without the permission of the labor office,[7] and in 1936 a similar regulation was applied to unskilled metalworkers as well.[8] In October, 1937, carpenters and masons, and shortly thereafter all building workers, were prohibited from leaving their jobs without the consent of labor offices.[9] After the introduction of general labor conscription in June, 1938, labor offices were endowed with powers to conscript workers for any work considered important for the state. Labor offices at first were authorized to draft workers for terms of six months, but in March, 1939, the term of service was made indefinite.[10] With the onset of hostilities, wages and salaries were frozen at the level prevailing on September 16, 1939, to avoid spiraling costs.[11] The necessary corollary of these measures was the introduction of rationing of foodstuffs, consumer goods, and floor space.

Postwar research has indicated that despite popular notions about the preparations for war and the well-advertised drive for self-sufficiency, Nazi economic and social goals were "in conflict with the notion of a total war." [12] Hitler's planning, based on the blitzkrieg strategy, did not involve huge outlays for armaments. His basic aim was immediate superiority over France and Great Britain, and he felt that fifty or sixty well trained and equipped divisions and some 2,000 planes would be adequate to subjugate Europe to his will. The first two years of fighting confirmed the efficacy of this strategy.[13]

When the war started Germany still had considerable manpower reserves. From 1939 to 1942 employment in war-strategic industries such as metalworking rose by roughly 20 percent and employment in non-war industries declined. But, unlike the United States or Great Britain, Nazi Germany "made no attempt to increase her manpower supply through an expansion of her gainfully occupied population."[14] One interesting indicator of labor reserves in 1942 is that the number of domestic servants was 1.4 million, only 100,000 less than in 1939, of which 97 percent were German nationals.[15] Another is that the total employment of German women was slightly lower in 1942 than in 1939.[16] These developments were probably a result of the Nazi doctrine that German women should stay home and bear racially superior children.

German expenditures for civilian consumption also remained considerably higher than those in the United Kingdom up to 1942. The Nazi government continued [17] to spend considerable sums on monuments, autobahns, and Party buildings, with the result that German war output remained considerably below its potential.

Only the defeat of the German armies at Stalingrad shattered Hitler's blitzkrieg concept. It became obvious that the Allies were outproducing the Axis nations in war matériel. The total mobilization of all German resources was the Nazi answer. To release as many men as possible for the armed forces and to supply the armament industries with more manpower became the two most important objectives. Yet, although far-reaching measures for the conscription of women were introduced, the employment of German women rose very slowly.

On July 25, 1944, after the Allied invasion of France, the Total Mobilization Decree gave Göring full powers to direct all phases of German life for total war.[18] Goebbels became the

Commissioner General of Total Mobilization. All activities considered unessential to the war effort were drastically cut in order to release the greatest possible manpower for war production and the armed services.

Sauckel, the wartime labor dictator, struck at shirkers—anyone who was nominally mobilized for war work but actually did nothing was to be either apprehended or put to work. All women from 17 to 45 years of age were subject to labor conscription. In September, 1944, Goebbels ordered the transfer of all domestics, including German women, to war production. Severe cuts were made in the postal services to release more manpower. All traveling entertainers were directed to war work. Newspapers were either amalgamated or suppressed. The minimum working week was extended to sixty hours. Some schools were closed.

In the course of the "combing out" operations of 1943 and 1944, 1.5 million workers were released for war work.[19] However, many of these measures remained on paper and were never carried out. On the whole, the Nazi mobilization of labor during the war, except for the last phase, was halfhearted and inadequate.

3. The Postwar Labor Control

CONTINUANCE OF LABOR CONSCRIPTION

As soon as the Allies took over their zones of occupation the military governments ordered all existing wage and labor controls continued. In the American zone the German *Land* governments were requested to continue the existing system of control, registration, and allocation of manpower through a system of regional and local labor offices. All males between the ages of 14 and 65 and all females from 16 to 45 were ordered to register.[20] In the British zone, where a similar order was issued,[21] food ration cards could not be obtained without "proof of registration." A Control Council order of January 17, 1946, also stipulated a general registration for Germany as a whole [22] and stated unequivocally that all labor offices were empowered to conscript workers. Jobs could be taken only with the approval of local labor offices.

A British Military Government ordinance affirmed on October 22, 1946, that general labor conscription was still in effect.[23] Under the terms of this directive, work was mandatory for the entire population of employable age. Due to an acute shortage of able-bodied men, women were not only conscripted but used for activities that previously had been the exclusive domain of male labor. A Control Council law also sanctioned a wide use of female labor for building and reconstruction work.[24]

THE WAGE FREEZE

Each Allied military government continued to enforce the Nazi wage freeze.[25] The Allied Control Council in Berlin, after it was established in the summer of 1945, ordered the 1938 wage freeze continued for Germany as a whole. Control Council Directive No. 14 of October 12, 1945, eliminated only the previously prevailing discrimination in wage rates on the basis of race, creed, and political affiliation.[26]

Collective bargaining on rates was also authorized within limits. In the future wages were to be determined by collective bargaining between employers and trade union representatives. For the time being, however, although wage rates could be renegotiated, average wages had to remain unaltered. The Allies believed that changes brought about by the war in the methods and nature of production would justify new piece and time rates of pay. Still, the general wage freeze within the framework of the directive left little room for the emergence of collective bargaining, and except in the coal-mining industry it was practically non-existent in the British and American zones of occupation until the end of 1947. And despite Directive No. 14, circumvention of the wage freeze was quite common in all zones.

Wage fixing hit particularly hard those persons working in industries where hourly rates were low. In some cases, as we shall see later, inadequate weekly earnings prevented people from buying even the meager food ration and the officially available consumer goods.[27] To eliminate these hardships, a supplement to Directive No. 14, adopted on September 13, 1946, permitted wages to rise to 50 pfennigs an hour in those industries where rates were less.[28]

More important, the regulation permitted certain exceptions to the wage freeze policy, particularly in the "problem industries." [29] Trade unions, employers associations, or *Land* ministries of labor could request this designation for industries that had been negatively affected by the political and economic goals of the Nazi government. The Nazis had raised the wages of metalworkers, for instance, to attract manpower at the expense of the building trades, forestry, mining, and agriculture. After the war, metalworking industries were in low gear because of the Allied policy of reducing Germany's war potential, but their hourly wage rates were considerably above those of the very industries where the demand for labor, due to urgent rehabilitation work, was greatest. The only way to attract sufficient manpower into other fields was to make a number of exceptions to the wage freeze.

The coal mining industry was the first to be designated as a "problem industry." The Allied Control Council in October, 1946, permitted miners' unions to negotiate for an average wage increase of not more than 20 percent.[30] The building trades and allied industries, including building materials, were next designated as "problem industries" in July, 1947.[31] The first state-wide agreement raising wages in the building trades no more than 20 percent was negotiated in Hesse early in 1948. It was made retroactive to October 15, 1947, and approved by the U.S. Military Government in February, 1948. During January, 1948, five additional industries were classified as "problem industries." The permissible wage increases were set at 15 percent for the textile industry, 12 percent for the clothing industry, 10 percent for forestry and railway workers, and 12.5 percent for mining other than coal.[32]

Wages and salaries in all other fields of activity remained nominally unchanged. Prices of all goods and services, however, had been rising slowly but constantly ever since the beginning of the occupation. To be sure, a wage-price spiral did not take place, but rising prices in conditions of almost stable wages and salaries led to a considerable deterioration of real wages. Despite controls, it was estimated that real wages were 30 percent lower in mid-June, 1948, than at the beginning of the occupation.[33]

To reverse this trend, bizonal area trade unions recommended a general 30 percent increase in all wages and salaries. As long as the Allied Control Council was in existence, however, the U.S. and U.K. Military Governments did not wish to take such an action without Soviet approval. Only after the Allied Control Council faltered in March, 1948, and the last pretense of Allied unity in Germany disappeared were the Americans and British willing to give serious consideration to the wage-price problem in their areas. It became urgently necessary to bring wages and prices into line again, although nobody wanted to admit it officially, to avoid jeopardizing the success of the impending currency reform. With this objective in mind, the U.S.-U.K. Military Government called on April 29, 1948, for an average increase of all wages and salaries as of May 1.[34] But the employers, also mindful of the approaching currency reform, showed considerable resistance to increasing wages. Employer and trade union organizations came to terms only after hard negotiations, and on May 31 a new contract was concluded calling for an across-the-board increase of 15 percent. However, the benefits of the wage hike were felt only after the currency reform of June 21.

4. Misallocation of Labor

Control Council Order No. 3 required all males 14–65 years of age and all females 15–50 to register with the labor offices. As in the British example, no one was entitled to a ration card unless registered. Job placements were to take place only through the labor offices and, with the continuance of labor conscription, the assigned jobs were mandatory upon the entire working-age population. But there were notable exceptions to this rule—mothers of school-age children, housewives, students, daughters helping in households, and convalescent prisoners-of-war repatriated from the Soviet Union. As a result the discrepancy between the total registered population of working age and the labor force was considerable, as shown in Table 17.

TABLE 17. Registered Working-Age Population, Bizonal Area of Germany. (In thousands)

	Population			
Date *	Total	Incapacitated	Exempt	% Available for Work
June, 1946	18,864	(combined total 4623)		75.5
Dec., 1946	22,473	596	6,057	70.4
June, 1947	23,314	600	6,525	69.4
Dec., 1947	23,822	626	6,751	69.0
June, 1948	24,249	612	6,771	69.6
Dec., 1948	24,610	566	6,706	70.5

* End of month.
Source: Control Commission for Germany (British Element), *Monthly Statistical Bulletin,* IV (February, 1949), 60.

From June, 1946, to June, 1948, the total registered population of the bizonal area of Germany rose 30 percent. During the same period the number of persons incapable of working because of poor health, lack of stamina, and malnutrition, and those exempt from work, such as housewives and students, rose by almost 60 percent. This development was primarily the result of the continuously deteriorating nutritional status and lack of incentives for legal work.

If to the number of these persons is added the number of unemployed, the total is roughly one-third of the total registered population.[35] The number of unemployed workers stood at 788,-000 at the end of June, 1946, while at the end of June, 1948, the number had gone down to 442,000.

Table 18 shows the composition of the labor force. The term labor force, by usual definition, means the total of all gainfully occupied plus the unemployed. But this concept of labor force and the occupation authorities' concept of working population were somewhat different. All men over 65 and women over 50

T A B L E 18. Estimated Total Labor Force, Bizonal Area. (In thousands)

| | | GAINFULLY OCCUPIED | | | | |
| | | | | Wage and Salary Earners | | Unemployed |
	Labor Force	Total	Self-Employed and Family Helpers	Number	% of Gainfully Employed	Number	% of the Labor Force
June, 1936	16,064	15,244	5,355	9,889	64.9	820	5.1
May, 1939	17,441	16,876	5,308	11,568	68.5	30	0.2
June, 1946	15,196	14,408	4,443	9,965	69.2	788	5.2
Dec., 1946	16,872	16,066	4,941	11,125	69.2	806	5.1
June, 1947	17,268	16,638	5,128	11,510	69.2	630	3.6
Dec., 1947	17,601	17,141	5,273	11,868	69.2	460	2.6
June, 1948	17,949	17,507	5,293	12,214	69.8	442	2.5
Dec., 1948	18,404	17,661	5,287	12,374	70.1	743	4.0

Sources: For 1936, Statistisches Amt des Vereinigten Wirtschaftsgebietes, *Wirtschaft und Statistik,* I (1949–50), p. 421; 1939–June, 1948, Control Commission for Germany (British Element), *Monthly Statistical Bulletin,* Vol. IV, No. 1 (January, 1949), p. 67; December, 1948, *ibid.,* Vol. IV (April, 1949), p. 59.

were outside the working population, while the labor force analyzed in Table 18 includes men over 65 and women over 50 in the "self-employed and family helpers" category. For this reason, the labor force is larger than it would be otherwise.

The table also shows that over a two-year period, from June, 1946, to June, 1948, the labor force of the two zones rose 18 percent, while the total of gainfully employed and unemployed rose 22 percent. Absorption of the formerly unemployed explains the divergence between the two figures. The low number of unemployed seems to indicate that during the first three postwar years unemployment was not an important economic issue. Unemployment in June, 1948, was 2.5 percent of the labor force, a situation generally associated with a fully employed economy. Another interesting aspect of the employment picture is that in June, 1947, and in June, 1948, the percentage of wage and salary earners out of all gainfully employed stood at 69.2 percent, while the respective figure for June, 1936, was 64.9 percent.

The nominal level of employment was high, but the aggregate output fluctuated at around 40 percent of the 1936 level. A number of factors may be cited to explain this anomalous situation. The fact that more than 30 percent of the total registered population was not working for money wages indicates that "the primary motive for working was not the need to meet living expenses but the desire to obtain a ration card." [36] Work evasion was widely practiced, and many people drew food ration cards without holding legitimate employment. Some people even made false entries in the labor books as to the nature and place of work. Others nominally held a job approved by the labor offices and an employer while actually they were doing something else or nothing. Another factor was employers' hoarding of manpower. Thousands of workers were listed as employed who, in fact, were trying to make a living somewhere else. In this fashion, the number listed as employed was greatly

TABLE 19. Employed Wage and Salary Earners by Major Economic Groups. (In thousands)

Period	Agriculture and Forestry	Index (% of 1936)	Industry and Handicrafts	Index (% of 1936)	Commerce and Transport	Index (% of 1936)	Public and Private Services	Index (% of 1936)	Domestic Service	Index (% of 1936)	Total	Index (% of 1936)
June, 1936	836	100	5,223	100	1,891	100	1,300	100	639	100	9,889	100
May, 1939	801	95.8	6,346	121.5	2,175	115.0	1,555	119.6	691	108.1	11,568	117.0
Mar., 1946	1,322	158.0	4,307	82.5	1,484	77.9	1,410	108.5	529	82.8	9,052	90.5
June, 1946	1,546	184.9	4,644	88.9	1,604	84.8	1,592	122.5	579	90.6	9,965	100.8
Sept., 1946	1,620	193.8	5,011	95.7	1,737	91.3	1,784	137.2	604	94.5	10,756	108.8
Dec., 1946	1,568	187.7	5,223	100	1,840	97.3	1,860	143.1	634	99.1	11,125	112.4
Mar., 1947	1,522	182.2	5,216	99.7	1,876	99.2	1,897	146.0	639	100	11,150	112.7
June, 1947	1,528	182.8	5,430	104.0	1,949	103.1	1,959	150.7	644	100.9	11,510	116.4
Sept., 1947	1,515	181.5	5,554	106.3	2,000	105.8	2,011	154.7	626	98.0	11,706	118.4
Dec., 1947	1,457	174.3	5,683	108.8	2,050	108.1	2,049	157.6	629	98.4	11,868	120.0
Mar., 1948	1,397	167.1	5,779	110.7	2,084	110.2	2,062	158.5	610	95.5	11,932	120.7
June, 1948	1,385	165.7	5,995	114.8	2,159	114.2	2,075	159.6	600	93.9	12,214	123.5
Sept., 1948	1,296	155.0	6,147	117.7	2,151	113.7	2,011	153.9	583	91.2	12,178	123.1

Source: Control Commission for Germany (British Element), *Monthly Statistical Bulletin*, Vol. IV, No. 1 (January, 1949), p. 70.

inflated [37] and concealed an extensive underemployment, or "hidden" unemployment. It has been estimated that in the second half of 1947 almost 40 percent of all wage and salary earners in the bizonal area would have been superfluous under normal economic conditions.[38]

The Allied policy of industrial disarmament was bound to alter the composition of the German gross national product and to induce shifts in the distribution of the labor force. Table 19 shows the extent to which labor nominally shifted from heavy industry to light and peaceful industry, including agriculture.

From 1939 to 1946, the first full postwar year, the number of wage earners in agriculture rose to 193.8 percent of the 1936 level. The large increase is not difficult to explain. Millions of hungry expellees and refugees settled in the villages, which were generally intact. Millions of city dwellers also flocked to the villages in the hope of finding more food and better shelter than in the ravaged cities. This "back to the country movement" was unique in recent German history; for almost two centuries Germany had experienced an uninterrupted exodus of country people into the cities. The extent of this phenomenon is set forth in Table 20.

TABLE 20. Total Population of Bizonal Area, Classified by Size of City: 1939, 1946, and 1948.

City Size	Population in 1939 (in thousands)	% Change in Population Compared to 1939	
		1946	1948
Less than 10,000	15,148.0	+41.0%	+48.3%
10,000–19,999	1,842.8	+20.7%	+33.0%
20,000–49,999	2,560.1	+12.1%	+23.8%
50,000–99,999	1,816.7	+ 1.6%	+11.5%
100,000 and up	12,714.9	−18.6%	−10.1%
	43,082.5	+13.4%	+21.9%

Source: H. Bartels, Grösse und Ursachen des Bevölkerungszuwachses im Vereinigten Wirtschaftsgebiet, *Wirtschaft und Statistik,* Vol. I, No. 1 (1949), p. 7.

In 1946 communities with populations of less than 10,000 had registered the greatest percentage increases, while cities over 100,000 had lost almost 20 percent of their 1939 population. By 1948 village population had continued to swell under the impetus of continued shortages, scanty housing, and industrial stagnation, and communities under 10,000 had almost 50 percent more inhabitants than in 1939. The trend halted only after the currency reforms in June, 1948, when the long-delayed reconstruction of Western Germany was initiated.

The high number of workers employed in agriculture and forestry shown in Table 19 is deceptive. Nominally the index rose until September, 1946, when it was almost twice as high as in 1936. From then on the index showed a small decline, but in June, 1948, was still 65 percent higher than in 1936. Despite the high level of listed employment the agricultural output of the bizonal area of Germany remained at two-thirds of the prewar level. Hundreds of thousands of people were merely registered as employed in agriculture to satisfy the requirements of the labor offices, while in fact they were either unemployed or greatly underemployed. The experience after the currency reform demonstrated that German industry could tap the huge reservoir of idle or underemployed labor available in the countryside to meet its requirements.[39]

The other sector of the German economy which showed a large increase in employment was public and private services. Employment in this sector mounted without interruption until the currency reform, although Western Germany had no armed forces. At the end of 1947, the employment index stood at 157.6 percent of the 1936 level.

The principal reason was the mushrooming bureaucracy in the local, state, and military governments. Another reason was the practice of the occupation authorities of employing large numbers of German servants. In December, 1947, roughly one-third of all people employed in public and private services were working for the occupation forces.[40] Military government jobs were particularly attractive because in almost all cases they meant more food and cigarettes. Thousands of skilled workers pushed brooms or performed other menial chores and ate better than they would have, had they worked in their regular occupation.[41] Only after the currency reform did better food, new currency, and availability of consumer goods restore specialization to its proper role in production.

The employment index for domestics held at the 1936 levels, but here again the index is deceptive because of "shadow jobs." Many girls and women were registered as maids at the labor offices without actually working as such. It is inconceivable that so many could have found employment in this field in such chaotic economic conditions.

The two fields of economic activity which in 1946 showed a reduction of employed wage and salary workers were industry and handicrafts, and commerce and transport.[42] As shown in Table 19, employment in industry in March, 1946, was roughly 20 percent below the 1936 level, while in commerce it was even lower. By the end of 1946 industrial employment matched the level of 1936, but industrial production lingered at 30 percent of the 1936 output. Employment in both industry and commerce continued to rise and in March, 1948, stood 10 percent higher than in 1936, but the high level of employment still was not reflected in high output.

Under the conditions described—underemployment, hoarding of labor, "shadow jobs," lack of incentives, and Allied restrictions and prohibitions—the bizonal economy before the currency reform had what might be called "full employment of misery." It was an economy without incentives, without a currency, and without clear-cut authority or administration. It was an economy in which the interests of producers were diametrically opposed to those of consumers. It was an economy that had even failed to solve the basic problems of what goods were to be produced, how they should be produced, and for whom they should be produced.

5. Working Hours and Earnings

A high level of employment, an acute shortage of skilled labor, and an oversupply of unskilled workers were the three principal features of the employment situation before the currency reform. Skilled, able-bodied men were short in supply while older men, youngsters without skills, and disabled veterans were numerous. From January, 1946, to June, 1948, the number of unfilled vacancies in the bizonal area of Germany fluctuated from 500,000 to 700,000.[43] Most of the job openings were in the iron and steel industry, construction, coal mining, repairs of railway rolling stock and roads, and cement. These industries were particularly unsuccessful in their bids for workers because of their primitive working conditions, heavy physical work, low food rations, lack of footwear and clothing, and wage inequities. People were looking for "easy" work, but even in these hard jobs it was impossible to earn a livelihood.

The expectation of the currency reform induced many people to live off their wartime accumulations of *Reichsmarks*. Others worked only part-time for money wages from lack of incentives and because of the grossly inadequate rationing level.

The low food allotments were the principal reason for an almost precipitous decline in labor productivity. Some estimates put the 1947 industrial output per man at 50 percent of the prewar level;[44] other official estimates put it as low as 40 percent.[45]

It was not unusual for firms to have an absence rate as high as 50 percent of all employees. On Saturdays and Mondays absences were particularly high because workers spent week-ends scouring the countryside for food. For this reason many companies introduced a five-day, forty-hour work week, although nominally the forty-eight-hour week was still in effect. Actually the yearly average work week in the British zone in 1946 was 40.3 hours, and in April, 1947, it was even less.[46] In the summer of 1947, Bavarian trade unions declared that the forty-hour week was necessary because of the "catastrophic rationing levels." [47]

Lack of proper work clothing and shoes also increased absenteeism; for a man with only one pair of shoes and a shirt or two, whose earnings would not replace them, it was much more rational to stay home and save them than to work for money. And another reason for the shorter work week was the general stagnation of German industry. Indices for bizonal industry of the average weekly hours worked, hourly wage rates, and gross average weekly earnings are shown in Table 21.

During the first three postwar years the index of average weekly hours was roughly 20 percent below the 1938 level. This was clearly reflected in gross weekly earnings, which in June, 1946, were 13.2 percent and in June, 1947, 7.5 percent lower than in 1938. As has been shown, the low level of industrial output raised unit costs of all products considerably although prices remained frozen at wartime levels. To minimize losses firms paid workers the lowest possible hourly rates of pay.[48] The index of gross weekly earnings rose to the 1938 levels only in June, 1948.

The index of gross hourly receipts, however, was considerably higher than in 1938. The 5 percent rise to June, 1947, was largely caused by the granting of increases in industries that had paid less than 50 pfennigs an hour, and much of the 7 percent increase to June, 1948, was due to higher wages in the "problem industries."

In terms of *Reichsmarks* the postwar average of weekly gross earnings in various industries is set forth in Table 22. Despite

TABLE 21. Indices of Average Weekly Hours and Earnings in Bizonal Area Industry. (1938 = 100)

Period	Average Weekly Hours			Gross Hourly Receipts			Gross Weekly Earnings		
	Males	*Females*	*All*	*Males*	*Females*	*All*	*Males*	*Females*	*All*
(Weights in %)	76.9	23.1	100.0	78.3	21.7	100.0	76.9	23.1	100.0
June, 1946	80.5	73.5	79.8	107.9	117.0	108.7	86.9	85.9	86.8
June, 1947	81.5	76.3	81.0	113.7	121.3	114.1	92.7	92.5	92.5
June, 1948	82.5	81.6	82.5	121.5	130.2	122.0	100.2	106.2	100.7

Source: Statistisches Amt des Vereinigten Wirtschaftsgebietes, *Wirtschaft und Statistik*, I (1949–50), 488.

Allied plans for the industrial disarmament of Germany the wartime wage structure was carried over. Logically, industrial disarmament would have seemed to call for reduction of wage rates in the steel and iron industries and increases in the consumer goods industries and the building trades. However, the average weekly earnings remained highest in those industries which formed the very core of German industrial war potential.

In June, 1946, the combined average weekly earnings for males and females in steel and iron production were RM 42.20, while in June, 1947, and in June, 1948, the comparable earnings were RM 47.35 and RM 52.19 respectively. The earnings in the typical "peaceful" industries, such as textiles, clothing, and building trades, remained almost 30 percent below the earnings of steelworkers. The situation was particularly acute in the building trades. Due to the severe bombing damage the demand for construction workers was heavy, but wage rates were too low to attract construction workers. The situation was remedied somewhat in 1947, when the building trades were designated "problem industries."

In June, 1946, the average weekly earnings of all industries stood at RM 35.22, while in June, 1948, the earnings level was RM 40.51, a rise of 15 percent. The 1948 earnings nominally were a fraction higher than comparable earnings in 1938. But to interpret monetary earnings it is necessary to examine what the money could buy and the postwar standard of living.

6. The Postwar Income-Expenditure Gap

One feature of any kind of repressed inflation is the excess of legal incomes over legal expenditures. Repressed inflation, by definition, implies two factors: the existence of excessive mone-

TABLE 22. Average Weekly Gross Earnings of Manual Workers in Manufacturing and Construction Industries, Bizonal Area. (in Reichsmarks)

Industry	June, 1946			June, 1947			June, 1948		
	Males	Females	Total	Males	Females	Total	Males	Females	Total
Iron and steel	43.33	24.22	42.20	47.75	29.57	47.35	52.64	33.48	52.19
Non-ferrous metals	39.91	20.98	39.21	41.88	23.70	41.02	46.68	30.89	46.04
Foundries	40.92	20.14	39.90	44.99	25.50	44.48	48.56	29.89	48.09
Metal fabricating	40.34	20.59	38.26	42.36	21.53	40.20	44.20	25.65	42.29
Chemical	40.64	20.33	35.24	43.76	22.68	38.23	49.67	26.66	43.50
Glass	39.84	21.83	36.94	42.95	20.47	38.90	46.98	24.06	42.97
Building and allied trades	33.27	18.28	32.99	36.80	20.28	36.50	42.53	27.86	42.37
Sawmills	32.65	13.20	31.89	34.86	16.31	34.15	39.20	21.28	38.69
Textiles	31.65	18.83	24.97	33.12	20.95	26.57	37.42	24.81	30.44
Clothing	38.67	18.90	25.33	38.85	21.21	25.75	40.87	24.10	28.40
Shoes	34.69	20.59	26.42	33.94	20.67	25.73	36.70	22.60	28.16
All industries	38.28	20.14	35.22	41.03	21.64	37.41	44.31	24.80	40.51

Source: Statistiches Amt des Vereinigten Wirtschaftsgebietes, *Wirtschaft und Statistik*, I (1949), 489.

tary demand and legal prohibitions on spending designed to stabilize prices of consumer goods and factors of production. Price, wage, and rent controls, rationing of goods and floor space, and direct allocations of factors to the producers are generally used to avoid the wage-price spiral of an open inflation.

During the first three postwar years the Western Allies unquestionably repressed the existing inflationary potential. In this period the bizonal economy was "one of the most tightly controlled in Europe." [49] Virtually all goods were rationed, except some of the "new" goods of the semi-luxurious variety already discussed.

But Allied tax legislation worked at cross purposes to the price-wage freeze. The Allied Control Council's most important tax actions were:

a) The wage tax was raised 25 percent in the fall of 1945 and was set even higher a few months later.

b) Property taxes rose 200 to 500 percent.

c) Turnover taxes were raised by 50 percent.

d) Tobacco taxes increased 200 to 600 percent.

e) The tax on alcohol rose by 2300 percent.

f) Taxes on beer and matches went up 30 to 900 percent.

g) The tax on sugar rose about 95 percent.[50]

The effect of these measures was to raise all German taxes by an average of roughly 50 percent. The incentive-killing effect of this should not be overestimated, however, since the prevailing low wages "held out little incentive in any case." [51] Corporation tax rates rose 35 percent to 65 percent.[52]

The elimination of food subsidies in the American zone of occupation and higher prices for "new" goods also pushed the cost of living up. Of the total increase, 60 percent was attributed to higher taxes, 20 percent to higher prices, and the remaining 20 percent to the elimination of food subsidies.[53]

Table 23 shows the rise of the postwar cost of living, includ-

TABLE 23. Cost-of-Living Index, Bizonal Area.* (1938 = 100)

Period	Total Index	Food	Stimu-lants **	Rent	Heat and Light	Clothing
1946 (July-December) †	125	118	199	100	108	168
1947 †	126	120	204	100	109	181
1948: January	126	118	204	100	110	192
February	127	119	204	100	110	193
March	127	120	204	100	110	194
April	128	122	204	100	110	198
May	131	127	204	100	110	201
June	134	136	204	100	111	204

* A provisional index pertaining to a bombed-out worker's family of five.
** Chiefly tobacco products.
† Monthly averages.
Source: U.S. Office of Military Government for Germany, *Monthly Report: Statistical Annex*, No. 20 (October, 1948), p. 136.

ing its most important components, from 1946 to June, 1948. Compared with increases in black market prices the rise in the cost-of-living index was quite small. Food was 15 percent higher and clothing 21 percent higher in 1948 than in 1946, but stimulants (chiefly tobacco products), heat, and light rose less than 3 percent and rent was almost unchanged.

The above data refer to a bombed-out worker's family of five persons. The total cost of living in the fall of 1945 stood 12 percent higher than in 1938. The cost of clothing and furniture, for instance, had risen by as much as 30 percent during the war, but most other items showed remarkable stability.[54] From the fall of 1945 to June, 1948, the increase came to another 20 percent, and compared to the prewar period living costs were 30 percent higher, a comparatively moderate increase.

Extreme caution is required, however, for a proper interpretation of the postwar standard of living in the bizonal area. For one thing, in 1938 the German standard of living was one of the highest in Western Europe; in 1947 it was the lowest.

The money wage bought virtually nothing except the 1550-calorie food ration—when that was available. The cost-of-living index measured merely "the changes in officially fixed prices and rationed quantities of food" and did not take into account the deterioration in quality of all goods sold.[55]

A mere reference to the cost of living does not throw enough light on the deterioration of the German "real wage" during the first three postwar years. One way to measure the decline of the "real wage" is to compare the weekly earnings of the various income and occupational groups with the legal expenditures. A number of Allied and German survey teams made serious attempts to correlate these factors.

An American survey showed that for a worker's family of three persons the legal rationing and living expenses came to RM 1504 per year while the average income was RM 1251 a year.[56] Of the earnings 46 percent, or RM 686, was spent for food; 13 percent, or RM 194, for shelter; 7 percent, or RM 104, for clothing; 9 percent, or RM 121, for fuel; 12 percent, or RM 179, for taxes; and 15 percent, or RM 218, for other items.[57] On the average, the legal expenditures of the sample households exceeded legal incomes by RM 253.

Another survey rendered similar findings. In 1946, the cost of a minimum standard of living in the U.S. zone for an average worker's family of four persons—a moderately heavy worker, his wife, and two children in the 6–10 and 10–18 age groups—came to RM 120 a month, or RM 1440 a year.[58] On the basis of a forty-hour work week, the highest wage category of the sample population had a net monthly wage of RM 172, the median wage group received RM 150, and the lowest wage group earned only RM 113 a month. A minimum of RM 120 a month was required to meet the cost of a minimum standard. Half of the families reportedly earned less than RM 35 gross a week, and widespread complaints of inability "to meet the cost of living out of earnings" were heard.[59] In practically all deficiency cases the gap between current incomes and legal expenditures "was bridged mostly by drawing on the past savings." [60]

A German survey in August, 1946, of twenty-two households in the Ruhr Valley also found no heads of households who earned sufficient incomes to maintain the family without using savings. The average income was RM 171.73 a month, and yet, on the average, only 41 percent of all expenditures could be met through current incomes.[61] To avoid misunderstanding, the above reference to *all* expenditures included, besides the legal expenditures on rationed food, housing, and utilities, the *associated* expenditures which arose out of the abnormal living conditions. For all income groups current earnings were sufficient to buy the legal food ration, but the grossly inadequate rationing levels made additional outlays for black market purchases of food, fares for countless trips to the countryside, and gardening virtually indispensable. Under the prevailing conditions it was quite difficult to determine what sort of expenditure was legal and what was not, and for this reason the survey data should be taken with some reservations. But Kurt Schumacher, the late leader of the West German Social Democratic Party, felt that the German working people "never worked for such a low wage as they did in mid-1947." [62]

An earlier German survey, conducted in the spring of 1946 in British-occupied Lower Saxony, also showed that current incomes of the households studied were insufficient to purchase all the necessary rationed and unrationed goods that were available on the market. This sample was limited to skilled workers with average incomes of RM 170 a month, but again workers spent considerable portions of their incomes on black market food and for this reason only 57 percent of all expenses came from current legal incomes.[63]

Furthermore, British-conducted surveys of miners' households in the Ruhr Valley showed that in 1946 the average miner's family spent 16 percent more than its current income, while in 1947 expenditures exceeded incomes by 11 percent.[64] Even though the Ruhr miners received a number of special incentive goods and considerably higher pay than other workers, abnormal economic conditions induced many associated expenditures. In the spring of 1947 the U.S. Military Governor also reported that "workers' legal incomes are insufficient to buy their rations and necessities at legal prices." [65]

Another valuable source of information on the prevailing trends of legal incomes and expenditures is the published expenditure records of German workers. For instance, in March of 1947, an unskilled building worker earned 64 pfennigs an hour and worked 45 hours a week. His family included a wife and three small children. His monthly income from wages was RM 106.92, his wife's income was RM 24 and his additional earnings came to RM 27, making the total RM 157.92 a month. In the same month—i.e., during the 99th rationing period—the legal expenditures, without the purchase of any furniture, came to RM 160.38, exceeding the legal income by RM 2.46. During the 100th rationing period his total legal income was RM 123 and legal expenditures were RM 135, and in the 101st rationing period his monthly legal expenditures exceeded the legal earnings by RM 20.27.[66] On the basis of such low earnings it was impossible to supplement the food ration from any source, legal or illegal.

A formal attempt to determine whether workers could buy the current food ration with current incomes indicated beyond doubt that even the lowest-paid income groups could.[67] But it must be kept in mind that the legal food ration was far below minimum standards of nutrition. Without additional food one was bound to succumb to starvation and the above-mentioned associated expenditures were necessary for life. Thus all of the above surveys show that legal expenditures plus the indispensable expenditures for additional food exceeded legal incomes.

Even though this unusual phenomenon under conditions of repressed inflation was reported, its significance was never evaluated.

Inadequate earnings posed no serious problems to those who had savings, assets, or simply something to sell. A non-smoker could easily dispose of his tobacco ration card and use the proceeds to meet necessary expenses,[68] and a ten-year-old radio might bring RM 3,000 on the black market.[69]

A congressional fact-finding mission recorded an anecdote illustrating the low status of money wages in the bizonal area of Germany prior to the currency reform. A coal miner working six days a week earned RM 60. He also owned a hen that laid five eggs a week. The miner ate one egg a week and swapped the other four for twenty cigarettes. The black-market price for a cigarette was RM 8, and the sale of twenty cigarettes brought him RM 160. Thus the miner's hen earned two and two-thirds times more for him than six days in the pit.[70]

To give the workers some kind of inducement to work, the German business community began paying workers *in kind* as well as in money.[71] This practice involved the retention of output for distribution to workers at legal prices. The workers, in turn, swapped the goods for food or sold them on the black market. In the fall of 1946 the German *Land* economic offices began permitting companies to use part of their output "for the satisfaction of internal requirements." [72] Similarly the U.S. military authorities, in an attempt to revive the traditional German export industries, permitted the use of 5 percent of the foreign exchange proceeds to buy food and consumer goods for workers in those industries.[73]

In this fashion a twentieth-century version of the "truck wage system" came into operation. The workers in a cutlery plant got pocket knives, a shoe manufacturer gave out shoes, a clothing producer paid in textiles, and electrical manufacturers paid in electric bulbs, and money wages were reduced by an amount representing the legal price of the goods received. In cigarette factories workers got 800 cigarettes a month as part of their wages,[74] and the sale of these in the black market easily brought an additional RM 20,000 a year.

As the "primitivization" of the German economy spread, wages in kind on the household level and approved barter, or compensation trade, on the corporation level went a long way to inflate the "semi-legal" sphere of economic activity. But since all transactions were conducted in terms of legal prices, these prices were not threatened, although their meaning as an approximate indicator of relative scarcities was destroyed. Industries paying wages in kind received a "clamor for transfers," while the steel industry and building activity, which had nothing to offer as wages in kind, had great difficulty in securing and holding workers.[75] It was obvious that such a primitive, almost moneyless system could not last long in the industrial heart of Western Europe.

7

RENT AND HOUSING CONTROLS

1. The Nazi Legislation on Rent and Housing Control

Control over housing and rents is part and parcel of a system of direct controls. In general, rent control strives to protect tenants from rising housing costs in the same fashion that price controls attempt to prevent price increases of goods and services. But price controls, *per se,* do not guarantee that consumers will be able to obtain consumer goods at a fixed price; rationing is necessary for that. Similarly, fixing rents does not guarantee housing to the tenant, so housing controls also assure some minimum of floor space by which tenants are protected against eviction. The control of floor space is as important in any effective system of rent control as rationing in price control.

In Germany, up to 1936 all buildings completed before July 1, 1918, were subject to the Reich Rent Act of 1922. This law fixed maximum rentals for floor space in terms of a percentage of the rental charged on July 1, 1914. But lack of controls on buildings completed after July 1, 1918, tended to push rent costs up. The Price-Stop Decree of 1936, which fixed prices and rents, closed this gap. Thereafter price control authorities had to approve any rent increase. A law dating from 1923 provided that no tenant could be evicted without the approval of a special tenants' court.

At the outbreak of war, existing rent and housing legislation was supplemented by the Reich Law on Exactions of September 1, 1939. This law authorized local housing authorities to requisition floor space for billeting purposes. Persons who were assigned housing under it could not be evicted except with the approval of the local housing office.

But as the war progressed, and especially after the Allied carpet bombing of cities turned millions of homes into heaps of rubble, the housing shortage became more acute. Additional measures to provide shelter for bombed-out families became necessary. The Decree for the Regulation of Housing Space of February 27, 1943, and the Decree for Supply of Housing Space for the Bombed-Out Population of June 21, 1943, became the emergency pillars in the field of housing during the final stages of the war.[1] Although rent control was formally the responsibility of the price control agencies, in practice rent control, housing allocation and evictions were handled by the housing offices in cities and villages.

The Nazi system of rent and housing control was highly decentralized, and for this reason allocation of floor space per person varied from locality to locality. In overcrowded communities housing was strictly rationed, and persons over 14 years of age could claim 4 square meters of floor space, excluding kitchen while children under 14 were entitled to only 2 square meters.[2]

To prevent overcrowding, housing offices were also authorized to refuse accommodations to strangers. The most effective way to achieve this aim was to refuse permits of residence. Without a permit nobody could claim a ration card and in this way the permits became more than just a tool in housing control.[3] As the housing situation deteriorated, finding a place to live became more important than the rate of rent.

2. *Housing Regulations in the Postwar Period*

The British and Americans preserved all Nazi housing legislation in their zones of occupation. The former posts of Reich Housing Commissioner and *Gau* Housing Commissioner were scrapped, but the Minister-Presidents of the newly formed German *Länder* were to enforce the housing and rent controls.[4]

The wartime mass bombing had eradicated huge areas in most towns, and the population had either to live in cellars and air-raid shelters or to crowd into the houses that remained standing. Never before had the buildings occupied by a population of over 30 million, with a Western standard of living, been in such devastated condition as when the British occupied the zone.[5]

In 1939 the bizonal area had an estimated population of 34.2 million. But later the population increased enormously, due mainly to the influx of German expellees from Poland, Hungary, Rumania, Austria, and Czechoslovakia and of refugees from Eastern Germany.[6] In early 1947 the bizonal population had swelled to 41.7 million and the housing situation was desperate. Yet the relentless influx of refugees, virtually without possessions, continued unabated. To provide shelter for the millions of homeless refugees was the immediate problem of the German housing authorities.

In 1945 and 1946 the finding of accommodations for homeless refugees took place without any central plan whatsoever. It was customary for military government officials to inform the German housing authorities of a particular community that so many refugees would be arriving in a day or two and that emergency quarters would have to be found by that time. To accommodate hungry and cold refugees and expellees, regardless of whether these people might be able to find employment in a given area, the housing authorities simply requisitioned rooms.[7] The legal basis for this was the 1939 Law of Exactions. In the postwar chaos this law was widely used, and with certain modifications it is still on the books.

The influx of expellees and refugees into different parts of Western Germany was not uniform. In some areas, like Schleswig-Holstein, the destitute refugee population simply piled up—in 1947, there were six refugees for every seven resident citizens. The refugee situation in Bavaria was grave but not as desperate as in Schleswig-Holstein. The French zone remained hermetically sealed and in the first postwar years hardly any refugees settled there.

To bring some order into the almost chaotic housing situation in all four zones of occupation, the Allied Control Council passed Law No. 18, known as the Allied Housing Law.[8] This law, superseding the Decree for the Regulation of Housing Space of 1943, provided that any person applying for housing must possess a ration card and an appropriate registration certificate from the labor office indicating his profession or employment.

Since the extent of the devastation of German cities was virtually unparalleled in history, the Allied Housing Law had to define the terms "housing space" and "a person." The former meant weatherproof space, adequately lighted and ventilated, with water supply and sanitary facilities. Bathrooms, halls, kitchens and stairways with an area of less than 10 square meters were not counted as "housing space." Anyone 14 years of age or over was considered "a person" and could claim, as in crowded areas under the Nazis, a minimum of 4 square meters of floor space.[9] A child between 1 and 14 years of age was entitled to only 2 square meters, and an infant under 1 was not legally entitled to any floor space at all.

Because of the considerable destruction nearly two-thirds of the population had to share accommodations, including cooking and toilet facilities. In the heavily industrialized British zone the bombing damage was particularly severe, and it was estimated that 50 percent of all prewar apartments had been destroyed.[10] To prevent further deterioration of living conditions, the Council provided that certain specified districts or localities could be designated as "critical areas." Declaration of a locality as a "critical area" authorized local housing authorities to take all necessary measures to prevent persons from taking up residence there. In extremely grave situations housing authorities could even compel residents not vital to the economy of the locality to move to other, less crowded areas. To have a better control over available housing the British military government decreed a general prohibition of change of residence.[11] This ordinance gave to local German housing authorities a legal basis for the system of "permits of residence." [12]

With housing controlled as well as jobs and consumption, the Germans' postwar lives were entwined in a forest of regulation. All jobs had to be approved by local labor offices and a person could claim ration cards and a certain amount of floor space from housing authorities only if he was working or excused from working. Except for a very few individuals, mostly black marketeers, postwar Germans had no difficulty in securing rationing cards, but housing was a different matter altogether. In most cases housing authorities could do little to cope with the legitimate demand.[13] The shortage was so acute that it would be more correct to speak of the program as control of shelter rather than control of housing.

3. The Postwar Housing Shortage

Roughly 25 percent of all urban housing in the bizonal area was destroyed by the war. In addition to the millions of refugees and expellees, the homeless indigenous population had to find shelter in the 75 percent of the housing remaining. Due to lack of coal, building materials, electricity, and transportation, very little damage was repaired immediately after the war. As the years went on millions of people continued to live in rubble, basements, bunkers, and camps. In 1947, the housing typically available consisted of a 12-foot square room for three persons. With such crowding, a rapid spread of tuberculosis and other diseases was inevitable. Former President Hoover, in his survey of the bizonal area, reported that the "housing situation in the two zones is the worst that modern civilization has ever seen." [14]

According to the 1939 census data, the number of apartments in Northern Germany, which after the war became the British zone, was 5.5 million and in the American zone 3.8 million, or 9.3 million combined. For Germany as a whole there were 19.5 million apartments; the number of family households was roughly the same, and the number of persons per apartment was from three to four.[15] In the British zone the occupancy was 3.5 persons per apartment.[16]

After the massive hail of bombs in 1944 and 1945 all German cities were in ruins and an unprecedented housing shortage marred the lives of the totally defeated people. The extent of housing destruction in the bizonal area is shown in Table 24.

Of 9.3 million apartments in 1939 only 4.8 million, or 52 percent, survived the war intact. The number of damaged apartments came to 2.7 million, or 29 percent of the total. The number of destroyed apartments was 1.7 million, or 18 percent.

All apartments with an estimated damage of 60 percent or

TABLE 24. Destruction of Apartments in Bizonal Area. (In thousands)

| | | | Undamaged | |
State	Available 1939	Totally Destroyed	Damaged	Number	% of 1939
Nordrhein-Westfalen	3,356	669	1,360	1,327	35
Niedersachsen	1,159	144	368	647	54
Hamburg	556	277	171	107	18
Schleswig-Holstein	435	47	49	340	78
Bayern	1,789	236	244	1,309	72
Württemberg-Baden	891	133	267	491	55
Hessen	956	133	236	587	61
Bremen	166	69	56	40	24
Total	9,308	1,708	2,752	4,849	52

Source: W. G. Harmssen, *Reparationen, Sozialprodukt, Lebensstandard* (Bremen: F. Trüjen Verlag, 1948), III, 95.

less were considered repairable. Apartments with an estimated damage of up to 15 percent could be relatively easily repaired. By the end of 1946 roughly 600,000 of these apartments had already been repaired in the British zone.[17] By the end of 1947 800,000 apartments had been repaired, although many repair jobs were temporary in nature.[18]

The chief handicap to appreciable progress in housing was the shortage of building materials. For the most part wartime stocks had been consumed by 1946, and with low production the entire official repair program slowed down. Disposal of rubble was another problem that hampered building operations. Many valuable housing sites were choked with rubble and debris, and removal was quite slow. It was estimated that at 1946 building and debris-clearing rates it would have taken eighty years to raise housing conditions of the bizonal area to reasonably adequate levels.[19]

The above figures, although reasonably correct, should be taken with certain reservations. The 1939 census recorded 9.28 million apartments in the two zones,[20] but postwar estimates list the total stock of apartments as 8.8 million,[21] or 500,000 apartments less. The later figure, based on the 1927 population census, appears to be rather on the low side, and the 1939 figure seems to be more reliable. The estimated number of totally destroyed apartments varies from 1.7 million to 2.1 million units.[22] In terms of percentages, the difference is between 18 and 22 percent of the 1939 figure.[23]

Although 52 percent of all apartments survived the war intact, the Allied requisitioning of housing aggravated the situation. In the British zone of occupation 250,000 apartments, 9 percent of the undamaged units, were requisitioned by the military government.[24] At one time 4.5 percent of all apartments in the American zone cities were reported requisitioned by the military, amounting to close to 100,000 apartments.[25] This figure may be low, for in some cities—Erlangen, Heidelberg, Schwabach, and Kitzingen—more than 10 percent of all available apartments were requisitioned by the military government.[26]

OVERCROWDING

With population swollen by refugees and housing gutted by bombs, finding a roof for everyone was possible only by herding more people into every available corner. Table 25 shows the extent of overcrowding.

In 1939 the average apartment was occupied by 3.61 persons; in 1948 occupancy had risen to 5.37 persons, or almost two persons more per apartment. Deterioration of living conditions was not uniform throughout the bizonal area because of differences in the degree of destruction, in the requisitioning of housing by the occupation forces, and in the influx of refugees. Schleswig-Holstein was accommodating more than three additional persons per apartment while Württemberg-Baden had only 1.2 persons more. In Schleswig-Holstein the increase of occupancy came to 85 percent, in Württemberg-Baden to 34

TABLE 25. Persons per Apartment, 1939 and 1948.

| State | 1939 | 1948 | Increase, 1939 to 1948 | |
			Number	%
Schleswig-Holstein	3.54	6.56	3.02	85
Hamburg	3.05	5.11	2.06	67
Niedersachsen	3.82	6.01	2.19	57
Nordrhein-Westfalen	3.53	5.21	1.68	48
Bremen	3.35	5.20	1.85	55
Hessen	3.58	4.85	1.27	35
Württemberg-Baden	3.54	4.75	1.21	34
Bayern	3.92	5.49	1.57	40
Total	3.61	5.37	1.76	49

Source: "Der Wohnungsbestand in den Ländern des Vereinigten Wirtschaftsgebietes am 1. Oktober 1948," *Wirtschaft und Statistik*, I (1949), 80–82.

percent. An important fact is that living conditions were considered worse in 1947 than in 1946 or 1945.[27]

The inevitable result was overcrowding, and this in turn had a direct bearing on labor productivity. It was estimated that in the early postwar years two persons, on the average, occupied every available room in the bizonal area.[28] Night-shift workers frequently found it impossible to obtain a place to rest. Members of thousands of families continued to live apart. Even in 1949 the overcrowding was almost unbelievable; a survey in the present-day Federal Republic showed that, on the average, 3.18 persons shared one bedroom. Moreover, 32.2 percent of those questioned did not have a bed of their own but only a place to sleep.[29]

4. Housing Construction: 1945–1948

During the first two years of occupation the main reconstruction effort concentrated on repairing damaged buildings to make them weatherproof and habitable. Repair work was slowly extended to more heavily damaged buildings, but progress was slow. Although the exact number of repaired apartments will never be known, it is reasonably safe to say that by the time the currency reform was carried out roughly 1.4 million damaged apartments had been repaired. If this estimate is correct, the total stock of apartments in the bizonal area then was around 6 million units.

Official statistics on building activity prior to the currency reform are not reliable. It is known that a great deal of activity was either "black" or "gray." Building "black" meant carrying out construction without a building permit. "Gray" building activity meant that authorities issued permits without allocating building materials. Anyone who said that he had the materials could get a building permit and German officials did not bother to ask how building materials were obtained. Consequently a great deal of legally licensed construction activity was done with black market materials. German statistics do not distinguish between black or gray building, alterations, partial reconstructions, or new buildings. In the second half of 1947 the total of illegal building cases penalized in the British zone was 2,611 and 4,072 cases were still pending.[30]

After December 1, 1946, housing legislation became the responsibility of the German *Land* governments, and local authorities were not too eager to prevent "gray" or even "black" building activity. Considering the desperate shortage, every additional apartment was viewed with approval, and considerable building activity took place. It is fairly safe to say that if the building materials had been used only to repair damaged houses, three or four times as many persons would have been accommodated. As it was, in 1948 the bizonal area was still short 5.32 million apartments.[31]

OUTPUT OF BUILDING MATERIALS

Production indices of principal building materials before the currency reform, contained in Table 26, do much to explain the inadequate building activity in the bizonal area. During 1946 and 1947 the production of cement, burnt lime, bricks, and roofing tiles fluctuated considerably below the 1936 levels. The output of cement lingered at around 30 percent and production of bricks was about 20 percent of the 1936 levels. Production of burnt lime and roofing tiles held at roughly 40 percent.

TABLE 26. Production of Building Materials, Bizonal Area, 1936–1948. (In thousands; 1936 = 100)

	Cement		Burnt Lime		Bricks		Roofing Tiles	
Date *	*Tons*	*%*	*Tons*	*%*	*Tons*	*%*	*Tons*	*%*
1936	625.7	100	365.0	100	343.3	100	56.3	100
1938	827.5	132			306.6	89		
1946	194.3	31	152.2	42	65.5	19	21.0	37
1947	224.6	36	171.5	47	74.6	22	22.6	40
1948	426.1	68	281.1	77	164.1	48	34.1	61

* Monthly average.
Sources: H. Kresling, *Statistisches Handbuch der Bauwirtschaft* (München: Institut für Wirtschaftsforschung, 1949), pp. 7, 12, 15, 16.

Inadequate allocation of coal to the building materials industry was unquestionably the most important single factor in the low output. In 1947, for instance, the average monthly allocation was 94,000 tons.[32] The bizonal building materials industry required roughly 400,000 tons of coal and coke a month for reasonably high level operations, but it actually received about 25 percent of its coal requirements.[33] An official British Military Government source estimated that to bring the bizonal building material factories into capacity operations, they "will need five times as much coal as they were allocated in 1947." [34]

Shortages and irregular supply of electric power was another factor which greatly increased coal consumption per unit of output. It was estimated that in 1946, on account of power shortages, 124 percent more coal was needed to produce 100 bricks than in 1936. The increase for a ton of burnt lime was 25 percent and for cement 37 percent.[35]

In January, 1948, production of building materials improved considerably, and in the last three months before the currency reform the monthly average output figures were roughly 70 percent above those of the previous year. The exact figures are impossible to obtain because underreporting was widely practiced. Wild rumors about the forthcoming currency reform were on everybody's lips, and it is known that hoarding was not only tolerated but occasionally even quietly recommended by German administrative agencies. After the currency reform considerable amounts of hoarded building materials were thrown on the market, but building activity could not be greatly increased for financial reasons.

5. Rent

After the defeat in 1945 all rents remained frozen at their prewar levels. The newly created German states took over the responsibility for enforcing rent control, but the almost fantastic housing shortage in the postwar period created new problems. Most apartments were shared by a number of families, and subletting of rooms was common. To block profiteering, German price control authorities decreed that the landlord must charge 1936 rates for a unit of floorspace. All hidden charges were to be avoided and an ordinance of November 18, 1947, gave a detailed listing of all factors—furniture, garage, and special privileges—which would justify additional charges.[36]

As a result, rents remained constant from 1936 to 1948, as shown by Table 27. The stability was truly remarkable for those who were fortunate enough to have a roof overhead at all. But it must be remembered there were millions of Germans who had neither an apartment, a room, nor, indeed, a bed of their own.

TABLE 27. Index of Rents, Western Germany, 1936–1948. (1913–14 = 100)

Year	Rents
1936	121.3
1938	121.2
1940	121.2
1942	121.2
1944	121.2
1945	121.2
1948	121.2

Source: Länderrat des Amerikanischen Besatzungsgebietes, *Statistisches Handbuch von Deutschland, 1928–1944* (München: F. Ehrenwirth Verlag, 1949), p. 463; data for 1945 and 1948, Deutsche Wohnungswirtschaft, *Wohnungswirtschaftliche Zahlen* (Düsseldorf: 1951), p. 43.

8

SUMMARY

During the first three years of Allied occupation the policy of industrial disarmament of Germany was vigorously pursued by the British and American military governments, not so much in terms of the removal of capital equipment as of a deliberate neglect of the industrial economy and an import embargo on raw materials. In the American zone the JCS 1067 directive, with its negative White-Morgenthau approach, provided the basic framework of occupation. JCS 1067 aimed at the creation of a new, peacefully oriented Germany without heavy industry but with a well-developed agriculture. By implication, this policy aimed at building an economically strong Europe with a weak Germany. In the prevailing "hate-the-Germans" milieu, the economic policy of JCS 1067 amounted to a pretense of restoring the German economy to the extent necessary to keep the Germans alive and free of disease (so that the victors would not catch typhus?).

In this rigid form, JCS 1067 guided the American policy for perhaps six months. As long as Americans put emphasis on economic chains for Germany the economic stagnation of Germany as well as the rest of Western Europe was inevitable. Americans slowly discovered that building an economically strong Europe by the economic destruction of Germany was a chimera. The onset of the cold war between East and West was primarily responsible for the reversal of the early policy, and by mid-1946 the policy drift was well on its course. However, Washington hesitated to make a clear-cut break with the Morgenthauist past and the Americans just "muddled through" for a whole year. By mid-1947 the German economic status was rapidly deteriorating. To undo the errors of the immediate past a new directive, JCS 1779, was issued July 17, 1947, stressing the economic rehabilitation and integration of Germany into the economic community of Western Europe.

The British never had anything like the JCS 1067 for their zone. Their responsible administrators and some influential public opinion makers viewed the White-Morgenthau policy as utter lunacy. Being partners in alliance, however, they accepted the Potsdam Agreement, which was also partially Morgenthau-inspired, with reservations. The British wanted essentially to achieve two objectives: the preservation of wartime unity among the Allies and the elimination of Germany as a potential trouble maker in the future. They never wavered from these two goals for more than brief periods.

Allied industrial disarmament was attempted within the framework of direct controls. In a war the aim of direct controls is to bring about speedy, efficient, and maximum utilization of available resources for the war effort. But in postwar Germany the Allies aimed not at the maximum utilization of industrial capacity but at precisely the opposite. Industrial disarmament of Germany required that only minimum industrial production be permitted. Thus, the reinstated direct controls were considered proper means to attain the envisaged retrogression of the German economic status for security purposes.

The economic prostration of Germany, in turn, disrupted the intra-European trade that was essential to the prosperity of other European nations. As long as German industrial capacity was kept idle the economic recovery of Europe was delayed. European economic deterioration brought further political complications. To nurse Europe back to economic health the Marshall Plan scrapped the early postwar economic chains of Germany.

The industrial disarmament policy worked at cross purposes to the policy of maximizing German agricultural production. Two policies were incompatible because agrarianization and industrialization of an economy are not simple alternatives but rather two different aspects of the same process. The population eked out an existence on food rations which were "too much to die on, but too little to live on." To escape the pangs of hunger the urban population took to scouring the countryside and bartering away their remaining household goods and other valuables for food. The farmers, in turn, received commodities they needed either to operate farms or for further barter transactions. A barter economy between the city and country thus came into being. Its existence reminded the occupation authorities as well as economists that when food rations fall below the indispensable minimum levels of sustenance the will-to-survive results in a considerable withdrawal of effort from industrial activity. The inability or unwillingness of the Western occupation powers to provide higher food rations for the Germans before the currency reform in mid-June, 1948, held in check even "permissible" industrial production and was thus partially responsible for the breakdown of the monetary economy.

The postwar monetary imbalance undeniably played a part in aggravating economic conditions. Uncertainty about the future value of the Reichsmark eliminated it as a store of value. Anticipation of the currency reform gave rise to widespread hoarding of goods by business to safeguard working capital, since it was generally expected that the reform would treat monetary claims much more harshly than material assets. The greatest portion of goods produced went into inventories. There was, in fact, a general flight into goods; everybody wanted to buy and nobody wanted to sell. Thus, in the final stages of repressed as well as open inflation a flight into goods results in the repudiation of the existing monetary system. In an open inflation the repudiation is complete, while in repressed inflation it is partial because food rations can still be bought for the existing currency.

Furthermore, the inability of manufacturers legally to obtain the amounts of coal, raw materials, and semifabricates needed for continuous operations and their desire to prevent the dissipation of their financial substance led to the establishment of the compensation activity. Like human beings, German business establishments coped with the situation by circumventing existing economic controls. Self-preservation of the firms made compensation trade an inescapable necessity, and this activity split the postwar German economic system into legal and illegal spheres. As conditions continued unimproved the legal sphere tended to shrink and the illegal tended to expand. But because compensation trade was conducted in terms of legal prices, similar to the barter between city and country, the stability of legal prices was not threatened.

For three years the Allies adhered strictly, with minor exceptions, to the policy of a price and wage freeze. As a result, the average weekly wages for all industries in the bizonal area of Germany were at the same levels in June, 1948, as in 1938. Prices of food, light, and fuel rose slightly, while the prices of consumer goods, including the "new" goods, rose substantially. The preservation of archaic prices of Nazi vintage meant that producers could not produce useful and needed goods, even though demand was high, because the prices generally did not cover the costs of production, let alone allow for profits. The easiest way out of the loss squeeze was the production of "new" commodities—formerly unproduced, semiluxurious items such as ash trays, fancy lamps, and dolls. The relative ease of obtaining higher prices for these goods meant that the available manpower and scarce raw materials were virtually squandered. For this reason the postwar price freeze constituted an integral part of the Allied policy of industrial disarmament of Germany.

In addition to the wage freeze the Allies preserved the Nazi system of labor conscription. All males between the ages of 14 and 65 and all females between the ages of 16 and 45 had to register at labor offices for an assignment. Holding a legal job, in turn, was a prerequisite to a food ration card. But on account of abnormal economic conditions, money earnings bought practically nothing except the 1,550-calorie food ration. To give workers some kind of inducement, and especially to raise productivity, the German business community began to pay workers in kind as well as in money. In this fashion the primitive "truck wage system" of the nineteenth century was revived in the trying circumstances in the mid-twentieth century. Wages in kind on the household level, and the compensation trade on the corporation level, tended to inflate the "real" flow at the expense of the "monetary." This feature negatively affected the social process of specialization and division of labor, with the result that the bizonal economy retrogressed more rapidly than had been deemed necessary for security purposes.

As long as the Western Allies persisted in the industrial disarmament of Germany, nowhere in Western Europe was the economic situation more desperate than in occupied Germany between 1945 and mid-1948. The cities were heaps of debris. The occupation authorities unquestionably established some semblance of order, but there was no hope, no future. The country remained partitioned and a relentless stream of refugees kept pouring into the Western zones. Food rations were insufficient to sustain life. Industrial production stagnated and the transportation system operated under serious strain. Legitimate work offered few incentives and productivity declined precipitously. The Reichsmark was heavily discounted as a unit of account, and hoarding of goods was widespread in the German business community.

The currency reform of June, 1948, changed the situation overnight. The long overdue economic and monetary reforms removed the economic chains, and thereupon West Germany launched its phenomenal economic upsurge.

Finally, one is tempted to wonder how it was possible for the United States to embark upon a policy of industrial disarmament of Germany which, in effect, amounted to a policy of fostering economic retrogression in the heart of Western Europe. Three reasons lend themselves as possible explanations. The Nazi atrocities created an understandable bias against Germany in everyone. And as a result many high-level policymakers in Washington were convinced that only harsh and repressive policies would be able to eliminate Germany as a threat to peace in the future. Furthermore, since the State and War Departments were virtually made subservient to the Treasury Department views on the planning work for German occupation, our German experts were overruled and bypassed. When an amateur, instead of an expert, makes policy, the result is likely to be disastrous. It was. The third possible explanation is that the vision of a deindustrialized Germany so blinded the principal policymakers in the Treasury to the realities of life that they inextricably confounded fact and fiction. Thus it seems reasonable that this fully developed plan for economic retrogression in the heart of Europe arose out of a mixture of bias, amateurism, and the failure to distinguish between positive and normative issues.

NOTES

CHAPTER 1

[1] S. U. Palme, "Politics and Economic Theory in Allied Planning for Peace," *The Scandinavian Economic History Review,* VII (1959), 87.

[2] The basic work on these matters is still J. M. Keynes, *The Scope and Method of Political Economy* (reprinted: New York: Kelley & Millman, 1955), pp. 34–36.

[3] K. Dönitz, *Zehn Jahre und zwanzig Tage* (Bonn: Anthenäum Verlag, 1958), p. 473. See also W. Lüdde-Neurath, *Regierung Dönitz* (Göttingen: Musterschmidt Wissenschaftlicher Verlag, 1951), pp. 117–24.

[4] Department of State, *Bulletin,* Vol. XII, No. 311 (1945), pp. 1051–55.

[5] *Ibid.,* Vol. XIII, No. 319 (1945), pp. 153–61.

[6] Clay, *Decision in Germany* (New York: Doubleday, 1950), p. 50.

[7] For an illuminating discussion of the different attitudes of the four powers at the Allied Control Council, see M. Balfour and J. Mair, *Four-*

Power Control in Germany and Austria (London: Oxford University Press, 1956), pp. 14–48. See also M. Gottlieb, *The German Peace Settlement and the Berlin Crisis* (New York: Paine-Whitman Publishers, 1960), pp. 85–100.

[8] The British held that a Germany without industry would paralyze the entire Western European economy. See *The Economist*, CIL, 321 (Sept. 8, 1945).

[9] For some instructive insights into the British policy in Germany see Balfour, *Some Aspects of the German Problem,* lecture delivered March 11, 1947, at the Chatham House, London (mimeographed; available at Hoover Institute).

[10] O. Strasser, *Germany in a Disunited World* ("Lifestream Controversy Series" [London: 1947]), pp. 5–7.

[11] For detailed discussion of French activities at the Allied Control Council, see Clay, *op. cit.,* pp. 104–62.

[12] The "socialistic transformation" of the Soviet zone is well described in "Die wirtschaftliche und soziale Entwicklung in der sowjetischen Besatzungszone Deutschlands, 1945–1949" (anonymous MS at the Hoover Institute).

[13] J. P. Nettl, *The Eastern Zone and Soviet Policy in Germany, 1945–1950* (London: Oxford University Press, 1951), p. 175.

[14] For the early Soviet tactics in their zone of occupation, see E. Davidson, *The Death and Life of Germany* (New York: Alfred A. Knopf, 1959), pp. 70, 140.

[15] K. Brandt, *Germany: Key to Peace in Europe* (Claremont, Calif.: Claremont College, 1949), p. 54.

[16] The "American fear of social changes implied in the Potsdam Agreement theme" has been fully developed in a perceptive book by Basil Davidson, *Germany: What Now?* (London: F. Müller, 1955), pp. 43, 48, 57, 75, 174, 178.

[17] G. S. Wheeler, *Die Amerikanische Politik in Deutschland, 1945–1950* (Berlin: Kongress-Verlag, 1958), p. 13. The author is a former official of the U.S. military government in Germany. For some time he was in charge of the denazification program in the U.S. occupied zone. He is now living in Czechoslovakia.

[18] J. P. Warburg, *Germany—Bridge or Battleground* (New York: Harcourt, Brace & Co., 1947), p. 32.

[19] *The Economist,* CLIV, 476 (March 27, 1948).

[20] For the postwar implementation of wartime agreements on Germany, see Department of State, *Agreements Reached at the Cairo, Teheran, Yalta, and Potsdam Conferences, Implementation and United States Policy* (mimeographed: 1948).

[21] The history of the matter has been the subject of many books and articles, e.g., J. L. Chase, "The Development of the Morgenthau Plan Through the Quebec Conference," *The Journal of Politics,* XVI (1954), 324–59; F. H. Gareau, "Morgenthau's Plan for Industrial Disarmament in Germany," *The Western Political Quarterly,* XIV (1961), 517–34; J. L. Snell, *Wartime Origins of the East-West Dilemma Over Germany* (New Orleans: the Hauser Press, 1959), pp. 67–125; G. Moltmann, *Amerikas Deutschlandpolitik im Zweiten Weltkrieg* (Heidelberg: C. Winter, 1958), pp. 118–65.

[22] A photostatic copy of this plan, entitled "Program to prevent Germany from starting World War III," is included in H. Morgenthau, *Germany Is Our Problem* (New York: Harper & Bros., 1945).

[23] House Select Committee on Foreign Aid, *Final Report on Foreign Aid* (1948), pp. 143–44.

[24] E. F. Penrose, *Economic Planning for the Peace* (Princeton: Princeton University Press, 1953), p. 250.

[25] House Select Committee on Foreign Aid, *loc. cit.*

[26] Senate Subcommittee on War Mobilization, *A Program for German Economic and Industrial Disarmament* (a study submitted by the Foreign Economic Administration, Enemy Branch [1946]).

[27] *Ibid.,* pp. 25, 285, 286.

[28] *Ibid.,* pp. 29–39.

[29] *Ibid.,* p. 377.

[30] *The Memoirs of Cordell Hull* (New York: Macmillan Co., 1948), p. 1616.

[31] N. I. White, *Harry Dexter White—Loyal American* (Waban, Mass.: B. [White] Bloom, 1956), pp. 251–57.

[32] Memo from H. D. White, written on September 7, 1944: "Is European Prosperity Dependent upon German Industry?" (H. D. White's collection at Princeton, file no. 22. A similar document reflecting a similar "Strong Europe, weak Germany" theme is to be found in a "Draft of Public Statement" in the same file.)

[33] Snell, *op. cit.*, p. 13.

[34] Penrose, *op. cit.*, p. 248.

[35] Harrod, *The Life of John Maynard Keynes* (New York: Harcourt, Brace & Co., 1951), p. 537.

[36] House Select Committee on Foreign Aid, *op. cit.*, p. 148.

[37] E. Davidson, *op. cit.*, p. 13. Similarly, Snell, *op. cit.*, p. 91.

[38] Department of State, *Germany 1947–1949: The Story in Documents* (1950), pp. 21–23.

[39] For an official interpretation of the actual occupational policies, see Department of State, *Occupation of Germany: Policy and Progress, 1945–46* ("European Series" [1947]), pp. 28–42.

[40] E. Varga, "Vozmeshchenija ushcherba gitlerovskoi Germaniyei i jeje soobchnikami," *Voina i Mir*, No. 10 (1943), 4–10.

[41] J. Schmelzer, "Die Geheimdirektive JCS 1067," *Wissenschaftliche Zeitschrift der Martin-Luther Universität Halle Wittenberg*, VIII (1958–59), 952.

[42] The entire text of the "Control Council Plan for Reparations and the Level of Postwar German Economy" has been reprinted in Beate Ruhm von Oppen, *Documents on Germany Under Occupation, 1945–1954* (New York: Oxford University Press, 1955), pp. 113–18.

[43] Gottlieb, *op. cit.*, pp. 93–94.

[44] The indispensable work for the day-to-day negotiations of the level of industry plan of 1946 is B. U. Ratchford and W. D. Ross, *Berlin Reparations Assignment* (Chapel Hill: The University of North Carolina Press, 1947), pp. 67–103.

[45] F. Grünig, *Industrieplan und künftige Leistungsfähigkeit der deutschen Volkswirtschaft* (mimeographed; Berlin: Deutsches Institut für Wirtschaftsforschung, May, 1946), p. 36.

[46] F. Seume, *Über die Durchführbarkeit des Industrieplanes der Alliierten* (mimeographed; Berlin: Deutsches Institut für Wirtschaftsforschung, June, 1946), p. 40.

[47] *Ibid.*, p. 41. For similar conclusions, see H. Meinhold, "Der Wirtschaftsplan vom 26, III, 1946" (typewritten; Ratzeburg: Institut für Weltwirtschaft, April 20, 1946), pp. 22–28.

[48] Ratchford and Ross, *op. cit.*, p. 69.

[49] *The Economist*, CL, 532 (April 6, 1946).

[50] International Chamber of Commerce, *The Economic Condition of Germany Today and Its International Repercussions* (Paris: 1947), p. 46.

[51] Statistisches Reichsamt, *Statistisches Jahrbuch für das Deutsche Reich 1937* (Internationale Übersichten, Aussenhandel, Berlin: 1937), pp. 123–24.

[52] Bank for International Settlements, *Seventeenth Annual Report, 1946–47* (Basel), p. 25.

[53] The Dutch, for instance, were stagnating on account of German industrial standstill. See *Auszug aus dem Memorandum der niederländischen Regierung v. 14. 1. 1947* in Sammelband von Veröffentlichungen zur Ruhrfrage in Kiel.

[54] F. Grünig, "Die innerdeutsche Wirtschaftsverflechtung, *Wirtschaftsprobleme der Besatzungszonen* (Berlin: Duncker & Humblot, 1948), pp. 65–95.

[55] A. Wolfers, *United States Policy Toward Germany* (New Haven: Yale Institute of International Studies, Memo No. 20, February 21, 1947), p. 8. See also F. Howley, *Berlin Command* (New York: G. P. Putnam's Sons, 1950), pp. 272–73.

[56] Very instructive was the testimony of the late Assistant Secretary of War, H. C. Petersen. See House Committee on Appropriations, *First Deficiency Appropriation Bill for 1947; Hearings,* February, 1947, p. 700.

[57] E. Kogon, "Das Jahr der Entscheidungen," *Frankfurter Hefte,* III (1948), 16–28.

[58] For a perceptive discussion of this matter, see S. Huddleston, *Popular Diplomacy and War* (Rindge, N. H.: R. R. Smith Publisher, 1954), pp.

237–38. See also J. S. Martin, *All Honorable Men* (Boston: Little, Brown & Co., 1950), p. 156.

[59] Printed in Department of State, *Germany 1947–1949: The Story in Documents,* pp. 33–41.

[60] *Ibid.,* p. 358.

[61] For an analysis of the two plans see Deutsches Büro für Friedensfragen, *Das Abkommen über verbotene und beschränkte Industrie vom 13, April 1949* (Stuttgart: 1949), pp. 5–11.

[62] Wirtschaftsvereinigung Nichteisen-Metalle, *Die NE-Metallindustrie im Industrieplan* (mimeographed; Altena: January, 1947), p. 31.

[63] House Committee on Foreign Affairs, *Plants and Parts of Plants Listed for Reparations from United States and United Kingdom Zones (of Germany)* (1947).

[64] W. O. Reichelt, *Demontageliste* (Hamburg: Drei Türme Verlag, 1947), p. 6.

[65] For a cogent criticism of the revised level of industry plan, see C. Emmet and F. Baade, *Destruction at Our Expense* (New York: Common Cause, 1947), pp. 7–11.

[66] Senate Committee on Foreign Relations, *Interim Aid for Europe: Hearings,* November, 1947, p. 240.

[67] House Committee on Foreign Affairs, *United States Foreign Policy for a Postwar Recovery Program: Hearings,* December, 1947-March, 1948, p. 364.

[68] *Ibid.,* p. 582.

[69] *Ibid.,* p. 1317.

[70] Senate Committee on Foreign Relations, *European Recovery Program: Hearings,* January-February, 1948, p. 269.

[71] *Ibid.,* p. 589.

[72] Former President Herbert Hoover, in his third report on Germany, assailed the Morgenthau-inspired U.S. policies in Germany by saying: "We can keep Germany in these economic chains but it will also keep Europe in rags." The President's Economic Mission to Germany and Austria, *Report No. 3* (March 18, 1947), p. 15.

[73] House Committee on Foreign Affairs, *op. cit.*, p. 1100.

[74] *Ibid.*, p. 392.

[75] Senate Committee on Appropriations, *European Interim Aid and Government and Relief in Occupied Areas: Hearings*, November, 1947, p. 662.

[76] Clay, *op. cit.*, p. 320.

[77] *Ibid.*, p. 322.

[78] Baade, "Demontage," *Handwörterbuch der Sozialwissenschaften*, II (1959), 570.

[79] Amt für Stahl und Eisen, *Coverage of the Iron and Steel Demand Within the Scope of the Marshall Plan With Due Regard to the Bottlenecks Caused by the Dismantling* (Düsseldorf: Verlag Stahleisen, 1948), pp. 5, 6, 26.

[80] For an industry-by-industry analysis, see W. Hasenack, *Dismantling in the Ruhr Valley: A Menace to European Recovery* (Köln and Opladen: Westdeutscher Verlag, 1949), pp. 49–76.

[81] For a careful quantitative analysis, see The Executive Committee of the Combined Economic Area, *Report on the Status of the Reparation Problem After the Washington Agreement* (July, 1949), pp. 20–28.

[82] Economic Cooperation Administration, Industrial Advisory Committee, *Report on Plants Scheduled for Removal as Reparations from the Three Western Zones of Germany* (January, 1949).

[83] Department of State, *op. cit.*, p. 425.

[84] "Protocol of Agreements Reached between the Allied High Commissioners and the Chancellor of the German Federal Republic at Petersburg" in Ruhm von Oppen, *op. cit.*, pp. 439–42.

[85] G. W. Harmssen, *Am Abend der Demontage* (Bremen: F. Trüjen Verlag, 1951), pp. 174–93.

[86] For a brief summary of the principal arguments for industrialization, see P. T. Bauer and B. S. Yamey, *The Economics of Under-Developed Countries* (Cambridge: Cambridge University Press, 1957), pp. 237–47.

[87] For a judicious discussion of this matter, see Penrose, *op. cit.*, pp. 275–92.

[88] For an illuminating work on war potential in terms of economic capacity, administrative competence, and motivation for war, see K. Knorr, *War Potential of Nations* (Princeton: Princeton University Press, 1956), p. 306.

[89] Statistisches Reichsamt, *Statistisches Jahrbuch für das Deutsche Reich 1937* (Internationale Übersichten), Berlin: 1937, pp. 123–24.

[90] U.S. Office of Military Government for Germany, *The European Recovery Program, U.S.-U.K. Occupied Area of Germany* (Joint Report; September, 1948), pp. 15–16.

[91] Keynes, *The Economic Consequences of the Peace* (New York: Harcourt, Brace & Co., 1920), p. 92.

[92] Knorr, *op. cit.*, pp. 278–80.

[93] U.S. Department of Commerce, Office of International Trade, *The Ruhr Area: Its Structure and Economic Importance* (1949).

[94] Senate Subcommittee on War Mobilization, *op. cit.*, pp. 167–89.

[95] For an interesting discussion of such a possibility, see D. Thorner, "De-Industrialization in India, 1881–1931," *First International Conference of Economic History* (Paris: Mouton, 1960), pp. 217–26.

[96] These factors may be regarded as an embryo outline of a general theory of economic retrogression. See *The Theory of Economic Growth* (Homewood, Ill.: R. D. Irwin, 1955), pp. 408–15.

[97] H. Zink, *American Military Government* (New York: Macmillan Co., 1947).

[98] W. Friedmann, *The Allied Military Government of Germany* (London: Stevens & Sons, 1947).

[99] For a good discussion of the administrative overlap, see C. J. Friedrich, "Organizational Evolution in Germany, 1945–1947," *American Experiences in Military Government in World War II* (New York: Rinehart & Co., 1948), pp. 197–210. See also H. O. Lewis, *New Constitutions in Occupied Germany* (Washington: Foundation for Foreign Affairs, 1958), pp. 63–72.

[100] For an excellent description of the German economic status at the end of 1947, see J. Müller-Marein, *Deutschland im Jahre 1, Panorama 1946–1948* (Hamburg: Nannen-Verlag, 1960).

CHAPTER 2

1 "Law No. 1" in *Amtsblatt der Militärregierung Deutschland* (Kontroll-Gebiet der 21. Armeegruppe), No. 1, pp. 11–12. This was the basic law for postwar direct controls in occupied Germany.

2 For example see A. Bourneuf, *Norway: Planned Revival* (Cambridge: Harvard University Press, 1958); R. Harrod, *Are These Hardships Necessary?* (London: Rupert Hart-Davis, 1947); J. Jewkes, *Ordeal by Planning* (New York: Macmillan Co., 1948).

3 U.S. Office of Military Government, *A Year of Potsdam: The German Economy Since the Surrender* (1946), p. 149.

4 H. Mendershausen, *The Economics of War* (New York: Prentice-Hall, 1940), p. 1.

5 K. Knorr, *War Potential of Nations* (Princeton: Princeton University Press, 1956), pp. 178–97.

6 J. K. Galbraith, *A Theory of Price Control* (Cambridge: Harvard University Press, 1952).

7 R. A. Dahl and C. E. Lindblom, *Politics, Economics and Welfare* (New York: Harper & Bros., 1953), p. 404.

8 L. Robbins, *The Economic Problem in Peace and War* (London: Macmillan, 1947), pp. 40–41.

9 C. Pigou, *The Political Economy of War* (New York: Macmillan Co., 1941), p. 118. See also W. K. Hancock and M. M. Gowing, *British War Economy* (London: HMSO, 1949), pp. 325–43.

10 For the mechanics of hyperinflation, see: C. Bresciani-Turroni, *The Economics of Inflation* (London: Allen & Unwin, 1953), p. 222.

11 F. Robinson, "Wartime Inflation," in her *Collected Economic Papers* (New York: M. Kelley, 1951), p. 92.

12 Robbins, *op. cit.*, p. 7.

13 M. Egle, "Wesen und Formen der Verbrauchsrationierung in Europa," *Weltwirtschaftliches Archiv*, LVIII (1943), 305–34.

14 W. B. Raddaway, "Rationing," *Lessons of the British War Economy,*

ed. D. N. Chester (Cambridge: Cambridge University Press, 1951), pp. 182–99.

[15] Pigou, *op. cit.*, pp. 137–50.

[16] A. Director, *Defense, Controls and Inflation* (Chicago: University of Chicago Press, 1952), p. 161.

[17] Dahl and Lindblom, *op. cit.*, p. 410.

[18] Knorr, *op. cit.*, pp. 111–12.

[19] E. A. G. Robinson, "The Overall Allocation of Resources," *Lessons of the British War Economy*, pp. 34–57.

[20] W. Röpke, "Offene und zurückgestaute Inflation," *Kyklos*, I (1947), 57–71.

[21] Galbraith, "The Disequilibrium System," *American Economic Review*, Vol. XXXVII, No. 3 (1947), pp. 287–302.

[22] R. Meimberg, "Kaufkraftüberhang und Kriegsfinanzpolitik," *Weltwirtschaftliches Archiv*, LVIII (1943), 99–107.

[23] For various types of repressed inflation, see H. K. Charlesworth, *The Economics of Repressed Inflation* (London: Allen and Unwin, 1956), pp. 35–48.

[24] J. M. Keynes, *How to Pay for the War* (New York: Harcourt, Brace & Co., 1940), p. 59.

[25] For a good discussion of the entire Nazi ideology see International Council for Philosophy and Humanistic Studies, *The Third Reich* (London: Weidenfeld & Nicolson, 1955).

[26] For a good introduction to the Nazi political system see F. Neumann, *Behemoth* (New York: Oxford University Press, 1942).

[27] For a typical account of Nazi property rights and qualifications see H. Hunke, *Grundsätze der deutschen Volks und Wehrwirtschaft* (Berlin: Hande & Spenersche Buchhandlung, 1938), pp. 78–81.

[28] C. B. Hoover, *The Economy, Liberty and the State* (New York: Twentieth Century Fund, 1959), pp. 160–77.

[29] L. Hamburger, *How Nazi Germany Has Controlled Business* (Washington: Brookings Institution, 1943), pp. 10–11.

30 H. Quecke, *Das Reichswirtschaftsministerium* (Berlin: Junker & Dünnhaupt, 1941), p. 26.

31 "Satzungen der Reichswirtschaftskammer" (mimeographed; Berlin: May 3, 1935 [4 pp.]).

32 For the specific subdivision of the thirty-one economic groups covering the activities of the entire manufacturing industry, see R. A. Brady, "Modernized Cameralism in the Third Reich: The Case of the National Industry Group," *The Journal of Political Economy,* Vol. L, No. 1, p. 80.

33 For a fuller discussion of the National Economic Chamber, see O. Nathan, *The Nazi Economic System* (Durham: Duke University Press, 1944), pp. 19–21.

34 A. B. Krause, *Organisation von Arbeit und Wirtschaft* (Berlin: Elsner Verlagsgesellschaft, 1935), p. 86.

35 "Der Aufbau der Organisation der gewerblichen Wirtschaft," *Der Wirtschaftsaufbau im neuen Europa* (Bad Oeynhausen: Verlag A. Lutzeyer, 1942), I, 1a/118.

36 Library of Congress, Legislative Reference Service, *Fascism in Action: A Documented Study and Analysis of Fascism in Europe* (Washington, 1947), p. 95.

37 Nathan, *op. cit.,* p. 24.

38 "Verordnung über die Vereinfachung und Vereinheitlichung der Organisation der gewerblichen Wirtschaft vom April 20, 1942," *Reichsgesetzblatt,* 1942, I, 189.

39 "Der Aufbau . . . Wirtschaft," *Der Wirtschaftsaufbau im neuen Europa,* Vol. I, pp. 1a/124–1a/156.

40 A. Pietzsch, *Der Aufbau der Gauwirtschaftskammern* (Berlin: n.p., 1942), pp. 14–19.

41 For a good discussion of Germany's raw material situation see H. G. Moulton and L. Marlo, *The Control of Germany and Japan* (Washington: Brookings Institution, 1944), pp. 22–23.

42 Hamburger, *op. cit.,* p. 29.

43 Nathan, *op. cit.,* pp. 47–49.

44 Quecke, *op. cit.,* p. 27.

[45] O. Long, *Die Reichsstellen* (Berlin: n.p. 1944).

[46] "Reichsnährgesetz" of September 13, *Reichsgesetzblatt*, 1933, I, 626.

[47] L. Münz, *Führer durch die Behörden und Organisationen* (Berlin: Duncker & Humblot, 1939), pp. 382–89.

[48] For some interesting observations of this relationship see L. Häberlein, *Das Verhältnis von Staat und Wirtschaft mit besonderer Hervorhebung der Selbstverwaltung des Reichsnährstandes und der landwirtschaftlichen Marktordnung* (Berlin: Verlag fuer Staatswissenschaften und Geschichte, 1938), pp. 22–33.

[49] *Der Wirtschaftsaufbau im neuen Europa* (Darstellung und Wiedergabe der wichtigen Aufbau- und Lenkungsmassnahem zur wirtschaftlichen Neuordnung Europas), Loseblattsammlung (1943), Vol. II, pp. 2b/47–2b/50.

[50] *Ibid.*, p. 2b/57.

[51] Nathan, *op. cit.*, p. 97.

[52] "Verordnung über das Verbot von Preiserhöhungen," *Reichsgesetzblatt*, 1936, I, 955. For a good summary of the Nazi experience of price fixing, see U.S. Office of Price Administration, *Price Control in Nazi Germany* (Mimeographed; 1943).

[53] J. Wagner, "Die Preispolitik im Vierjahresplan," in *Kieler Vortraege* (Jena: G. Fischer, 1938), p. 7.

[54] H. H. Bormann, *Der Reichskommissar für die Preisbildung: Amt—Aufgaben—Organisation* (Berlin: Deutsche Industriebank, 1943), p. 18.

[55] For an excellent summary discussion of Nazi price fixing, see U.S. Office of Strategic Services, *Price and Rent Control in Germany* (issued as confidential War Dept. Pamphlet No. 31–154, July 22, 1944), pp. 4–6.

[56] *Vierjahresplan*, vols. for 1937–38.

[57] W. Rentrop, *Preisbildung und Preisüberwachung in der gewerblichen Wirtschaft* (Hamburg: Hanseatische Verlagsanstalt, 1937), p. 17.

[58] U.S. Office of Price Administration, *op. cit.*, p. 15. See also W. Rentrop and H. Kayser, *Preispolitik und Preisüberwachung* (München & Berlin: C. H. Beck, 1941), p. 46.

[59] Bormann, *op. cit.*, p. 28. This pamphlet is an extremely useful exposition of the structure of wartime price control in Germany. The respective numbers of the subordinate price control agencies were taken from this study.

[60] J. Wagner, *Gesunde Preispolitik* (Dortmund: Westfalen-Verlag, 1938), p. 49.

[61] Bormann, *op. cit.*, p. 30.

[62] For another recent testimony of the remarkable price stability see B. Klein, *Germany's Economic Preparations for War* (Cambridge: Harvard University Press, 1959), p. 154.

[63] *Reichsgesetzblatt*, 1939, I, 1495.

[64] Deutsches Institut für Wirtschaftsforschung, *Die deutsche Industrie im Kriege 1939–1945* (Berlin: Duncker & Humblot, 1954), pp. 25–38.

[65] Quecke, *op. cit.*, p. 54.

[66] For the over-all operation of the Ministry of Economics during the war, see "Das Reichswirtschaftsministerium unter der nationalsozialistischen Diktatur 1933 bis 1945," F. Facius, *Wirtschaft und Staat* (Boppard am Rhein: A. Boldt-Verlag, 1959), pp. 124–76.

[67] H. J. Riecke, "Ernährung und Landwirtschaft im Kriege," in *Bilanz des zweiten Weltkrieges* (Oldenburg: G. Stalling Verlag), pp. 334–35.

[68] *Der Wirtschaftsaufbau im neuen Europa*, Vol. II, pp. 2b/64–2b/67.

[69] Riecke, *op. cit.*, p. 343.

[70] For more data on the actual rationing levels, see U.S. Department of War, Strategic Bombing Survey, *The Effects of Strategic Bombing on the German War Economy* (1945), p. 132.

CHAPTER 3

[1] One hectare equals 2.4711 acres.

[2] An indispensable source on this matter is U.S. Office of Military Government for Germany, *Title 12: Food and Agriculture* ("U.S. Military Government Regulations"). For some typical examples of how the previous sys-

tem was restored after the defeat see *Lübecker Nachrichten*, No. 1, May 10, 1945.

[3] L. D. Clay, *Decision in Germany* (New York: Doubleday, 1951), p. 263.

[4] The German title of the agency was *Zentralamt für Ernährung und Landwirtschaft*. Hereafter it will be referred to as ZEL.

[5] K. Passarge, *Zentralamt für Ernährung und Landwirtschaft in der britischen Zone, 1945–1948; Ein Rückblick* (mimeographed; Hamburg: ZEL, 1948), pp. 1–5.

[6] For examples of this development see "Das Molkereiwesen in Niedersachsen seit dem Waffenstillstand," *Neue Molkerei-Zeitung*, Vol. I, No. 4 (1946), p. 34.

[7] For the history of this agency see "Landwirtschaftliche Verwaltung unter deutscher Führung," *Neue Mitteilungen für die Landwirtschaft*, I (1946), 126.

[8] ZEL, *Amtsblatt*, Vol. I, No. 1 (1946).

[9] *Ibid.*, No. 2.

[10] The number of economic boards varied from state to state. See Agrarwerbung, *Land- und ernährungswirtschaftliche Organisation in Norddeutschland* (Hamburg: 1948), pp. 8, 28.

[11] Verwaltung für Ernährung, Landwirtschaft und Forsten des Vereinigten Wirtschaftsgebietes, *Die Überwindung des Hungers* (Frankfurt: 1949), p. 5.

[12] ZEL, *op. cit.*, Vol. I, No. 2 (1946).

[13] For a more detailed account of the postwar import boards see H. Schlange-Schöningen, *Im Schatten des Hungers* (Hamburg: P. Parey-Verlag, 1955), pp. 55, 67.

[14] General Clay's chapter on food and agriculture in *Decision in Germany*, especially p. 271, provides a good over-all view of some of the difficulties arising from the democratization of the German food collection system.

[15] For the effects of denazification on the efficiency of postwar German food collection, see Schlange-Schöningen, *op. cit.*, pp. 53, 55, 111.

[16] Institut für landwirtschaftliche Arbeitswissenschaft, Imbshausen, *Imbshäuser Hefte, No. 2, Erzeugung und Erfassung* (Hannover: 1947). See also Allied Control Authority, Joint British and U.S. Zone Food and Agriculture Conference, "Decision No. 2." *Report on Conference in Hamburg, June 13 and 14, 1946* (mimeographed).

[17] For an excellent account of the administrative loopholes in the postwar agricultural delivery system see Hütterbräuker, "Anbauplanung und Ablieferungsveranlagung," *Neue Mitteilungen für die Landwirtschaft,* I (1946), 250–51.

[18] Schlange-Schöningen, *Possibilities of Increasing Agricultural Production in Germany* (Frankfurt: 1948), pp. 24–25.

[19] L. Härtel, *Der Länderrat des amerikanischen Besatzungsgebietes* (Stuttgart: W. Kohlhammer, 1951), pp. 133–38. See also G. Weisser, ed., *Der Zonenbeirat der britisch besetzten Zone* (Göttingen: Verlag O. Schwartz, 1953), pp. 89–98.

[20] W. Bauer, "Der allgemeine wirtschaftliche Charakter der Zonen," *Wirtschaftsprobleme der Besatzungszonen* (Berlin: Duncker & Humblot, 1948), p. 17.

[21] U.S. Office of Military Government, *Economic Data on Potsdam Germany* (1947), Table 7, p. 16.

[22] For a detailed account of the evolution of the postwar German administration, see R. H. Slover, "The Bizonal Economic Administration of Western Germany" (Doctoral dissertation, Harvard University, 1950). See also J. F. J. Gillen, *State and Local Government in West Germany, 1945–1953, with special Reference to the U.S. Zone and Bremen* (Bad Godesberg: Office of the U.S. High Commissioner for Germany, 1953).

[23] A. Kohn-Brandenburg, "Das System der Provisorien," *Europa Archiv,* Vol. I, No. 11 (1947), pp. 576–77.

[24] Schlange-Schöningen, *op. cit.,* pp. 105, 133, 153.

[25] Appendix of "British Military Government Ordinance No. 88: Agreement for Reorganization of Bizonal Economic Agencies," reproduced in B. Ruhm von Oppen, *Documents on Germany under Occupation, 1945–1954* (New York: Oxford University Press, 1955), pp. 227–31.

[26] U.S. Office of Military Government, *German Government Organization and Civil Administration,* No. 23 (April-May, 1947), p. 5.

[27] E. Köhler, *Ohne Illusionen, Politik der Realitäten* (Wiesbaden: n.p., 1949), p. 15. Köhler was the Chairman of the Economic Council and his volume offers many useful insights into its work.

[28] For some extremely interesting points on this conflict see Slover, *op. cit.*, pp. 102–5.

[29] "Gesetz über die öffentliche Kontrolle der landwirtschaftlichen Ablieferungen" of September 5th, 1947; "Gesetz zur Sicherung der Kartoffelversorgung im Wirtschaftsjahr 1947–48" of October 3rd, 1947, and "Gesetz zur Sicherung der Fleischversorgung im Wirtschaftsjahr 1947–48," of October 3rd, 1947; see Verwaltung für Ernährung, Landwirtschaft und Forsten, *Amtsblatt*, 1947–48, pp. 3–7.

[30] For details of the "potato and meat wars" between the states and the bizonal agencies, see Schlange-Schöningen, *op. cit.*, pp. 168–69 and 174–76.

[31] P. W. Bidwell, "What Is Happening in Germany?" *Harper's Magazine*, Vol. CLXXXVI, No. 2 (1948), pp. 173–79.

[32] L. H. Brown, *A Report on Germany* (New York: Farrar, Straus & Co., 1947), p. 185, also estimated that "Western Germany's farm production [was] now only about 70 percent of prewar." The appendix on food, pp. 182–203, provides a good description of the food situation then prevailing in the Anglo-American zones.

[33] F. Ahlgrimm, "Düngerwirtschaft und Ernährungskrise," *Niederschrift über die Sitzung des Ausschusses für allgemeine Wirtschaftspolitik der Arbeitsgemeinschaft der deutschen Bauernverbände am 19, Juni, 1946*, pp. 7–8.

[34] *Ibid.*, p. 8.

[35] Schlange-Schöningen, *Denkschrift über die Möglichkeiten der Aufhebung bzw. Auflockerung der Zwangsbewirtschaftungsbestimmungen bei landwirtschaftlichen Erzeugnissen u. landwirtschaftlichen Produktionsmitteln* (Frankfurt: 1948), p. 13.

[36] *Loc. cit.* For comparable data on fertilizer supply, see Verwaltung für Ernährung, Land- und Forstwirtschaft, *Statistik der Landwirtschaft, U.S.-Britisches Besatzungsgebiet Deutschland, 1935–1947*, I (1948), 190.

[37] For an excellent account of the early postwar chaos in the fertilizer industry, see F. Baade, *Amerika und der deutsche Hunger* (Braunschweig: A. Limbach, 1948), pp. 12–17.

[38] Landesbauernschaft Weser Ems, *Landwirtschaftsblatt*, No. 6 (December, 1945).

[39] Britische Militarbehörden, *Neue Mitteilungen für die Landwirtschaft*, II (1947), 131.

[40] O. Lattemen, "Betriebswirtschaftliche Fragen der Nachkriegszeit," *Archiv der Deutschen Landwirtschafts-Gesellschaft, Vorträge der Frühjahrstagung, Wiesbaden, 1948* (Hannover: 1948), p. 119.

[14] J. P. Nettl, *The Eastern Zone and Soviet Policy in Germany, 1945–1950* (London: Oxford University Press, 1951), p. 178.

[42] P. M. Raup, "Postwar Recovery of Western German Agriculture," *Journal of Farm Economics*, XXXII (1950), 5.

[43] Verwaltung für Ernährung, Land- und Forstwirtschaft, *op. cit.*, pp. vi–vii. For another source see E. Pagenstecher, *Anbau- und Erntestatistik nach dem zweiten Weltkrieg* (mimeographed diss.; Bonn: 1953).

[44] Rheinischer Landwirtschafts-Verband, *Landwirtschaftliche Zeitung*, CXIV (1947), 161.

[45] Schlange-Schöningen, *Possibilities . . . in Germany*, pp. 41–42.

[46] Rheinischer Landwirtschafts-Verband, *op. cit.*, Vol. CXV, No. 1 (1948), p. 13.

[47] Verwaltungsamt für Wirtschaft, *Mitteilungsblatt*, Vol. 1, No. 18, PR 86/47, pp. 249–50.

[48] Britische Militärbehörden, *op. cit.*, I. (1946), 221.

[49] Verwaltungsamt für Wirtschaft, "Begründung zur Anordnung Nr. 56/47 über Erzeugungspreise für Getreide im Getreidewirtschaftsjahr 1947/48," *op. cit.*, Vol. I, No. 13–14, p. 179.

[50] Rheinischer Landwirtschafts-Verband, *op. cit.*, CXV (1948), 29.

[51] K. Padberg, "Die Verkaufserlöse der Landwirtschaft," *Neue Mitteilungen für die Landwirtschaft*, Vol. II, No. 21 (1947), p. 294.

[52] M. Frey, *Demontage der Landwirtschaft* (Opladen: Westdeutscher Verlag, 1948), p. 8.

[53] W. Meinhold, *Volkswirtschaftliche Preis- und Kreditprobleme der*

westdeutschen Agrarwirtschaft (München: R. Pflaum Verlag, 1949), pp. 22–23.

[54] Testimony of Colonel W. H. Draper, Undersecretary of War. See Senate Committee on Appropriations, *European Interim Aid and Government and Relief in Occupied Areas: Hearings*, November, 1947, p. 515.

[55] Schlange-Schöningen, *op. cit.*, p. 21.

[56] K. Werba, "Die Preisschere in der Landwirtschaft," *Landwirtschaftliche Praxis*, No. 4 (München: Bayerischer Landwirtschaftsverlag, 1948), pp. 12–14.

[57] Padberg, *Geld-Naturalumsatz und Rentabilität der landwirtschaftlichen Betriebe im Vereinigten Wirtschaftsgebiet* (Hannover: Landbuch Verlag, 1949), pp. 12–13.

[58] A. Münzinger, "Preisgestaltung in der Landwirtschaft," *Niederschrift über die Sitzung des Ausschusses für allgemeine Wirtschaftspolitik der Arbeitsgemeinschaft der deutschen Bauernverbände am 19. Juni, 1946*, pp. 13–21. Münzinger, *Die Erzeugungskosten der württembergischen Landwirtschaft* (Stuttgart: E. Ulmer, 1948).

[59] A. Hanau, "Preisprobleme auf dem Agrarmarkt," *Archiv der Deutschen Landwirtschafts-Gesellschaft*, III (1949), 279–81.

[60] Verwaltung für Ernährung, Land- und Forstwirtschaft, *op. cit.*, p. 192.

[61] For some cogent observations on the effects of hyperinflation on the German farming community, see C. Bresciani-Turroni, *The Economics of Inflation* (London: Allen & Unwin, 1937), p. 299.

[62] Testimony of John H. Hildring, Director of Civil Affairs Division, War Department. House Committee on Appropriations, *Military Establishment Appropriation Bill for 1946: Hearings*, May, 1945, p. 53.

[63] For an example see *Lübecker Nachrichten*, No. 5, May 18, 1945.

[64] H. Zink, *The United States in Germany, 1944–1955* (Princeton: D. Van Nostrand, 1957), p. 176.

[65] E. Woerman, "Der mögliche Anteil der Inlandserzeugung an der Versorgung Deutschlands mit Nahrungsmitteln," *Die Vortrage der KTL-Tagung*, I (1949), 5. For comparable data see U.S. Office of Military Gov-

ernment, Economics Division, *A Year of Potsdam: The German Economy Since the Surrender* (1946), p. 8.

[66] K. Brandt, *Germany: Key to Peace in Europe* (Claremont, Calif.: Claremont College, 1949), p. 49.

[67] House Select Committee on Foreign Aid, *Final Report on Foreign Aid* (1948), p. 121.

[68] F. S. V. Donnison, *Civil Affairs and Military Government North-West Europe, 1944–1946* (London: HMSO, 1961), pp. 338–39.

[69] Schlange-Schöningen, *op. cit.*, p. 310.

[70] H. Hoover, The President's Economic Mission to Germany and Austria, *Report No. 1: German Agriculture and Food Requirements* (1947), p. 20.

[71] G. Stolper, *German Realities* (New York: Reynal & Hitchcock, 1948), p. 67.

[72] Annex to the *Hague Convention of October 19, 1907,* Article 43, Section III.

[73] Very instructive are: Senate Committee on Appropriations, *op. cit.*, p. 551; House Committee on Foreign Affairs, *United States Foreign Policy for a Post-War Recovery Program: Hearings,* December, 1947-March 1948, p. 362.

[74] Control Commission for Germany (British Element), *Monthly Statistical Bulletin,* III (August, 1948), 7; Schlange-Schöningen, *op. cit.*, p. 189; Clay, *op. cit.*, pp. 264–73.

[75] Schlange-Schöningen, *Im Schatten des Hungers,* p. 140.

[76] House of Commons Select Committee on Estimates, *The Control Office for Germany and Austria: Expenditure in Germany* (London: HMSO, 1946), pp. iv–v.

[77] U.S. Office of Military Government, *Monthly Report,* No. 30 (December, 1947), p. 40. See also Slover, *op. cit.*, Chapter V. Also very informative is M. Gottlieb, *The German Peace Settlement and the Berlin Crisis* (New York: Paine-Whitman Publishers, 1960), pp. 80–83.

[78] W. A. Brown and R. Opie, *American Foreign Assistance* (Washington: Brookings Institution, 1953), p. 121.

[79] U.S. Department of Commerce, *Foreign Aid by the U.S. Government, 1940–1951* (1952), pp. 16–17.

[80] W. Niklas, *Ernährungswirtschaft und Agrarpolitik* (Bonn, 1949), p. 13. See also Schlange-Schöningen, *op. cit.*, p. 192, and G. Thiede, "Die Ernährungshilfe für Westdeutschland von 1945–46 bis 1952–53," *Berichte über Landwirtschaft,* XXXII (1954), 241.

[81] W. Bauer, "Kurzer Überblick über die Gruppierung der Verbraucher bei der Lebensmittelrationierung in Deutschland, 1939–1945" (typewritten; Berlin: Deutsches Institut für Wirtschaftsforschung, 1946).

[82] H. Schmitz, *Die Bewirtschaftung der Nahrungsmittel, 1939–1950* (Essen: 1956), pp. 7, 60.

[83] Beginning with the 97th rationing period.

[84] Donnison, *op. cit.*, pp. 327–28.

[85] P. Martini, "Über die gesundheitliche Lage in Deutschland," *Die soziale und gesundheitliche Lage in Deutschland* (Berlin: Urban & Schwarzenberg, 1947), p. 30.

[86] U.S. Office of Military Government, *op. cit.*, No. 42 (December, 1948), p. 1.

[87] L. Pakenham, *Born to Believe* (London: J. Cape, 1953), p. 170.

[88] National Research Council, *Recommended Dietary Allowances* ("Reprint and Circular Series" No. 115 [January, 1943]).

[89] Nutrition Board of the German Medical Profession, *The German Medical Profession on the State of Nutrition in Germany* (1947), p. 2.

[90] F. Paetzold, "Beobachtungen zur Ernährungslage," *Arbeitsblatt für die britische Zone,* II (1948), 256.

[91] Testimony of D. A. Fitzgerald, Secretary General of the International Emergency Food Council. See House Committee on Appropriations, *First Deficiency Appropriation Bill for 1947: Hearings,* p. 793.

[92] U.S. Office of Military Government, *op. cit.*, No. 16 (October, 1946), p. 16.

[93] Some indispensable German sources on postwar food rationing are: J. Simon, *Die Entwicklung der Lebensmittelzuteilungen in Hamburg seit*

Anfang 1945 und ihre Folgen (Hamburg: 1947); A. Beck, *Die Bedeutung der Unterschreitung des Eiweiss- und Fettminimums in unserer Volksenährung* (1946); H. Harmsen, *Gegenwartsprobleme unseres Gesundheitwesens (1946–1950)*, (Hamburg: Akademie für Staatsmedizin) I; Institut für Weltwirtschaft an der Universität Kiel, *Deutsche Wirtschaft und Industrieplan* (Essen and Kettwig; West Verlag, 1947), pp. 199–201; Verwaltungsamt für Ernährung, Landwirtschaft und Forsten des Vereinigten Wirtschaftsgebietes, *Europas Ernährungsstandard nach dem Kriege* (mimeographed; 1949).

[94] President's Committee on Foreign Aid, *European Recovery and American Aid* (1947), p. 121. For similar estimates see Martini, *op. cit.*, p. 34.

[95] H. Mendershausen, "Prices, Money and the Distribution of Goods in Postwar Germany," *American Economic Review,* XXXIX (1949), 653.

[96] "Die Mitwirkung des Arbeitsamtes bei der Lebensmittelkartenausgabe," *Arbeitsblatt für die britische Zone,* II (1948), 212–13.

[97] For an interesting account of such activities, see W. Eucken and F. W. Meyer, "The Economic Situation in Germany," *Annals of the American Academy of Political and Social Science,* CCLX, 53–62.

[98] For a highly illuminating work see K. Zentner, *Aufstieg aus dem Nichts* (Köln and Berlin: Kieperheuer & Witsch, 1954).

[99] U.S. Office of Military Government, *Monthly Report: Statistical Annex,* No. 29 (July, 1949), p. 282.

[100] Freie und Hansestadt Hamburg, Behörde für Ernährung und Landwirtschaft, "Jahresbericht 1947" (unpublished), pp. 60–64.

[101] V. Gollancz, *Leaving Them to Their Fate: The Ethics of Starvation* (London: V. Gollancz, 1946).

CHAPTER 4

[1] *The Economic Consequences of the Peace* (New York: Harcourt, Brace & Howe, 1920), p. 81.

[2] U.S. Department of War, Strategic Bombing Survey, *The Effects of Strategic Bombing on the German War Economy* (1945), p. 90.

3 B. H. Klein, *Germany's Economic Preparations for War* (Cambridge: Harvard University Press, 1959), p. 123.

4 For the 1938, 1945, 1946, and 1947 data, Deutsche Kohlenbergbau-Leitung, *Zahlen zur Kohlenwirtschaft,* III (April, 1948), 3; for 1948, *ibid.,* January, 1949, p. 3. See also Statistisches Amt des Vereinigten Wirtschaftsgebietes, *Wirtschaft und Statistik,* II (1950), 1383.

5 Potter-Hyndley Mission to North West Europe, *The Coal Situation in North West Europe* (June, 1945).

6 F. S. V. Donnison, *Civil Affairs and Military Government North-West Europe, 1944–1946* (London: HMSO, 1961), p. 406.

7 G. Boldt, *Staat und Bergbau* (München and Berlin: C. H. Beck, 1950), pp. 69–70.

8 "General Order No. 5: Collieries and Associated Undertakings in the British Zone," *Military Government Gazette Germany* (British Zone of Control), pp. 64–67.

9 For a brief summary of this episode see M. Balfour and J. Mair, *Four-Power Control in Germany and Austria* (London: Oxford University Press, 1956), pp. 155–56.

10 F. Haussmann, *Der Neuaufbau der deutschen Kohlenwirtschaft im internationalen Rahmen* (München and Berlin: C. H. Beck, 1950), p. 27.

11 "Ordinance No. 112; German Coal Organization," *Military Government Gazette Germany* (British Zone of Control), No. 21, pp. 631–32.

12 U.S. Department of Commerce, *The Ruhr Area, Its Structure and Economic Importance* (1949), p. 11.

13 For an indispensable work on the postwar food situation in the Ruhr Valley, see H. Schmitz, *Die Bewirtschaftung der Nahrungsmittel, 1939–1950* (Essen: Stadtverwaltung, 1956). This information appears on pp. 463–65.

14 K. Heller and R. Regul, "Der Kohlenbergbau in Nordrhein-Westfalen," *Staat und Wirtschaft,* 2 (1950), pp. 326–28. Another reporter on the grave food shortages in the Ruhr observed that while miners were taking a shower he "could count their ribs" from a distance of eight yards; V. Gollancz, *In Darkest Germany* (Hinsdale, Ill.: H. Regnery Co., 1947), p. 51.

15 U.S. Office of Military Government, *Monthly Report,* No. 9 (April, 1946), p. 6.

[16] E. Deissmann, *Bericht an die Mitglieder des Verwaltungsrats für Wirtschaft des amerikanischen und britischen Besatzungsgebietes über das Bergarbeiter-Punktsystem* (March, 1947).

[17] Nutrition Board of the German Medical Profession, *The German Medical Profession on the State of Nutrition in Germany* (1947), p. 5.

[18] *Die Zeit*, No. 20, May 14, 1947.

[19] For some penetrating observations on the food crisis see *The Manchester Guardian*, LVI, May 21, 1947.

[20] H. Schlange-Schöningen, *Im Schatten des Hungers* (Hamburg: P. Parey, 1955), pp. 87, 128.

[21] H. Apelt, *Schwarzschlachtung* (Hamburg: ZEL and Region Food Office, 1947).

[22] "Mehr Kohle mit besserer Ernaehrung," *Wirtschaftszeitung*, No. 31, August 1, 1947.

[23] U.S. Office of Military Government, *op. cit.*, No. 25 (September, 1947), p. 15.

[24] *Wirtschaft und Statistik* No. 12 (March, 1950), p. 1356.

[25] U.S. Department of Commerce, *loc. cit.*

[26] U.S. Department of War, Strategic Bombing Survey, *op. cit.*, p. 98.

[27] F. Busch, "Transportation in Postwar Germany," *The Annals of the American Academy of Political and Social Science*, CCLX (1948), 82. See also Donnison, *op. cit.*, pp. 425–34.

[28] Deutsches Kohlenstatistisches Amt, *Die Kohlenwirtschaft der britischen Zone im Jahre 1946* (Mimeographed; Essen-Bredeney, 1947), p. 9.

[29] *Loc. cit.*

[30] C. M. Weir, "The Coal Campaign," *British Zone Review*, Vol. I, No. 32 (1946), pp. 10–11.

[31] Exekutivrat des Vereinigten Wirtschaftsgebietes, *Die Wirtschaftslage im Vereinigten Wirtschaftsgebiet* (Stand Herbst, 1947), pp. 55, 79.

[32] Deutsche Kohlenbergbau-Leitung, *Die Kohlenwirtschaft im Jahre 1947 und gegen Ende des Winters 1947–48* (Essen, 1948), p. 26.

[33] H. Hildebrand, "Aktuelle Verkehrsprobleme," *Kohlenwirtschafts-zeitung,* No. 6 (March 3, 1948).

[34] J. Semler, Speech on January 4, 1948 at Erlangen, p. 6 (Hoover Institute Collections).

[35] Hilfswerk of the Evangelical Churches in Germany, *Living Conditions in Germany, 1947* (Stuttgart: June, 1947), p. 48.

[36] Deutsche Kohlenbergbau-Leitung, *loc. cit.*

[37] L. D. Clay, *Decision in Germany* (New York: Doubleday, 1950), pp. 191–92.

[38] *Potsdam Agreement,* Section B, Paragraph 17*b.*

[39] *Handelsblatt,* special appendix of December 30, 1946.

[40] G. Gebhardt, *Ruhrbergbau, Geschichte, Aufbau und Verflechtung seiner Gesellschaften und Organisationen* (Essen: Verlag Glückauf, 1957), p. 58.

[41] Verwaltung für Wirtschaft des Vereinigten Wirtschaftsgebietes, *Bericht über die Auswirkungen der vorgesehenen Demontagen und die dadurch entstehenden Engpässe in der Wirtschaft der vereinigten amerikanischen und britischen Besatzungszone,* May 15, 1948, p. 9.

[42] Donnison, *op. cit.,* pp. 410–11.

[43] U.S. Office of Military Government, *A Year of Potsdam: The German Economy Since the Surrender* (1946), p. 70.

[44] U.S. Office of Military Government, *The German Forest Resources Survey* (1948), p. 11. For similar observations see G. W. Harmssen, *Reparationen, Sozialprodukt, Lebensstandard* (Bremen: F. Trujen Verlag, 1948), I, 48.

[45] A. Heinrichsbauer, *Der Ruhrbergbau in Vergangenheit, Gegenwart und Zukunft* (Essen: Verlag Glückauf, 1948), p. 42.

[46] Verwaltung für Wirtschaft des Vereinigten Wirtschaftsgebietes, *Die Wirtschaftslage der Vereinigten Zone, November-Dezember und im Jahre 1947,* p. 5.

[47] U.S. Office of Military Government, *Industry (Including Coal),* No. 31 (1948), p. 11.

[48] Heller and Regul, *op. cit.*, pp. 335–36.

[49] Hess, Heller and Deist, *Gutachten über die Kosten- und Ertragslage des Westdeutschen Steinkohlenbergbaus* (Essen: 1949), p. 39.

[50] For a summary of Moses' report see *Herald Tribune* (New York), August 1, 1947.

[51] Industrieverband Bergbau, *2. Generalversammlung, Recklinghausen 1948* (Bochum: 1949), pp. 55, 84.

[52] Deutsches Kohlenstatistisches Amt, *op. cit.*, pp. 3–4.

[53] Deutsche Kohlenbergbau-Leitung, *Ruhr-Almanach* (Köln: Verlag E. A. Seemann, 1950), p. 57. For some curious practices of the British military in recruiting miners, see F. Brockway, *German Diary* (London: V. Gollancz, 1946), pp. 100–1.

[54] Deutsche Kohlenbergbau-Leitung, *Die Kohlenwirtschaft im Jahre 1947 . . .* , p. 11.

[55] Deutsches Kohlenstatistisches Amt, *op. cit.*, p. 4.

[56] Deutsche Kohlenbergbau-Leitung, *op. cit.*, p. 14. Balfour and Mair, *op. cit.*, estimate that desertions of freshly recruited miners in the British zone came to be 50–60 percent, p. 149.

[57] Deutsche Kohlenbergbau-Leitung, *loc. cit.*

[58] Heller and Regul, *op. cit.*, p. 323.

[59] Deutsche Kohlenbergbau-Leitung, *op. cit.*, p. 20.

[60] Department of State, *Bulletin*, Vol. XIII, No. 338 (December 16, 1945), p. 964.

[61] Keynes, *op. cit.*, p. 228.

[62] U.S. Office of Military Government, *op. cit.*, p. 7. *The Economist*, CLI, 406 (September 14, 1946) estimated the stocks to have been 5 million tons.

[63] N. Samuels, "The European Coal Organization," *Foreign Affairs*, XXVI (1947–48), 728–36.

[64] Balfour, *Some Aspects of the German Problem*, address given at Chatham House, London, on March 11, 1947 (mimeographed; available at Hoover Institute), p. 6.

[65] A. C. Tittmann, *Incredible Infamy* (Middlebury, Vt.: 1948), p. 14.

[66] *Ibid.*, p. 15.

[67] Department of State, *Germany, 1947–1949: The Story in Documents* (1950), pp. 481–82.

[68] Deutsche Kohlenbergbau-Leitung, *Zahlen zur Kohlenwirtschaft*, No. 7, pp. 53–59.

[69] Deutsche Kohlenbergbau-Leitung, *op. cit.*, p. 54.

[70] For a respectable refutation of this charge see E. Nölting, *Wo bleibt unsere Kohle?* (Düsseldorf Verlag, 1947).

[71] U.S. Office of Military Government, *Monthly Report*, No. 10 (May, 1946), p. 13.

[72] *Ibid.*, No. 35 (May, 1948), p. 55.

[73] E. Effert, "Probleme der Finanzierung und Sanierung des Kohlenbergbaus," in *Fragen der Kapitalerhaltung und Finanzierung* (Wolfenbüttel: Heckners Verlag, 1949), p. 62.

[74] Senate Committee on Appropriations, *European Interim Aid and Government and Relief in Occupied Areas: Hearings*, November, 1947, p. 547.

[75] Semler, *Kommentare zu Meiner Erlanger Rede* (mimeographed; 1948), pp. 34–36.

[76] Keynes, *op. cit.*, p. 92.

[77] Semler, *Anlagen zum Kommentar meiner Erlanger Rede* (1948), appendix 6.

[78] Deutsche Kohlenbergbau-Leitung, *op. cit.*, p. 32.

[79] Deutsches Kohlenstatistisches Amt., *op. cit.*, p. 17.

[80] Oberbürgermeister of Frankfurt, *Mitteilungen der Stadtverwaltung*, No. 5 (January 28, 1946), p. 19.

[81] Deutsche Kohlenbergbau-Leitung, *op. cit.*, pp. 47–48.

[82] For the actual distribution see Verwaltung für Wirtschaft des Vereinigten Wirtschaftsgebietes, *Statistischer Hausdienst*, No. 18 (mid-December, 1947), Table 5.

[83] *Loc. cit.*

[84] Wirtschaftsrat des Vereinigten Wirtschaftsgebietes, *Wörtlicher Bericht über die Vollversammlung,* No. 2 (July 22–24, 1947), p. 16.

[85] H. C. Wallich, *Mainsprings of the German Revival* (New Haven: Yale University Press, 1955), p. 65.

[86] Arbeitsgemeinschaft der Verbände Deutscher Maschinenbauanstalten, *Produktionswirtschaftliche Gesichtspunkte zum Industrie- und Demontageplan* (October, 1947). See also Wirtschaftsvereinigung Eisen- und Stahlindustrie, *Der deutsche Eisen- und Stahlbedarf* (1946).

[87] P. W. Bidwell, "What Is Happening in Germany?" *Harper's Magazine,* Vol. CLXXXVI, No. 2 (1948), p. 173.

[88] Verwaltung für Wirtschaft des Vereinigten Wirtschaftsgebietes, Amt für Stahl und Eisen, *Statistisches Vierteljahresheft,* January–March, 1948, pp. 14, 16, 18.

[89] Verwaltungsamt für Stahl und Eisen, *Bericht über die Tätigkeit des Verwaltungsamtes für Stahl und Eisen (VSE) im 1. Quartal 1946,* p. 2.

[90] Verwaltungsamt für Stahl und Eisen, *Bericht über die Tätigkeit des Verwaltungsamtes für Stahl und Eisen im 2. Halbjahr 1946, p. 1.*

[91] Verwaltungsamt für Wirtschaft des amerikanischen und britischen Besatzungsgebiets, Amt für Stahl und Eisen, *Bericht über die Tätigkeit des Verwaltungsamtes für Wirtschaft, Amt für Stahl und Eisen (VSE), 1. Quartal, 1947,* p. 2.

[92] For an excellent discussion of the postwar decartelization see G. Stolper, *German Realities* (New York: Reynal & Hitchcock, 1948), pp. 172–96.

[93] "List of Companies to which General Order No. 5 applies," *Military Government Gazette Germany* (British Zone of Control), 5 (1945), pp. 65–67.

[94] "General Order No. 7: Iron and Steel Undertakings," *Military Government Gazette Germany* (British Zone of Control), No. 11, pp. 308–9.

[95] O. Deissmann, R. Gielen, and H. G. Rautmann, *Die Auswirkungen der Entflechtung der Eisenschaffenden Industrie* (mimeographed; September, 1948), p. 16.

[96] For an appraisal of this operation see B. Davidson, *Germany: What Now?* (London: F. Müller, 1950), pp. 199–201.

[97] Deissmann, Gielen, and Rautmann, *op. cit.*, p. 18.

[98] *Wirtschafts- und Finanzzeitung*, Vol. I, Nos. 23–24 (December 18, 1947), p. 1.

[99] German Iron and Steel Producers of the British Zone, *Die Massnahmen zur Entflechtung und Neuordnung der Eisenschaffenden Industrie* (Duisburg: K. Brinkmann, 1948), pp. 32–33.

[100] For a more detailed discussion of this matter, see Wirtschaftsrat des Vereinigten Wirtschaftsgebietes, *op. cit.*, p. 15.

[101] Semler, speech, p. 15.

[102] Klein, *op. cit.*, p. 57.

[103] K. Dönitz, *Zehn Jahre und zwanzig Tage* (Bonn: Athenäum, Verlag, 1958), p. 397.

[104] Beate Ruhm von Oppen, *Documents on Germany under Occupation, 1945–1954* (New York: Oxford University Press, 1955), pp. 114, 242.

[105] Verwaltung für Wirtschaft des amerikanischen und britischen Besatzungsgebietes, Amt für Stahl und Eisen, *Bericht über die Tätigkeit des Verwaltungsamtes für Wirtschaft, Amt für Stahl und Eisen (VSE), 4. Quartal, 1947*, p. 3.

[106] *Loc. cit.*

[107] U.K. House of Commons, Select Committee on Estimates, *Purchase and Collection of Scrap in Germany* (London: 1948), p. vii.

[108] *Ibid.*, p. 55.

[109] *Ibid.*, pp. 53–54.

[110] Verwaltungsamt für Wirtschaft des amerikanischen und britischen Besatzungsgebietes, Amt für Stahl und Eisen (VSE), *op. cit.*, p. 18.

[111] *Wirtschafts- und Finanzzeitung*, II (April 15, 1948), 1.

[112] *Ibid.*, p. 4.

[113] U.K. House of Commons, Select Committee on Estimates, *British Expenditure in Germany* (London: 1947), p. 306.

[114] Amt für Stahl und Eisen, *Statistisches Vierteljahresheft,* January–March, 1950, p. 61.

[115] Verwaltungsamt für Wirtschaft des amerikanischen und britischen Besatzungsgebietes. Amt für Stahl und Eisen (VSE). *Bericht über die Tätigkeit des Verwaltungsamtes für Wirtschaft, Amt für Stahl und Eisen (VSE), II. Quartal, 1947,* pp. 6–9.

[116] For another discussion of the postwar steel and iron production, see U.S. Office of Military Government, *op. cit.,* No. 30 (November, 1947), p. 20.

[117] U.S. Office of Military Government, *The European Recovery Program, US/UK Occupied Area of Germany* (1948), pp. 15–16.

CHAPTER 5

[1] M. Gottlieb, *The German Peace Settlement and the Berlin Crisis* (New York: Paine-Whitman Publishers, 1960), p. 94.

[2] M. Gottlieb, "The German Economic Potential," *Social Research,* XVII (1950), 78.

[3] L. H. Brown, *A Report on Germany* (New York: Farrar, Straus & Co., 1947), p. 85. See also: Exekutivrat des Vereinigten Wirtschaftsgebietes, *Die Wirtschaftslage im Vereinigten Wirtschafsgebiet (Stand Herbst, 1947)* (mimeographed; 1948), p. 66.

[4] *Report of the Secretary-General for the Year 1947* (Brussels: Inter-Allied Reparation Agency, 1948), p. 4.

[5] U.S. Office of Military Government for Germany, *Monthly Report: Reparations and Restitution,* No. 11 (June, 1946), p. 1.

[6] *Report of the Secretary-General for the Year 1946* (Inter-Allied Reparation Agency), pp. 63–67.

[7] *Ibid.,* p. 7.

[8] *Report of the Secretary-General for the Year 1947* (Inter-Allied Reparation Agency), p. 20.

[9] For details of the crippling effects of the program see Verwaltung für Wirtschaft des Vereinigten Wirtschaftsgebietes, "Multilateral Deliveries BIOS und FIAT Aktion" (typewritten; 1948).

[10] J. Semler, *Kommentare zu meiner Erlanger Rede* (mimeographed; 1948), pp. 44–47.

[11] Verwaltung für Wirtschaft des Vereinigten Wirtschaftsgebietes, *op. cit.*, p. 4.

[12] *Report of the Secretary-General for the Year 1947* (Inter-Allied Reparation Agency), p. 4.

[13] For a perceptive treatment of the German reparations problem after World War II, see Gottlieb, "The Reparations Problem Again," *Canadian Journal of Economics and Social Science*, XVI (1950), 40.

[14] *Bericht der Industrie- und Handelskammer München über die wirtschaftliche Lage (Jahreswende 1947–48)* (mimeographed; 1948), p. 16.

[15] *Report of the Secretary-General for the Year 1948* (Inter-Allied Reparation Agency), p. 16.

[16] *Report of the Assembly of the Inter-Allied Reparation Agency to its Member Governments* (1951), p. 15. See also G. W. Harmssen, *Am Abend der Demontage* (Bremen: F. Trujen Verlag, 1951).

[17] Verwaltung für Wirtschaft, des Vereinigten Wirtschaftsgebietes, *Protokoll über die Tagung mit Firmenvertretern und Sachverständingen am 16. Juni 1948 in Königstein zum Thema: "Bewertung des von den Allierten entnommenen geistigen Eigentums"* (mimeographed; 1948). See also M. Bunke, *"Zur Bewertung weggenommenen geistigen Gutes, insbesondere der Auslandspatente"* (Mimeographed; 1948), pp. 11–12.

[18] G. Colm, J. M. Dodge, and R. W. Goldsmith, *A Plan for the Liquidation of War Finance and the Financial Rehabilitation of Germany* (Tübingen: 1955), p. 5.

[19] Harmssen, *Reparatienen, Sozialprodukt, Lebensstandard* (Bremen: F. Trujen Verlag, 1948), p. 86. For other estimates see G. Stolper, *German Realities* (New York: Reynal & Hitchcock, 1948), p. 102.

[20] F. Lütge, "An Explanation of the Economic Conditions which contributed to the Victory of National-Socialism," *The Third Reich* (London: Weidenfeld and Nicolson, 1955), pp. 420–24.

[21] *Potsdam Agreement,* Section B, Paragraph 14c.

[22] A. Bourneuf, *Norway: The Planned Revival* (Cambridge: Harvard University Press, 1958), pp. 14–15.

23 E. Liefmann-Keil, *Die wirtschaftliche Verarmung Deutschlands: Verarmungsprozess oder Aufbau?* (Mimeographed; Stuttgart: 1947), pp. 18–19. See also J. Gimbel, *A German Community under American Occupation: Marburg, 1945–1952* (Stanford: Stanford University Press, 1961), pp. 117–32; J. Joesten, *Germany: What Now?* (Chicago: Ziff-Davis Publishing Co., 1948), pp. 168–90.

24 G. Reddeweg, "Anpassung und Lenkung der Währung in Deutschland," *Probleme zur Neuordnung der Währung* (Berlin: Deutscher Betriebswirte-Verlag, 1947), pp. 78–79.

25 E. Wolf, "Geld- und Finanzprobleme der deutschen Nachkriegswirtschaft," *Die Deutsche Wirtschaft zwei Jahre nach dem Zusammenbruch* (Berlin: A. Nauck, 1947), p. 221.

26 W. W. Heller, "Tax and Monetary Reform in Occupied Germany," *National Tax Journal*, II (1949), 216.

27 H. Sauermann, "The Consequences of the Currency Reform in Western Germany," *The Review of Politics*, XII (1950), 178–79.

28 For examples see U.S. Office of Military Government, *op. cit.*, No. 8 (March 1946), p. 44; No. 31 (January, 1948), p. 16.

29 Köln Industrie- und Handelskammer, *Bericht für das Jahr 1947*, p. 5; Ludwigsburg Industrie- und Handelskammer, *Denkschrift: Grundsätzliche und aktuelle Probleme unserer wirtschaftspolitischen Aufgabe* (1947), p. 20.

30 Senate Committee on Foreign Relations, *Interim Aid for Europe: Hearings*, November, 1947, p. 126. See also F. H. Sanderson, "Germany's Economic Situation and Prospects," *The Struggle for Democracy in Germany*, ed. G. A. Almond (Chapel Hill: University of North Carolina Press, 1949), pp. 137–45; J. Müller-Marein, *Deutschland im Jahre I* (Hamburg: Nannen-Verlag, 1960), pp. 183–90.

31 IFO-Institut für Wirtschaftsforschung, *Fünf Jahre Deutsche Mark* (Berlin and München: Duncker & Humblot, 1954), p. 32.

32 F. A. Burchardt and K. Martin, "Western Germany and Reconstruction," *Bulletin of the Oxford University Institute of Statistics*, Vol. IX, No. 12 (1947), p. 405. See also Wirtschaftsrat des Vereinigten Wirtschaftsgebietes, Amerikanisches und Britisches Besatzungsgebiet in Deutschland, *Wörtlicher Bericht über die Vollversammlung*, No. 7 (October 29–30, 1947), p. 229.

[33] U.S. Office of Military Government, *op. cit.*, No. 27 (September, 1947), p. 19.

[34] Stolper, *op. cit.*, p. 99. See also A. J. Brown, *The Great Inflation, 1939–1951* (London: Oxford University Press, 1955), p. 32.

[35] C. Bresciani-Turroni, *The Economics of Inflation* (London: Allen & Unwin, 1953), p. 174.

[36] T. Balogh, *Germany: An Experiment in "Planning" by the "Free" Price Mechanism* (Oxford: Blackwell, 1950), p. 12. See also Heller, *op. cit.*, p. 217.

[37] "Die Stagnation und ihre Gründe," *Der Wirtschaftsspiegel*, III (1948), 105–7.

[38] W. Schneider, *Das Warenverkehrsrecht der gewerblichen Wirtschaft und die Organisation der Wirtschaftsverwaltung in den vereinigten Westzonen* (Frankfurt: Kommentator-Verlag, K. Allmayer, 1948), pp. 109–26.

[39] G. Keiser, *Die Neuordnung des Bewirtschaftungssystems, Bewirtschaftung und Wirtschaftssystem* (mimeographed; 1947), pp. 2–3.

[40] *Nachkriegsbericht der Handelskammer Bremen über die Jahre 1945–1947,* pp. 25–26.

[41] G. Weisser, *Thesen zur Ordnung der Wirtschaft nach der Sanierung der Währung* (mimeographed; 1948), p. 17. A slightly altered version of the above may be found in "Leitsätze zur Ordnung der Wirtschaft nach der Währungsreform," *Finanzarchiv*, N. F., XI (1948–49), 429–78.

[42] The basic proposal was presented by W. Kromphardt, "Marktspaltung und Kernplanung in der Volkswirtschaft," *Dortmunder Schriften zur Sozialforschung*, No. 3 (1947).

[43] *Bericht der Industrie- und Handelskammer München* . . . , p. 5.

[44] For some perceptive insights into the effects of hoarding on the general public, see K. Schumacher, "Von der Freiheit zur sozialen Gerechtigkeit," *Turmwächter der Demokratie*, ed. A. Scholz and W. G. Oschilewski (Berlin: Verlags GmbH), II, 112–13. See also Schumacher, *Nach dem Zusammenbruch* (Hamburg: Phönix Verlag, 1948).

[45] Keiser, *op. cit.*, p. 12.

[46] U.S. Office of Military Government, *Monthly Report: Trade and Commerce,* No. 21 (February-March, 1947), p. 19.

[47] For an illuminating analysis of the compensation trade see F. Reger, *Zwei Jahre nach Hitler* (Hamburg: Rowohlt Verlag, 1947), pp. 40–41.

[48] The yearly reports of the various German chambers of trade and commerce are particularly revealing on the general state of German industry after the end of hostilities. See, for instance, Reutlingen Industrie- und Handelskammer, *Wohin führt der Weg. Eine sehr nüchterne Betrachtung zur Wirtschaftslage anlässlich der Jahreswende* (1947), p. 5; *Nachkriegsbericht der Handelskammer Bremen über die Jahre 1945–1947*, p. 5.

[49] See Chapter IV for the steel industry's example.

[50] H. Mendershausen, "Prices, Money and the Distribution of Goods in Postwar Germany," *American Economic Review*, XXXIX (1949), 655.

[51] F. H. Klopstock, "Monetary Reform in Western Germany," *The Journal of Political Economy*, LVII (1949), 279.

[52] An indispensable source for the legal background of the compensation trade is U.S. Office of Military Government, Trade and Commerce Branch, *Compensation Trade in Court* (mimeographed; 1947).

[53] *Wirtschafts- und Finanzzeitung*, January 8, 1948, p. 8.

[54] U.S. Office of Military Government, *op. cit.*, No. 25 (June-July, 1947), p. 2.

[55] "Law No. 50: Punishment for the Theft and Unlawful Use of Rationed Foodstuffs, Goods and Rationing Documents," *Official Gazette of the Control Council for Germany*, No. 14 (March 31, 1947), p. 266.

[56] U.S. Department of War, *The Statutory Criminal Law of Germany* (1946), pp. 209–11. For similar observations see K. Mehnert and H. Schulte, *Deutschland Jahrbuch 1949* (Essen: West Verlag, 1949), p. 96.

[57] Wirtschaftsrat des Vereinigten Wirtschaftsgebietes, Amerikanisches und Britisches Besatzungsgebiet in Deutschland, *op. cit.*, No. 8 (November 21, 1947), p. 209.

[58] The German literature on this question is meager and scattered. See P. Becker, *Rechts- und Steuerfragen des Schwarzen Markts* (Köln: A. Wolters, 1948); R. Fischer, *Der Betrug auf dem Schwarzen Markt* (Meissner Verlag, 1948); H. Apelt, *Schwarzschlachtungen* (Hamburg: P. Parey. 1947).

59 "Spinnfaser A. G. Prozess," *Wirtschafts- und Finanzzeitung*, Vol. I, Nos. 11–12 (1947), p. 10.

60 U.S. Office of Military Government, Trade and Commerce Branch, *op. cit.*, p. 6.

61 U.S. Office of Military Government, *Monthly Report: Trade and Commerce;* No. 29 (1947), p. 16.

62 For a good description of the entire complex of the compensation trade, see Gewerkschaftszeitung, II (München: 1947). No. 10, p. 13 mentions that 90 percent of the entire output of German industry went into compensation channels.

63 Keiser, *op. cit.*, p. 12.

64 W. Kromphardt, "Marktspaltung und Kernplanung in der Volkswirtschaft," *Dortmunder Schriften zur Sozialforschung,* No. 3 (1947), p. 3.

65 L. D. Clay, *Decision in Germany* (New York: Doubleday, 1950), p. 202.

66 H. Mendershausen, *Two Postwar Recoveries of the German Economy* (Amsterdam: North-Holland Publishing Co., 1955), p. 37.

67 U.S. Office of Military Government, *Monthly Report,* No. 10 (May, 1946), p. 13.

68 Senate Committee on Appropriations, *European Interim Aid and Government and Relief in Occupied Areas: Hearings* (1947), p. 549.

69 U.S. Office of Military Government, *op. cit.*, No. 8 (March, 1946), p. 52.

70 F. Schily, *Grundsätzliche Fragen der Produktion* (mimeographed; Wuppertal; 1946), p. 10.

71 U.S. Office of Military Government, *Monthly Report: Trade and Commerce,* No. 8 (March, 1946), pp. 8–10.

72 Frankfurt/Main Industrie- und Handelskammer, *Bericht für die Jahre 1948/49,* p. 785; *Nachkriegsbericht der Handelskammer Bremen über die Jahre, 1945–1947,* p. 100.

73 U.S. Office of Military Government, *op. cit.*, No. 23 (April-May, 1947), p. 14.

[74] U.S. Office of Military Government, *op. cit.*, No. 15 (1946), p. 6.

[75] U.S. Office of Military Government, Trade and Commerce Branch, *op. cit.*, p. 6.

[76] Frankfurt/Main Industrie- und Handelskammer, *op. cit.*, p. 785.

[77] U.S. Office of Military Government, *Monthly Report*, No. 35 (May, 1948), pp. 31, 35.

[78] H. Deist, F. Lauter, and H. Wüsten, *Gutachten über Kosten und Preise der Eisenschaffenden Industrie in der britischen Zone* (1946).

[79] Calculated from data published in U.S. Office of Military Government, *Monthly Report: Trade and Commerce*, No. 27 (August-September 1947), pp. 7–8.

[80] U.S. Office of Military Government, Manpower Division, *Unemployment und Underemployment in the Bizonal Area of Germany* (mimeographed; 1949), p. 18.

[81] W. Eucken and F. W. Mayer, "The Economic Situation in Germany; *The Annals of the American Academy of Political and Social Science*, CCLX (1948), 59. See also Eucken, "Deutschland vor und nach der Währungsreform," *Vollbeschäftigung, Inflation und Planwirtschaft*, ed. A. Hunold (Zürich: E. Rentsch Verlag, 1953), pp. 134–83.

[82] This and similar cases are presented in Wirtschaftsrat des Vereinigten Wirtschaftsgebietes, Amerikanisches und Britisches Besatzungsgebiet in Deutschland, *op. cit.*, No. 7 (October 29–30, 1947), p. 163.

[83] International Chamber of Commerce, *The Economic Conditions of Germany Today and its International Repercussions* (Paris: 1947), p. 33.

[84] W. Röpke, "Das Deutsche Wirtschaftsexperiment Beispiel und Lehre," in Hunold, *op. cit.*, p. 271.

[85] H. Mendershausen, "Prices, Money . . . ," p. 653.

[86] J. A. Schumpeter, *The Theory of Economic Development* (Cambridge: Harvard University Press, 1934). See also Schumpeter, "Unternehmer," *Handwörterbuch der Staatswissenschaften*, VIII, p. 481.

[87] U.S. Office of Military Government, *Monthly Report*, No. 37 (July, 1948), p. 2.

[88] F. A. Lutz, "The German Currency Reform and the Revival of the German Economy," *Economics,* XVI (1949), 122.

CHAPTER 6

[1] U.S. Office of Military Government, *A Year of Potsdam: The German Economy Since the Surrender* (1946), p. 149.

[2] For the best treatment of the German industrial concentration during the hyperinflation in the early 1920's, see C. Bresciani-Turroni, *The Economics of Inflation* (London: Allen & Unwin, 1953), pp. 107–207.

[3] Senate Committee on War Mobilization, *A Program for German Economic and Industrial Disarmament* (1946), pp. 578–79.

[4] For a good exposition of the tripartite wage control system in postwar Norway, see M. W. Leiserson, *Wages and Economic Control in Norway, 1945–1957* (Cambridge: Harvard University Press, 1959), pp. 21–40.

[5] H. K. Charlesworth, *The Economics of Repressed Inflation* (London: Allen & Unwin, 1956), pp. 26–27.

[6] Leiserson, *op. cit.,* pp. 25 and 39.

[7] *Reichsgesetzblatt,* 1934, I, 202.

[8] *Ibid.,* 1936, I, 311.

[9] *Ibid.,* 1937, I, 248.

[10] *Ibid.,* 1938, I, 652; 1939, I, 126.

[11] "Kriegswirtschaftsverordnung of September 4, 1939," *ibid.,* p. 1609; "Durchführungsbestimmungen zur Kriegswirtschaftsverordnung," *ibid.,* p. 2028. For some general observations of the Nazi wartime price and wage controls, see U.S. Office of Price Administration, *Price Control in Nazi Germany* (Mimeographed; 1943).

[12] B. Klein, *Germany's Economic Preparations for War* (Cambridge: Harvard University Press, 1959), p. 200.

[13] *Ibid.,* p. 27.

[14] N. Kaldor, "The German War Economy," *The Review of Economic Studies,* Vol. XIII, No. 33 (1945–46), p. 37.

[15] Klein, *op. cit.*, p. 143.

[16] Kaldor, *op. cit.*, p. 39.

[17] *Ibid.*, p. 47.

[18] *Reichsgesetzblatt*, 1944, I, 161–62.

[19] "Total Mobilisation in Germany," *International Labour Review*, Vol. LI, No. 1 (1945), pp. 82–83.

[20] U.S. Office of Military Government, *Title 15: Manpower Administration* ("Military Government Regulations").

[21] *Lübecker Nachrichten*, June 19, 1945.

[22] "Order No. 3: Concerning a Registration of the Population of Employable Age, Registration of Unemployed and Their Placement at Work," *Military Government Gazette Germany* (British Zone of Control), No. 6 (1946), pp. 82–83.

[23] "Ordinance No. 54: Compulsory Direction to Work," *ibid.*, No. 14 (1946), pp. 327–28.

[24] "Law No. 32: Employment of Women in Building and Reconstruction Work," *ibid.*, No. 12 (1946), pp. 277–78.

[25] U.S. Office of Military Government, *op. cit.*, pp. 15–592, 15–600a; M. Balfour and J. Mair, *Four-Power Control in Germany and Austria* (London: Oxford University Press, 1956), pp. 147–48.

[26] "Directive No. 15: Wage Policy," *Military Government Gazette Germany* (British Zone of Control), No. 9 (1945), pp. 188–89. For the early history of postwar wage controls, see M. A. Kelly, "Allied Policy on Wages in Occupied Germany," *International Labour Review*, Vol. LV, No. 5 (1947), pp. 352–57.

[27] W. Schmidt, "Grundprobleme der Preispolitik," *Der Wirtschaft Spiegel*, III (1948), 113–15.

[28] U.S. Office of Military Government, *Manpower, Trade Unions and Working Conditions*, No. 22 (March-April, 1947), p. 6.

[29] For a brief account of the "problem" industries, see *ibid.*, No. 32 (1948), pp. 20–21.

[30] "Directive No. 41: Increase of Wages in the Coal Mining Industry," *Official Gazette of the Control Council for Germany*, No. 11 (October 31, 1946), p. 213.

[31] D. Müller, *Die Lohnpolitik in Deutschland in den Jahren 1945 bis zur Währungsreform* (Wien: Westkulturverlag A. Hain, 1952), pp. 40–42.

[32] U.S. Office of Military Government, *op. cit.*, pp. 20–21.

[33] Der Deutsche Gewerkschaftsbund, *Die Gewerkschaftsbewegung in der britischen Besatzungszone (Geschäftsbericht 1947–1949)* (Köln: Bund Verlag, 1949), p. 179.

[34] *Ibid.*, pp. 180–81.

[35] For similar findings see H. Wander, *Bevölkerung, Arbeitspotential und Beschäftigung im britisch-amerikanischen Besatzungsgebiet* (Kiel; 1948), p. 31.

[36] U.S. Office of Military Government, *Monthly Report*, No. 36 (June, 1948), p. 6.

[37] F. Rupp, "Die Beschäftigung in Deutschland," *Europa-Archiv*, III (1948), 1411.

[38] Wander, *op. cit.*, p. 51.

[39] This conclusion is borne out by a more detailed statistical analysis in U.S.-U.K. Bipartite Control Office, *Food and Agriculture Statistics, Bizonal Area of Germany, 1935–1947*, II, 12.

[40] Control Commission for Germany (British Element), *Monthly Statistical Bulletin*, IV (January, 1949), 73.

[41] H. R. Bernsdorff and R. Tüngel, *Auf dem Bauche sollst Du kriechen* (Hamburg: C. Wegner Verlag, 1958), pp. 96–100. See also P. Schmidt, *Der Statist auf der Galerie, 1945–1950* (Bonn: Athenäum Verlag, 1961), p. 158.

[42] Whether one compares these developments in terms of employed wage and salary earners or in terms of all gainfully employed persons the results are similar. See Wander, *op. cit.*, pp. 26–27.

[43] Control Commission for Germany (British Element), *op. cit.*, p. 80.

[44] Siebert, *Arbeitsmarkt und Arbeitsmarktpolitik in der Nachkriegszeit* (Stuttgart: W. Kohlhammer, 1956), pp. 15–16.

[45] Statistisches Amt für die britische Besatzungszone, *Berechnung einer Indexziffer der Arbeitsleistung für die Industrie der britischen Zone* (Mimeographed; Minden: January, 1948), p. 2.

[46] Exekutivrat des Vereinigten Wirtschaftsgebietes, *Die Wirtschaftslage im Vereinigten Wirtschaftsgebiet (Stand Herbst 1947)*, p. 153.

[47] Bayerische Gewerkschaften, *Gewerkschafts-Zeitung*, Vol. II, June, 1947.

[48] Niedersächsisches Institut für Wirtschaftsforschung, *Löhne und Preise* (Clausthal-Zellerfeld, 1946), pp. 11–12.

[49] U.S. Office of Military Government, *op. cit.*, No. 42 (December, 1948), p. 63.

[50] Control Council Laws Nos. 3, 12, 13, 15, 26, 27, 28, 30, in *Official Gazette of the Control Council for Germany*, Nos. 1, 4, 7, 8.

[51] H. C. Wallich, *Mainsprings of the German Revival* (New Haven: Yale University Press, 1955), p. 67.

[52] M. Newcomer, "War and Postwar Development in the German Tax System," *National Tax Journal*, Vol. I, No. 1 (1948), p. 6. See also J. van Hoorn, "Postwar Changes in German Taxation," *Bulletin for International Fiscal Documentation*, I (1946–47), 164.

[53] Müller, *op. cit.*, p. 46.

[54] Statistisches Amt für die britische Besatzungszone, *Indexziffern für die Lebenshaltungskosten, Basis 1938 = 100 (Neues Schema) für Oktober 1945 und Juli-Dezember 1946.*

[55] U.S. Office of Military Government, *Monthly Report: Statistical Annex*, No. 29 (June, 1949), p. 96. See also Niedersächsisches Institut für Wirtschaftsforschung, *op. cit.*, pp. 21–22.

[56] U.S. Office of Military Government, *Incomes and Expenditures of Workers' Families in Urban Areas in American-Occupied Germany, 1946* (mimeographed), p. 1.

[57] *Ibid.*, p. 9.

[58] Kelly, *op. cit.*, p. 363.

[59] *Ibid.*, p. 366.

[60] U.S. Office of Military Government, *op. cit.*, p. 13.

[61] M. Rohlfing, "Lohn und Lebenshaltungskosten," *Dortmunder Schriften zur Sozialforschung*, I (1947).

[62] "Von der Freiheit zur sozialen Gerechtigkeit," *Turmwächter der Demokratie*, ed. A. Scholz and W. G. Oschilewski (Berlin: VerlagsGmbH, 1953), II, 118.

[63] Niedersächsisches Institut für Wirtschaftsforschung, *op. cit.*, p. 25–27, 37.

[64] Control Commission for Germany (British Element), *The Ruhr Miner and His Family, 1947* (1948), p. 13.

[65] U.S. Office of Military Government, *Monthly Report: Trade and Commerce*, No. 21 (February-March, 1947), p. 21.

[66] Bayerische Gewerkschaften, *op. cit.*, No. 14, p. 6.

[67] K. H. Katsch, "Was Kostet heute die Lebenshaltung," *Statistische Monatshefte Württemberg-Baden*, Vol. I, No. 6 (1947), pp. 135–41.

[68] A. Grabowsky, "Deutsche Währung und Wirtschaft," *Schweizer Rundschau*, Vol. XLVII, No. 6 (1947), p. 443.

[69] U.S. Office of Military Government, *op. cit.*, No. 27 (August-September, 1947), p. 2.

[70] Senate Committee on Appropriations, *European Interim Aid and Government and Relief in Occupied Areas: Hearings*, November, 1947, p. 532. For other interesting examples see H. L. Brown, *A Report on Germany* (New York: Farrar, Straus & Co., 1947), pp. 232–43.

[71] W. Hasenack, *Betriebsraubbau und Wirtschaftslenkung* (Wolfenbüttel: Heckners Verlag, 1948), p. 24.

[72] U.S. Office of Military Government, *Compensation Trade in Court* (Mimeographed; 1947), p. 4.

[73] U.S. Office of Military Government, *Monthly Report*, No. 34 (April, 1948), p. 17.

[74] W. Eucken and F. Meyer, "The Economic Situation in Germany," *The Annals of the American Academy of Political and Social Science*, CCLX (1948), 53–62.

[75] U.S. Office of Military Government, *op. cit.*, p. 22.

CHAPTER 7

[1] For an excellent exposition of German rent controls see U.S. Office of Strategic Services, *Price and Rent Control in Germany* (issued as a confidential pamphlet in 1944), pp. 16–17.

[2] K. A. Bettermann and W. Haarmann, *Des öffentliche Wohnrecht* (Köln: Verlag O. Schmidt, 1947), p. 36.

[3] F. Lütge, *Wohnungswirtschaft* (2d ed.; Stuttgart: Piscator Verlag, 1949), pp. 398–401.

[4] U.S. Office of Military Government for Germany, "Part IV: Housing," *Title 15: Manpower Administration* ("Military Government Regulations"), pp. 15–400.1–20.2.

[5] H. H. D., "Housing: The Reconstruction Problem," *British Zone Review* (July-August, 1948), p. 4.

[6] For background information on the postwar German refugee problem see Federal Republic of Germany, Ministry for Expellees, Refugees, and War Victims, *Documents on the Expulsion of the Germans from Eastern-Central-Europe* (4 vols.; Bonn: 1954). Also highly instructive, although a bit one-sided, is R. F. Keeling, *Gruesome Harvest* (Chicago: Institute of American Economics, 1947). Another good source is G. Karweina, *Der Grosse Treck* (Stuttgart and Wien: E. Wancura Verlag, 1958).

[7] R. Petz, "Wohnungs- und Flüchtlingsprobleme," *Arbeitsblatt für die Britische Zone,* Vol. I, Nos. 7–8 (1947), p. 288.

[8] *Official Gazette of the Control Council for Germany,* No. 5 (March, 1946), pp. 117–21.

[9] *Loc. cit.*

[10] P. Wiel, *Überlegungen und Berechnungen zum Wiederaufbau der Wohnungen in den Ruhrgebietsstädten* (Essen and Kettwig: West-Verlag, 1947), p. 11.

[11] "Ordinance No. 16," *Military Government Gazette Germany* (British Zone of Control), No. 7 (1946), pp. 123–26.

[12] Petz, "Wohnungs- und Aufenthaltswechsel," *Arbeitsblatt für die Britische Zone,* Vol. I, No. 9 (1947), p. 336. An indispensable work for post-

war housing legislation is K. A. Bettermann and W. Haarmann, *Das öffentliche Wohnungsrecht* (Köln: Verlag O. Schmidt, 1947).

[13] For an insight into the nature and the acuteness of the problem faced by all postwar German housing authorities, see Kiel, Wohnungsamt, *Jahresbericht des städtischen Wohnungsamtes für die Zeit vom 1. Januar bis 31. Dezember 1948* (mimeographed).

[14] H. Hoover, The President's Economic Mission to Germany and Austria, *Report No. 1* (February, 1947), p. 3.

[15] W. G. Harmssen, *Reparationen, Sozialprodukt, Lebensstandard* (Bremen: F. Trüjen Verlag, 1948), p. 92.

[16] Exekutivrat des Vereinigten Wirtschaftsgebietes, *Die Wirtschaftslage im Vereinigten Wirtschaftsgebiet* (Stand Herbst, 1947) (mimeographed), p. 154.

[17] P. Fuchs, "Gedanken zum Wiederaufbau," *Arbeitsblatt für die Britische Zone*, Vol. I, Nos. 4–6, p. 226.

[18] E. C. T., "Housing: the Target and Future Prospects," *British Zone Review*, April 24, 1948, p. 8.

[19] Fuchs, *loc. cit.*

[20] "Der Wohnungsbestand in den Ländern des Vereinigten Wirtschaftsgebietes am 1. Oktober 1948," *Wirtschaft und Statistik*, I (1949–50), 80.

[21] H. Kresling, *Statistisches Handbuch der Bauwirtschaft* (München: Institut für Wirtschaftsforschung, 1949), p. 63.

[22] "Der Wohnungsbestand in den Ländern . . . ," *Wirtschaft und Statistik, loc. cit.*

[23] Kresling, *op. cit.*, p. 67, estimated the total loss of apartments to have been 23 percent.

[24] Exekutivrat des Vereinigten Wirtschaftsgebietes, *loc. cit.*

[25] "Die Wohnungslage in den Grossstädten der U.S.-Zone am 31. März 1946," *Europa Archiv*, I (1946–47), 233.

[26] For a listing of apartments occupied by the two military governments in principal cities of the bizonal area, see B. Mewes, *Der Lebensstandard in den Städten* (Schwäbisch-Gmünd: A. Bürger Verlag, 1949), p. 38.

[27] Haarmann, "Notmassnahmen auf dem Gebiete der Raumbewirtschaftung in Nordrhein-Westfalen," *Arbeitsblatt für die Britische Zone,* II (1948), 236.

[28] G. Müller, "Aufgaben und Problems der Wohnungsstatistik," *Arbeitsblatt für die Britische Zone,* Vol. I, Nos. 4–6 (1947), p. 146.

[29] E.M.N.I.D., "Untersuchung No. 12," *Jeder Dritte hat kein Bett* (mimeographed; July, 1949).

[30] "Black Market Building," *British Zone Review,* May 29, 1948, p. 11.

[31] Deutsche Wohnungswirtschaft, *Wohnungswirtschaftliche Zahlen* (Düsseldorf: 1951), p. 15. See also R. Proske, "Der Kampf gegen das deutsche Wohnungselend," *Frankfurter Hefte,* IV (1949), 686.

[32] Deutsche Kohlenbergbauleitung, *Zahlen zur Kohlenwirtschaft,* No. 3 (April, 1948), pp. 22–23.

[33] Harmssen, *op. cit.,* p. 96.

[34] H. H. D., *op. cit.,* p. 5.

[35] Harmssen, *loc. cit.*

[36] *Mitteilungsblatt der Verwaltung für Wirtschaft des Vereinigten Wirtschaftsgebietes,* I (1948), 23.

INDEX